W9-AWA-838

April, 1945. Elements
of Company G, 23rd U.S. Infantry,
Second Infantry Division,
bringing the war home to Germany.

Painting by Ed Valigursky

Captain Charles B. MacDonald
led his men through some
of the toughest, bloodiest
infantry fighting of World War II ...

COMPANY COMMANDER

Read this book to find out what it's like to be
afraid. How it feels to be responsible for men's
lives. What happens when a company retreats
against orders. What a man thinks while he's
fighting. Why men are willing to die for their
fellow soldiers. Why atrocities are committed.
How it feels to be wounded. What happens when
mistakes are made in battle ...

"Can go down as not only the finest narrative to
come out of the war but one that can't be beat
... *Company Commander*."

—*Detroit Free Press*

THE BANTAM WAR BOOK SERIES

This is a series of books about a world on fire.

These carefully chosen volumes cover the full dramatic sweep of World War II. Many are eyewitness accounts by the men who fought in this global conflict in which the future of the civilized world hung in balance. Fighter pilots, tank commanders and infantry commanders, among others, recount exploits of individual courage in the midst of the large-scale terrors of war. They present portraits of brave men and true stories of gallantry and cowardice in action, moving sagas of survival and tragedies of untimely death. Some of the stories are told from the enemy viewpoint to give the reader an immediate sense of the incredible life and death struggle of both sides of the battle.

Through these books we begin to discover what it was like to be there, a participant in an epic war for freedom.

Each of the books in the Bantam War Book series contains a dramatic color painting and illustrations specially commissioned for each title to give the reader a deeper understanding of the roles played by the men and machines of World War II.

COMPANY
COMMANDER
by Charles B. MacDonald

*This low-priced Bantam Book
has been completely reset in a type face
designed for easy reading, and was printed
from new plates. It contains the complete
text of the original hard-cover edition.*
NOT ONE WORD HAS BEEN OMITTED.

RL 8, IL 8-up

COMPANY COMMANDER
A Bantam Book

PRINTING HISTORY
*First published by the United States Army
Bantam edition / August 1978
2nd printing .... March 1979*

*Drawings by Tom Beecham.
Maps by Alan McKnight.*

*All rights reserved.
Copyright 1947 by Charles B. MacDonald
Illustrations copyright © 1978 by Bantam Books, Inc.
This book may not be reproduced in whole or in part, by
mimeograph or any other means, without permission.
For information address: Bantam Books, Inc.*

ISBN 0-553-12916-3

Published simultaneously in the United States and Canada

Bantam Books are published by Bantam Books, Inc. Its trademark, consisting of the words "Bantam Books" and the por-
trayal of a bantam, is Registered in U.S. Patent and Trademark
Office and in other countries. Marca Registrada. Bantam
Books, Inc., 666 Fifth Avenue, New York, New York 10019.

PRINTED IN THE UNITED STATES OF AMERICA

*In humble appreciation
to the Combat Infantrymen
those who live and those who died
of Companies I and G, 23d Infantry
and their counterparts in the other Infantry
Regiments of the United States Army, who
contributed so much to victory
in World War II*

PREFACE

THE CHARACTERS in this story are not pretty characters. They are not even heroic, if lack of fear is a requisite for heroism. They are cold, dirty, rough, frightened, miserable characters: GIs, Johnny Doughboys, dogfaces, footsloggers, poor bloody infantry, or, as they like to call themselves, combat infantrymen. But they win wars.

They are men from Companies I and G, 23rd Infantry, but they might be men from Companies A and K, 16th Infantry or they might be men from Companies C and E, 254th Infantry. For their stories are relatively the same. Some may have fought the Germans longer than others, or some may have fought the Germans less. For all it was an eternity.

The characters in my story are not fictional, and any similarity between them and persons living or dead is intentional, and some of them are dead.

This is a personal story, an authentic story. And to make a story of a war authentic you must see a war—not a hasty taste of war but the dread, gnawing daily diet of war, the horrors and the fears that are at first blunt testimony that you are a novice and then later become so much a part of you that only another veteran, through some sixth sense, may know that those same horrors and fears are yet there.

I was an officer in the war, a captain and company commander of Companies I and G, and because I was a captain my lot was easier somtimes than that of Joe Private, and Joe Private First Class, and Joe Sergeant, and Joe Lieutenant. But when my lot was easier physically it might be harder mentally, because I knew Joe Private, and Joe Private First Class, and Joe Sergeant, and Joe Lieutenant, and I could not suppress my love and admiration for them. But physical suffering can be worse sometimes, and when the GIs' lot was harder than mine I shall try to tell you that, because I am not the hero of my story.

The heroes are the men from Companies I and G —the lead scouts, the riflemen, the machine-gunners, the messengers, the mortarmen. Companies I and G are called rifle companies in the Army, and when you call a company a rifle company, you are speaking of the men who actually *fight* wars.

I did not fight the Germans as long as some of the characters in my story. Some of them had been meeting the enemy since D plus 1—June 7, 1944—when I joined them in September as a replacement company commander. They had completed the capture of a stubborn enemy garrison at Brest, France, the day before I joined them. They rested in an open field on the Brittany Peninsula for five days, and then they took a train ride on French freight cars across France to meet the Germans again.

C.B.M.

CONTENTS

BOOK ONE

COMPANY I

1
MEET COMPANY I

Dusk was approaching when the French locomotive, whistling shrilly to announce its arrival, wheezed into the station hidden sedately among the green-clad mountains along the French–Belgian border. The little moustached Frenchman who had jolted and jostled us across the whole of France jumped from his dominating perch in the engine and ran beside the train to join a cohort in chattering and gesticulating wildly. It was not too dark to read the faded black and white sign hanging above the station platform—Longuyon.

I gathered my equipment and stepped from the train. Already hundreds of men in olive drab uniforms, loaded with the variety of equipment and weapons that characterizes the American soldier, were disentangling themselves from the freight cars.

I decided that the little engineer must have thought we had not played fair with his forty-and-eight cars. There was not a car in my section of the train which did not disgorge at least forty-three men, plus equipment. The equipment would more than make up for the absence of the eight horses.

"I Company over here," I shouted above the noise of the detrainment. "Column o' twos facing this way. Headquarters, first, second, third, fourth."

The milling around began to take on a semblance of unity of purpose. I signalled "forward," and the column began an accordion-like action of moving off, a man here and there making a last-minute adjustment of his pack or overcoat.

We moved through the gate in the dirty concrete fence of the station yard and out to the main street of the town.

Dropping back from my position at the head of the column, I surveyed the long line of men . . . tall ones, short ones; not unlike similar companies I had commanded in the US before coming overseas. Perhaps there *was* something about the way these men walked—the confident swagger, perhaps. I think I would have known even had I been one of the silent, stone-faced civilians staring at us from the open doorways and windows along the way, that underneath those stubbly growths of beard and those wisps of straw from the boxcars clinging to the unpressed uniforms lay a wealth of battlefield experience.

"Company I, 23rd Infantry," I thought. "You fought your way ashore in Normandy on D plus one. You battled to the top of Hill 192 to pave the way for the St. Lô breakout. You stormed the ring of pillboxes at Brest and had your number reduced to fifty in the explosion as the Germans blew them up in your faces. And now they give you a company commander fresh from the States. They ask you to put your faith in me . . ."

I felt weak and ineffectual.

Quickening my pace, I regained my place at the head of the column as we crossed a temporary US Army bridge which had replaced the demolished ancient stone structure over the gurgling mountain stream which ran through the center of the village. We approached the last houses on the edge of the town, and the road began its steep ascent to the hilltop beyond. Now a dirty little French boy came running out to yell some newly learned Yankee curse word at us as we passed. Now a little girl bashfully thrust a bouquet of flowers into a soldier's hands and turned to disappear behind her mother's skirts in a doorway.

Our column plodded slowly up the hill, the full field packs beginning to assert their weight. Sweat formed on my body, and I wished that I had carried my heavy GI overcoat instead of wearing it. My nose began to run from the cold acquired on the long train ride, but I couldn't reach my handkerchief through the bundlesome overcoat and equipment.

The road made a sharp bend to the left as we reached the crest. It was light enough to see the deep valley to the right with its roving stream following the contour of the railroad track on the mountainside beyond.

"Damn," a heavily-breathing soldier in my headquarters group exclaimed between clenched teeth, "I sure hope it levels off before we reach the front. It'd be a sonofabitch to fight in this kind of country."

"We're still a helluva ways from the front," another said. "How far you reckon it is, Cap'n?"

I looked back. It was Private First Class Henry Croteau, of East Hartford, Conn. He had been the company interpreter and the company commander's runner through the campaign in France. "About twenty or thirty miles, the Colonel says," I replied.

The road continued upgrade and we walked on in silence. The cold wind felt good to my face. I was conscious of a heavy mist about us which slowly turned into a fine rain, which, coupled with the overcast that had plagued us all day, boded no good for a bivouac in the open.

A mile down the road we met the battalion commander, Lieutenant Colonel Paul V. Tuttle, of San Antonio, Texas. He was a tall, handsome young West Pointer. His short brown hair was beginning to grey slightly at the temples, and his face had a ruddy glow from the wind as he waited for us beside the road. He motioned me to a field a few hundred yards down the road and designated a spot on the right for my company.

"We'll bivouac here for the night, Mac," he said. "There's a haystack over there. Let the men heat K-rations with the boxes but leave off the other fires. There might be some little birds around, you know."

I congratulated myself upon the good fortune that had given me such an understanding battalion commander for my first combat experience and turned off the road at the place he had designated. I directed the platoons to their respective areas in the field and noted that K, L, M and Battalion Headquarters Companies were following us in.

Our arrival seemed to be the signal for the clouds to burst. The mist that had become a drizzle now became a torrent. The men scrambled madly to get their packs undone and shelter halves spread over equipment. Then followed the rush for the haystack. The field was already a soggy mass of mud, and the downpour of rain was making it muddier by the minute.

I joined my headquarters group in heating the cans of K-rations over the oblong cardboard boxes they came in.

The rain and wind made it hard to get the fires started at first but the rain soon slackened. I wondered how I could force down another K-ration meal after five days of the same monotonous food aboard the train, but I found that anything edible tasted good after the hike from the station.

Colonel Tuttle sent a messenger with the message for me to report to him for instructions for the morning. My executive officer said he would fix up our tent and put my equipment in out of the rain while I was gone. He was First Lieutenant Rudolph A. (Sparky) Flaim, of Rosati, Mo., a husky young officer who had already qualified for three Purple Hearts and was on his way to flirt with the fourth. When I returned he was snoring loudly on his own side of the little pup tent, and most of the company had turned in for the night.

I walked through the disorderly rows of tents and the thick mud made sucking noises as it pulled at my overshoes. Seeking out the platoon leaders, I found First Lieutenant Long H. Goffigon, of Cape Charles, Va., my 1st Platoon leader, and First Lieutenant Alfred Antey, of Evansville, Ind., my 3d Platoon leader, sleeping in the same tent. First Lieutenant Thomas D. Brock, of Plymouth, Mich., my 2d Platoon leader, and First Lieutenant Robert H. Glasgow, of Arlington, N. J., weapons platoon leader, were together. I told them the plans for the morning and walked to the end of the field where I found two guards huddled in their raincoats. I told them to pass the word on to the guards who relieved them to awaken the company at five o'clock. We would have another K-ration breakfast before loading on trucks to continue the move.

I went back to my tent and pulled off my muddy overshoes and crawled inside but I couldn't go to sleep. Sparky had pushed well over toward my side of the tent in his sleep and a mound of dirt positioned itself squarely in the small of my back; it had seemingly escaped the softening process of the heavy rain.

My mind began to peruse the duties that were before me. In perhaps one day, and at the most, three days, I would be leading these men against a team of trained killers. I wondered how I would react. These men so deserved the best in leadership. Could I give it to them? They could boast a glorious combat record already and I knew nothing. Suddenly, all my long hours of training for just such a role as this seemed pitifully inadequate. If only there were some way I could know just what "it" was like. It seemed incredible that this group of hardened combat veterans could accept an inexperienced youth of twenty-one to lead them into battle simply because he happened to come to them wearing a set of flashy bars on his shoulders. If only I could look into their minds to see what they were thinking!

I was awakened the next morning by someone rapping on my tent and shouting that it was five o'clock. It was dark but the rain had stopped. That would make it slightly less disagreeable to roll up wet shelter-halves and damp equipment to strap to one's back. We had scarcely enough time to heat a K-ration meal before battalion headquarters sent a runner to tell us to load on the trucks.

The truck ride took us through a portion of Belgium before we crossed the border into the Duchy of Luxembourg. Civilians began to come to their doors to greet us with enthusiastic cheers and two fingers upraised in the "V"-for-victory sign. In one town an effigy of Adolf Hitler hung suspended by the neck from a rope above the road. Everywhere there were spontaneous expressions of gratitude. I felt a surging feeling of pride within me that for the moment pushed my fears of the future into the background. If war but consisted of only travel and cheers from a grateful populace!

We crossed the Luxembourg border and entered Belgium once again, noticing an increase in the military traffic. As our trucks rolled into Schönberg, Belgium, numerous command post and hospital installations, the increased number of German shop signs, and the apathy of the civilians told us we could not be far from Germany.

Our convoy turned off the highway at Schönberg and wound slowly up a sandy dirt road leading into the thick fir forests beyond the town. We rode on and on, and the forest seemed of an impenetrable depth. The sandy road gave out eventually and we found ourselves on an unimproved trail that had become a morass of mud from unaccustomed heavy traffic. Our convoy came to a halt. We had reached the spot for our bivouac.

Beneath the dense covering of the fir trees our kitchens

were already set up. They had arrived from France by
motor the evening before. An appetizing supper of hamburgers and vegetables awaited us, but it proved too much
for my stomach after the week's diet of K-rations and I
suffered pains from overeating.

Darkness had fallen and the company was beginning to
turn in for the night when I was called to battalion headquarters. The Colonel had set up a small command post
tent in the woods. A gasoline lantern took some of the
chill off the night air inside. The other company commanders were already there.

I was handed five maps, one for myself and one for
each of my platoon leaders. The Colonel did not waste
much time. He said, "I'd like to give you the information
I have so you can get back and get some sleep."

My pulse quickened. "So this is it," I said to myself,
using a phrase that every replacement uses a thousand
times before he ever actually reaches combat. I would
soon know if I could "take it." I would soon know if I
could justify the faith of the men from Company I.

"It looks as if we've finally drawn a good assignment,"
Colonel Tuttle continued, and I breathed somewhat easier. Already whirling visions of attacking formidable Siegfried Line pillboxes had been flashing through my mind.
"We're to relieve the 28th Division in the defense of a
stretch along the Siegfried Line. It's supposed to be a
quiet sector—so they tell us. There've been a few small-
scale German counterattacks in the area and some artillery and SP[1] fire, but at least it's quieter than the attack."

There were questions and a general discussion.

"Now," the Colonel continued, "we leave in the morning at seven o'clock. Have your kitchens prepare a hot
breakfast. They'll move up later under Lieutenant Koch.[2]
We'll go to a forward assembly area back of the line
where you can issue more ammunition. Then we'll have
time for reconnaissance, and the actual relief will take
place tomorrow night."

We dispersed to our company areas. In the darkness
outside the tent I noticed the flashes of artillery to the

---

[1] Self-propelled guns.
[2] First Lieutenant Verner C. Koch, of San Antonio, Texas, battalion supply officer.

east and the deep rumble of the big guns came from the distance. A voice in my brain kept repeating, "This is it! This is it!" I stumbled blindly through the dark forest in the direction of the company.

I stopped by the first sergeant's tent where I found First Sergeant Henry D. Albin, of Houston, Texas, huddled in his tent with a raincoat over the entrance as a blackout curtain. He was a young auburn-haired, red-faced Texan who drawled pleasantly when he talked. He was preparing the company morning report by flashlight. "How does it look?" he asked.

"Not too bad," I answered. "It's the defense."

"Could be worse then, I guess," he said. "If it ain't bad it'll be the first time this outfit ever drew a good assignment."

I asked him to send for the platoon leaders to receive the information I had about the situation. They soon gathered around the tent. I was beginning to give them the information when a soldier stepped from the darkness.

"Is the first sergeant 'round?" the soldier asked.

"Right here," Sergeant Albin answered.

"I'm from the 9th Infantry, Sergeant," the soldier said. "We're bivouacked just across the way, and I got a ride over so I figured I'd stop by to see my brother. I haven't seen him in some time but he's in this company."

"What's the name?"

"Wagram,[3]" the soldier answered. "Wagram. His first name's—"

The feeble light from the flashlight inside the tent shone briefly on the soldier's face.

"Yeah. Yeah, I know," Sergeant Albin interrupted. "In the 3d Platoon. With us at Brest. Killed in action there."

---

[3] Soldier's name in this instance is fictitious.

2
INTO THE LINES

Our truck convoy wound its way back through the thick forest into Schönberg the next morning and out again over the highway leading east. As we neared the German border the road began a steep ascent to the mountains to our front. A big white signboard with glaring black letters told us what we were near. "You are now entering Germany, an enemy country. Be on the alert." I looked at my watch. It was 11:15 on the morning of October 3, 1944. We were entering the country at a point approximately twelve miles east of St. Vith, Belgium, in the Schnee-Eifel forest. The old iron border gate stood open, mud-splashed by the Army traffic.

The road twisted and turned like some giant snake slithering up the steep slopes. The boom of big artillery pieces grew nearer. We turned from the highway on a freshly-plowed dirt road to the left, and the drivers shifted gears as the big trucks sank into the mud. The artillery pieces that had heralded our approach appeared in a deep valley to our right behind grey puffs of smoke as they belched their big noise into the spaces beyond.

Our convoy pulled to a halt, and the driver cut the ignition and jumped out to open the tailgate. I gathered my equipment and stepped out on the muddy ground. This was Germany!

We lined up in the familiar column of twos on either side of the muddy road for the two-mile walk to the forward assembly area. The overcast skies with perpetual threat of rain made a sticky murkiness of the atmosphere despite the nipping cold, and the accustomed perspiration of road marches appeared beneath our overcoats.

We reached the assembly area in a thick scrub-oak

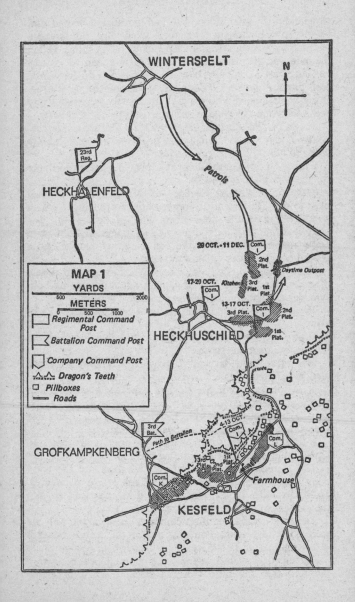

WINTERSPELT

N

23rd
Reg.

HECKHALENFELD

Patrols

29 OCT. - 11 DEC.
Com.
I

2nd
Plat.

Daytime Outpost

17-29 OCT.
Com.
I

Kitchen

3rd
Plat.

1st
Plat.

13-17 OCT.
Com.
I

2nd
Plat.

3rd Plat.

1st
Plat.

HECKHUSCHIED

MAP 1
YARDS
500   2000
METERS
0   500   1000

⬡ Regimental Command
Post

◀ Battalion Command Post

⬡ Company Command Post

⌃⌃⌃⌃ Dragon's Teeth

◻ Pillboxes

── Roads

3rd
Bat.

Path to Battalion

4-13 OCT.
Com.
I

Com.
L

GROFKAMPKENBERG

3rd
Plat.

2nd
Plat.

1st
Plat.

Farmhouse

Com.
K

KESFELD

woods shortly after noon. We had no sooner halted and begun to disentangle ourselves from the burdensome packs than Captain Jimmie Anderson, of Cushing, Okla., the battalion operations officer, rode up in a jeep.

"Turn your company over to your exec and have him feed dinner," he said. "Your kitchen should be up shortly. Bring what officers you want to go on reconnaissance and come with me. The old man's ready to go right now."

Be calm. Be business-like. This is the same as maneuvers. Give some orders. Start things moving. You're going to have a look at the German Army.

I turned and mumbled instructions to Sparky and sent for the four platoon leaders.

Sergeant Raymond Savage, of Mobile, Ala., walked over to me. He was my communications sergeant, a small, good-looking young Southerner who spoke slowly in a matter-of-fact Alabama drawl. I had come to know him better than anyone else in the company thus far; he had a friendliness that was difficult to resist.

"You going up, Captain?" he asked. Savage had a way of never slurring the title of captain but pronouncing both syllables clearly despite his deep Southern accent.

"Yeah," I said, making an effort at nonchalance. "Right away."

"Can I go with you?" he asked. "I'd like to check on the communications set-up."

"I'm afraid not, Savage," I answered. "There's only one jeep, and I have to take the platoon leaders."

"OK," he said as if he had half expected a refusal, "but watch yourself, Captain." His face looked worried. "Don't go sticking your neck out the first thing. . . . and for God's sake hide those damned captain's bars!"

I looked at the shiny objects on my shoulders and hastily pulled them off and stuffed them into my pockets.

The platoon leaders arrived. We climbed into the company jeep driven by Private First Class James Earnhardt, of Mooresville, N. C., and moved down the trail to join the other company commanders.

The road to the battalion command post of the unit we were to relieve twisted in and out of the woods beneath low-hanging limbs. We reached a clearing. A sign said: "Windshields covered beyond this point." We crossed a hill and saw the little German farming town of Grof-

kampkenberg with its closely clustered houses and barn-
yards and the inevitable manure piles. We plowed through
the black filth of mud that covered the road and pulled up
to a white house in the center of the town. Here and there
an artillery shell had plunged through a roof or knocked
off the corner of a chimney. A dead cow—dead cows had
become for us a sort of symbol of the war in France—
lay with legs upstretched in the open field to the left of
the road.

A guide from the company we were to relieve joined us,
and I heard Colonel Tuttle admonishing us to return by
3:30 P.M. and the guide was saying "Ready?" and I was
swallowing and answering "Yes."

We had come as far as we could by vehicle but the
guide said we had a mile and a half yet to go. We ran
across an open hill on the east edge of town because the
guide said the enemy could observe us from the towering
blue hills to our front. We continued in a narrow valley
and I tried to note each terrain feature as we passed. It
would be night when I would lead the company over the
route. I noted that the terrain was no longer mountain-
ous but had given way to a series of rolling hills and
valleys.

We crossed a slight knoll and the antitank wall of the
Siegfried Line came suddenly into view. It looked like a
prehistoric monster coiled around the hillsides; the concrete dragon's-teeth were like scales upon the monster's
back—or maybe headstones in a kind of crazy cemetery.
We crossed the antitank wall. The open mouths of two
pillboxes yawned at us from the slope ahead.

We passed the pillboxes and skirted the left edge of a
thick patch of fir trees. The ground was covered with
black holes where shells had hit and exploded. The
dragon's-teeth coiled across our path again, and we
crossed them again. Tucked into the slope of a higher hill
to our front was a row of eight concrete pillboxes, completely dug into the hillside except for their faces.

"We'll have to run again here," the guide said and
pointed to a high slope to our right front peopled by a
similar row of pillbox giants. "That's *theirs!*"

We ran across the plowed field and halted for breath at
the entrance to a pillbox at the crest of the slope. The
entrance had been filled in with dirt. Two soldiers rose up

to view us from shallow slit trenches dug near the entrance.

"You better keep low," one of them said. "They been shootin' here all day."

"This is part of L Company," our guide announced, ignoring the warning except for a quick look toward the speaker that must have said "thanks."

We imitated our guide's half-crouch as we ran from the pillbox to a thin hedge that ran parallel with the ridge along its crest. I could still see the enemy pillboxes in the distance to our right and they could very evidently see us, but I realized as I looked around that our guide had taken the only concealment the ground afforded us. I could discern the general outline of the defensive position we were to occupy. The battalion's position was to be in the shape of a giant horseshoe with Company I embedded in the center of the arc. We would have been exposed from the other side of the hedge as well.

I imitated the guide's cautiousness as we advanced but I was strangely unafraid. I was a bit awed by the momentousness of it (*you are inside the Siegfried Line!*), but thus far it had been child's play.

We continued for two hundred yards when the guide suddenly veered into the hedge, and we found ourselves in the shaded back yard of a two-story farmhouse. We followed the guide in a back window, and I knew we had reached our destination.

We found the company commander, a first lieutenant, in a small, low cellar illuminated only by a dim kerosene lantern that needed its shade washed. There were men in every conceivable sleeping position all over the floor. The lieutenant suggested that we move upstairs where we could talk, and we made our way again up the dark, narrow staircase that led from the cellar.

When we reached the light of the first floor, I saw that the lieutenant's eyes were blood-shot and a half-week's growth of beard covered his face. His voice trembled slightly when he talked and he would start at the slightest noise. He asked if I had my platoon leaders with me and I indicated my lieutenants. He sent two runners for his own platoon leaders.

"I can't get the 3d Platoon leader now," he said. "Can't reach the 3d Platoon in daylight, but he can go with the

2d Platoon. He can see the positions from there." He interrupted himself to admonish two soldiers to move more quietly when they walked. "By the way, they're all sergeants. I have only one officer left besides myself." He flinched perceptibly at the sound of a door closing.

I conferred with my platoon leaders and we set our time for reassembly at the company command post in the farmhouse at three o'clock. The company commander and I went upstairs to the forward room on the second floor.

From the upstairs window I could see a towering ridge rising to our front, spotted with poorly camouflaged pillboxes and patches of trees. A small farming town lay in a valley between us and the high ridge.

"It's not too bad a position," the lieutenant said. "You all have winter clothes and we haven't had a chance to get ours yet. That'll be a helluva big help."

"Jerry throws quite a bit of artillery and mortars at you," he continued, "and we've had some casualties, but it was their own fault for moving around in the daytime when they knew they shouldn't. We haven't had any counterattacks or patrols hit us yet, and we've been here fifteen days. K Company on our right got the living hell knocked out of them two nights ago. Swarm of Kraut infantry hit 'em along with a flame-throwing halftrack. Caught a lot of men in a pillbox and stampeded the company. My right platoon started falling back until I got 'em stopped. They counterattacked the next morning, however, and got their positions back. They found some of the men who hadn't run still holding their foxholes."

The attack against K Company with the loss of the men in the pillbox was the basis for a battalion order to move out of all pillboxes, the lieutenant said. That was the reason for the I Company CP being in the farmhouse. It had originally been in a bunker-type pillbox to the right rear of the house, and since there was no other spot available, it was necessary to move into the crowded farmhouse, even though it was in L Company's area. I decided immediately that I would take the chance and move my CP into the pillbox when we came up that night. The farmhouse was too crowded.

A closer look through the window revealed a line of foxholes a few yards in front of the house. The lieutenant explained that these belonged to the right flank platoon of

L Company. A small trail running along the right of the farmhouse was the dividing line between the companies and led down into the valley to the German-held town which my map labeled Kesfeld. The three rifle platoon positions my men would occupy extended five hundred yards to the right of the trail.

There were no windows on the right side of the farmhouse, so we moved downstairs and out into the back yard to view the platoon positions.

"Your 3d Platoon on the right has it worst," the lieutenant said, pointing toward the outline of foxholes on a small knoll to the right front. "They're completely exposed. Can't even raise their heads out of their holes in daylight without some goddamned Kraut taking a shot at them. We can't contact them by runner except at night. There's a two-hundred-yard gap on their right before K Company starts . . . which ain't good, of course."

Over the entire area the Germans from the high ridge to the front and right front had perfect observation of our positions. Their view was supplemented by that of those who occupied the high ridge on our left, but the observation from the left was restricted by the foliage surrounding the farmhouse.

I decided to dispose my company initially as the lieutenant had done. We could make changes later. I would have preferred holding one of my rifle platoons in a support position; but it seemed unwise, for our company frontage was great.

My platoon leaders reassembled at the farmhouse. Our guide had waited to go back with us, and upon his suggestion we moved back in groups of two to give the enemy a less profitable target. I decided to wait until the last to leave. Lieutenant Brock, my 2d Platoon leader, elected to remain with me. I was filled with misgivings about the return trip until we should reach the concealment of the patch of fir trees, but when the other platoon leaders drew no fire as they crossed the open space my fears partially subsided.

Brock and I made our way in a half-crouch beside the hedge, more conscious now that our only concealment from the enemy depended upon our blending with the foliage on our right. We reached a point opposite the pillbox where we had encountered the men in the slit trenches on the trip forward, and started out on a run across the crest of the hill.

I had almost reached the cover of the pillbox when the projectiles from a 20mm antiaircraft gun began to crack overhead. I hit the ground instinctively. I found myself behind a small knoll formed by the embedded pillbox and was thus protected from the enemy fire. I was beginning to congratulate myself on choosing the position when I looked to my right. Five feet from me lay a German soldier, crumpled as he had fallen and bloated in death.

It was my first view of a dead man and I tried to avoid the revulsion that filled me by quickly turning my eyes away.

We crawled down to the face of the pillbox and paused a moment to catch our breath. I started the journey again by dashing across the plowed field that led to the first row of dragon's-teeth, expecting at any moment to see the bullets from the antiaircraft gun kick up the dirt around my feet. I could hear Lieutenant Brock panting as he ran behind me.

But the sound of bullets did not come. In its stead came the sharp crack and heavy explosion that I knew must be mortar fire falling behind me. It sounded as if the shells were falling on the crest of the ridge we had so recently left, but I took no time to look back. I increased my speed and dived behind a clump of bushes next to the outer row of dragon's-teeth. There would be no protection from those bushes against the mortar shells, but I was comforted by their concealment. I lay there panting.

It could not have been more than a minute before Brock joined me but it seemed like ten. I sighed in relief. His face was white and his breath came in gasps but he was unhurt. When he had regained his breath he stammered out his story.

"Those damn mortars," he said. "The concussion must have thrown me at least three feet into the air and then flat on my face on the ground!"

We made an effort to laugh at his narrow escape, and continued the journey past the patch of fir trees and into Grofkampkenberg.

In Grofkampkenberg Colonel Tuttle told me that my company would be the first to move up that night. We would leave our assembly area around ten o'clock in order to begin effecting the relief at midnight. The other two rifle companies would leave at two-hour intervals thereafter; thus one company would be completely on position before another had begun.

We rode our jeep back to the company assembly area. The mess sergeant, Staff Sergeant Lee W. Threadgill, of Franklin, Texas, had saved dinner for us but the company was eating supper when we arrived. We ate the two meals together and I gave final instructions to the platoon leaders as we ate. The men were to carry three meals of K-rations and their blanket rolls with them. They would leave their gas masks and duffel bags to be transported by Service Company. I arranged to have my jeep driver follow L Company's jeep to the L Company CP after darkness, and bring with him a load of ammunition and our heavier weapons, the light machine-guns and 60mm mortars.

Darkness had fallen and a misty rain was coming down when I completed the arrangements. I climbed into the back of the kitchen truck and smoked a cigarette and listened to the slow tick of my watch as ten o'clock rolled nearer.

"This is it! This is it!" my brain kept repeating madly, over and over. I must not appear afraid. I must give these men confidence in me despite the fact that they know I'm inexperienced. They were playing their parts well. I had been unable to detect any attitude of distrust in their actions, and I had searched their faces for long periods at a time. I must keep that confidence. I *must!* I *must!*

"Scared, Captain?" Sergeant Savage asked.

"A little," I admitted. I took a long, slow drag on my cigarette.

"We all are," Savage said. "We always are."

The rain had stopped and somewhere there was a moon that was hidden by the clouds as we collected our equipment and set out on the night march to "the front." It was a slow, fatiguing march under the burden of the mounting tension and the heavy equipment. Our guide of the afternoon joined us in Grofkampkenberg. I was surprised because I had not expected he would be with us.

After we had passed the patch of fir trees the guide led

us in a more direct line toward our objective than we had
traveled on the reconnaissance. We crossed the dragon's-
teeth and began the ascent of the slope beyond, and I
made out the outline of the slight rise which would be
the pillbox I was to use for a command post.

I stumbled and looked down at my feet. An American
soldier, fully clothed even to his helmet, lay on his back
with glassy eyes turned skyward, his arms outstretched.
His body was almost twice its normal size. I shuddered
involuntarily. The shock of almost stepping upon the body
before seeing it left me weak inside.

The guide stooped down and retrieved the automatic
rifle that lay beside the body, swinging the weapon over
his shoulder.

"Must be one of our BAR[1] men," he said, casually. "He
headed for battalion the other day. There was a mortar
barrage. We hadn't heard from him since."

We reached the entrance to the pillbox in the rear of
the farmyard a few moments later. Guides from the rifle
platoons of the 28th Division company asked in hoarse
stage whispers what platoon it was.

I directed my company headquarters group to the pillbox and dispatched the rifle platoons with their guides into the darkness beyond, telling them that we would have
telephone lines to them as soon as possible. I grew openly
nervous lest we be caught by an enemy artillery barrage
with a large number of men on the exposed hilltop.

The lieutenant from the 28th Division appeared and we
moved together down the incline that led to the circuitous
entrance of the pillbox. A giant hole had been dug into
the ground on the crest of the hill and the massive concrete emplacement had been constructed within, its entrance facing the rear of the farmhouse across the trail.
Its roof was constructed of four feet of reinforced concrete with three feet of dirt making a slight mound above.
The walls were six feet thick.

I noted the size of the big bunker as we entered. It was
sixteen feet square and eight feet high. The men from my
headquarters were arranging their equipment on three

---

[1]Browning Automatic Rifle.

rows of iron-frame bunks with laced rope bottoms that were suspended in tiers of three each from the ceiling along each side. In the left front corner an iron door led to a small concrete storage room.

A candle burned on a table at the front of the pillbox; it cast flickering shadows on the walls and revealed a hand-operated ventilation device against the left wall. On the right next to the floor was a small door that open revealed a fireplace that ended in the tin chimney I had seen silhouetted against the sky outside. Signs and mottos in German script were on each wall. The concrete floor was littered with empty cardboard cartons and K-ration tins. The air was cold and damp and stale and smelled of dust and dried man-sweat.

Sergeant Albin was busy with the morning report. Private First Class Lupe Naranjo, of Aquadulce, Texas, and Private First Class Walter Zellin, of Boston, Mass., the two men who served as messengers from the battalion CP, waited to take the report back with them. Sergeant Savage was attaching the company's field telephone to a line that entered the room through a small slit which commanded a view of the entrance and could be closed by pushing a small concrete block across it, thus blacking-out the pillbox completely.

"I ought to have communication with battalion in a couple of minutes, Captain," Savage said. "I'm using the 28th Infantry's old line."

He soon made contact with battalion, and there was a call waiting for us.

"It's L Company," he said. "Neafach[2] has got our mortars and machine guns and some ammunition at their CP."

He told him that we would have someone there to pick them up in a few minutes and then he gathered up his wire-laying equipment. Private First Class Luther T. Blackburn, of Oklahoma City, Okla., one of the SCR[3]-300 operators, would assist him. They would lay telephone wire to the forward platoons.

A man from the 28th Division came in to report to his

---

[2] Staff Sergeant Harold L. Neafach, of Altoona, Pa., the company supply sergeant.
[3] Signal Corps Radio.

company commander that messengers from all four of his platoons had reported outside with the information that the platoons had all pulled out. The lieutenant turned to me. "Is there anything else, then, Captain?" he asked.

"No, I think not," I said, trying in vain to think of something I might have forgotten and a bit alarmed that soon I would be entirely on my own.

I reported our progress to Colonel Tuttle, and the lieutenant talked with his own battalion commander and asked me to tell his CO that I was satisfied. I did so and the lieutenant prepared to leave, taking my two battalion runners with him.

He seemed overjoyed at the prospect of leaving and I wondered if someday I would be just as happy to leave this area. And how long would that someday be? A week, two weeks, a month, two months? There was no way of knowing. We might sit here until the war ended. Or we might leave tomorrow.

I closed my eyes for a brief moment and murmured a silent prayer.

The lieutenant was gone. I was on my own.

3

ELEVEN MEN IN A PILLBOX

Lieutenant Glasgow (Scotty), my weapons-platoon leader-er, whose love for Scotch whiskey and insistence that his name was pronounced with a *g* and not a *c* were standing jokes in the company, came in a few minutes after the lieutenant from the 28th had left. He said his platoon CP was in the back room of the house across the trail. He was setting up one mortar in the rear of the house and the other two beside the rearmost and smaller of the two wooden sheds behind the house. The positions afforded no cover, only concealment, but they were the only available positions. L Company was using all the pillboxes to our rear.

I told him that the machine guns and mortars were at L Company's CP and directed him there. He asked for several men from my company headquarters to help him carry ammunition and left with his mortar section to bring up the equipment.

Sergeant Savage called over the sound-powered telephone from the 1st Platoon and then from the 2d and the 3d. I was glad when I heard the first whistle over the phone that indicated that the lines were in. A whistle, plus the call sign of the party desired, was the signal, since all platoons were on a party line. We had adopted the same call signs for both telephone and SCR-536, the famed little walkie-talkies, using nicknames of the platoon leaders, or their last names, plus the numerical designation of the platoon—*Long One* for the 1st Platoon, *Brock Two, Antey Three, Scotty Four,* and merely *CP* for the company command post.

I was greatly relieved that the communications were in.

SCR–536

I wondered how the lieutenant from the 28th Division
had endured the nervous tension of the pillbox positions
for fifteen days without communications to his platoons.
One platoon, or all platoons, might have been completely
overrun by the enemy before a foot messenger could get
back to the command post—if he got back.

First Sergeant Albin made up a guard roster from the
company headquarters group. Each man would guard outside the pillbox in two-man shifts that would change every
two hours. Savage and Blackburn would split the night on
the telephones. Sparky went to sleep early so that he
could take over from me later, thus insuring that one of
us would be awake at all times.

Scotty returned with the machine-guns and mortars at
two o'clock. I didn't like the prospect of hand-carrying all
our supplies from the L Company CP, exposing the carry-

ing detail to enemy shelling for long periods, but it seemed impractical to bring a jeep as far forward as my command post.

I didn't plan to sleep at all the first night. Now that we were on position and the difficulties of moving in no longer worried me, I was filled with a growing fear that the Germans might hit us with a counterattack. I decided that the enemy must surely know that new troops were moving in and would attempt to dislodge us while we might still be disorganized.

Despite my fears I was confident that Company I would meet with little difficulty in holding the positions. Already we had communications which far surpassed those of the unit we had relieved; and where they had had no antitank defenses except a small string of mines on the trail running along our left flank, we had seven rocket launchers (bazookas). I had placed two of the launchers with each forward platoon and kept one for the protection of the CP. And already I was thoroughly imbued with the spirit common among all infantrymen that "my outfit is the best damned outfit in the whole damned Army." It could boast of a record to prove it. I was certainly not a veteran in combat but I was no novice in my esteem for Company I.

I talked with the three rifle-platoon leaders over the telephone. They were thoroughly dissatisfied with their positions. The foxholes were little more than depressions in the ground, they said, and poorly disposed. Both the 1st and 2d Platoons wanted to occupy two pillboxes in their areas. Already they had begun to dig out the entrances which the preceding unit had covered with a bulldozer to prevent the Germans from re-occupying them if they were retaken. The 3d Platoon was changing the disposition of a few foxholes but little could be done to lessen the daylight vulnerability of their position.

The platoon leaders said there were about fifteen corpses in different spots over the company area—both German and American dead. Sergeant Savage said he was sliding under a fence while laying the wire to the platoons when he reached out and grasped the bare chest of a dead German. I told them I would call battalion the next day in an effort to get a graves-registration unit to remove the dead.

Lieutenant Brock said his platoon had discovered a US tank destroyer seventy-five yards in front of his position. A two-man crew that had been there three days since their vehicle had become stuck in the mud in the draw still occupied the TD. The 4th Platoon said there was another TD a few yards to the left of the shed occupied by two of the mortar squads, but it had been knocked out by a German shell.

The short candle in the pillbox flickered and went out. The command post settled down to an extravaganza of snores, an occasional ring of the battalion telephone, and low conversation between Savage and me. The routine was broken occasionally by the surprised comments of a sleeper as another man awakened him to go on guard. Savage began to nod from sleepiness and his head fell forward on the table. I did not awaken him. I was alone with my thoughts in the cold, damp darkness.

Eleven men in a pillbox! Eleven men who must live from day to day, never thinking of the immediate future but only of the infinity when the war would someday be over.

There was Sparky, and First Sergeant Albin, Savage, Blackburn, Croteau and me. There was Private First Class Willie Hagan, the tobacco-chewing thirty-nine-year-old Army regular who kept us laughing with sage tactical wisdom and served as 1st Platoon runner. Then there was Private First Class Angelo Butare, of Boston, 2d Platoon runner who had lost two brothers already in the war; Private First Class Hubert Berger, of Memphis, Tenn., 3d Platoon runner who was eighteen years old and read his Bible every night; Private First Class Kenneth Lampton, of Detroit, Mich., weapons-platoon runner who was also eighteen and corresponded with college girls from Michigan; and Private First Class Earling G. Salberg, of Fargo, N. D., who was nineteen and cleanly good-looking and the headquarters bazooka man. The cooks and jeep drivers, the supply sergeant and the mail orderly had been left behind with Service Company to keep us supplied.

The changing of the guard at four o'clock revealed that it was raining outside, a slow, cold, miserable drizzle. I thought of the men in the forward platoons in their exposed foxholes with no protection from the elements except shelter halves stretched across their holes and nothing between them and the hostile killers in front of us but the muzzles of their own rifles. I had admired the unglamorous infantry soldier before, but as the rain continued to fall and the night grew colder my pride at being a part of this dirty, miserable infantry knew no bounds.

The night wore on, quiet but for the pounding of our own artillery on the ridges to our front, sometimes a distant rumble, sometimes a heavy cracking explosion not far away. I nodded as the urge for sleep protested against denial, but then I would moisten my eyelids with saliva or pound my knuckles against my forehead, and the remembrance of the deep-rooted fear of a German counterattack would bring me back to my senses.

Around six o'clock I stepped across the trail to the shed behind the farmhouse to urinate and I saw that faint vestiges of dawn were appearing across the distant hills. There was something spooky about it. I returned to the pillbox and woke up Savage. We opened a breakfast K-ration and devoured its chopped-ham-and-egg mixture with a cup of coffee between us which Savage heated in his canteen cup. The long night was over.

We awakened Sparky and Blackburn and changed places with them. I slept with all my clothes on to combat the damp chill of the underground pillbox and to be prepared for any eventuality.

Daylight would be no detriment to sleep I realized as I climbed into the bunk. The pillbox was as dark in daytime as it had been at night.

I slept well except for occasional awakenings from the noise of someone sweeping out the pillbox or to cough from the acrid smoke of burning K-ration cartons as the men awoke and heated their breakfasts. One of the men from the TD in the 2d Platoon area came in around nine o'clock to use the telephone. He wanted permission from his outfit to abandon the TD and return. He got his permission and I went back to sleep. Twelve rounds of enemy mortar fire fell a hundred yards in rear of the pillbox around noon, but I scarcely noticed it as I turned over in my sleep. I heard Sparky talking with the platoon leaders in an effort to pick up the location from which the enemy weapons were firing when twelve more rounds fell to the rear of the 3d Platoon at one o'clock.

I got up at three o'clock and dusted from my hair the

loose dirt and straw that had fallen from the bunk above me and wiped the sleep from my eyes with my hand. I had not shaved since the day we detrained at Longuyon and the stubble felt rough on my face. I had difficulty finding a breakfast K-ration, since they were the least evil of the three meals and disappeared more quickly than the dinners and suppers, but I found one and stepped to the entrance of the pillbox to heat it. Rain continued to fall in a thin, needlepoint spray.

I talked with the platoon leaders again over the sound-powered telephone and got a list of the items that they wanted brought up with the rations after dark. I added a list of my own and called it in to the battalion supply officer. The main request was for several types of ammunition, including 60mm mortar shells adapted for firing from the M1 rifle with the aid of a grenade launcher. My

M1 Rifle with Grenade Launcher

men had found the expedient to be most effective in street fighting in Brest and swore that it was more effective than either hand grenades or fragmentation rifle grenades. It, in effect, put the equivalent of 60mm mortars in the forward foxholes.

I was standing a few feet outside the entrance to the pillbox when one of our own artillery shells whistled menacingly overhead. I started instinctively toward the safety of the pillbox. The men laughed at me and said, "That's ours." I felt foolish and wondered if I would ever be able to tell the difference between incoming and outgoing shells.

An enemy artillery piece fired ten rounds into the area around five o'clock. The barrage centered one hundred yards to the rear of the CP in relatively the same position as the mortar barrage at noon but the shells did no damage.

The rain stopped around six, but the weather stayed damp and cold and the skies showed no signs of clearing. Night began to fall and I yearned for the long days of summer when the sun had not set until ten or eleven o'clock. Night with its long hours of mysteries and uncertainties was the time to fear.

Colonel Tuttle telephoned from battalion. He was planning to send a platoon of 57mm antitank guns into position around the farmhouse during the night and wanted to know if I thought it possible to tow the guns all the way forward with jeeps. I was elated. A dread fear of the enemy's terror-provoking flame-throwing halftrack had persisted since my initial conversation with the nervous lieutenant from the 28th Division. The presence of the antitank guns would practically wipe away the danger of the halftrack. Yes, I thought it possible to tow the guns forward. Yes, yes, yes!

When darkness came Sergeant Albin rounded up the carrying detail to go for the rations and supplies at the L Company CP. He left only a skeleton force at the CP, two men on guard, Savage on the phones, and Lieutenant Flaim and myself. But the detail was still too small. I called Scotty and he sent two squads of mortarmen and left only a skeleton crew on the third gun.

The carrying detail had been gone only five minutes

when a call came from the 2d Platoon. It was Technical Sergeant Rupert L. Middlebrook, of Long Beach, Calif., the platoon sergeant.

"There's some sort of track vehicle out to our front, Cap'n, about six hundred yards, and it's headed this way!"

The phone seemed to be a conductor that sent an electric thrill through my body. The flame-throwing halftrack I had so recently shelved into the back of my mind suddenly reared up before my eyes and began spurting hideous orange, deadly flame over the area. A wave of fear possessed me. My body began to shake uncontrollably. My voice trembled despite my efforts to control it. I felt foolish at being afraid, and I hoped the others did not notice it, but I could not stop my body from trembling.

"Get battalion," I cried to Savage. I turned again to the sound-powered phone. "I'm getting battalion. We'll try to get artillery." And then, when that seemed inadequate, "Just what does it sound like?"

"I can't tell exactly," Middlebrook said. "It might be a tank or a halftrack. But the sonofabitch is headed this way. We've been hearing it some time, but I wanted to be sure before I called."

Willie Hagan, on guard outside the CP, burst into the pillbox. "There's a f——g tank headed this way, Cap'n! We can hear it plain out here. It's in front of the 1st Platoon."

I nodded to Willie and Savage told him I was on that now.

"Can you get a light to look at your map?" I asked Middlebrook. "I want you to tell me what artillery concentration you think might get it."

"I can't use a light," he answered, "but it sounds like it's on that road that runs up through the town. Maybe you can figure close to it from your map and I can adjust."

I adjusted my map to the faint light of the kerosene lantern we had borrowed from the L Company platoon in the farmhouse earlier in the day. Concentration Number 221 was on the road leading out of the town. I would try that one first and Middlebrook could adjust it by sound from his position.

Savage handed me the battalion phone. I grasped it with one hand, keeping the platoon phone glued to the opposite ear. "I'm getting battalion now," I said into the sound-powered phone.

"Make it snappy," a voice cut in that I knew was Lieutenant Goffigon. "This is Long, Cap'n. We can hear it plain now, and it's headed right this way. Coming pretty fast."

Captain Anderson was at the other end of the battalion wire. I made a desperate effort to control my trembling voice but I knew that I failed. I outlined our situation hurriedly and called for the concentration.

"Coming right up," Captain Anderson said. "Hold on."

I waited for what seemed an interminable period. Long and Middlebrook discussed the situation in one ear. Lieutenant Antey, the 3d Platoon leader, joined the discussion. He could hear the vehicle now although he hadn't heard it at first. The battalion switchboard operator spoke in a voice that was maddening with its politeness, "Have you finished, sir? Have you finished, sir?" I said, "Waiting," and my mind echoed the words . . . "waiting, waiting, waiting."

I glanced at my watch. It had been only two minutes since I first talked with Captain Anderson but it seemed more like two hours. My God! Would the artillery never come?

Long was talking again on the platoon phone.

"What do you think now, Middlebrook? Sounds like it's stopped to me."

A reprieve! A reprieve! I felt weak with relief inside.

"Yeah, I think so too," Middlebrook answered. "It seems to have . . . no, no . . . there she comes again. It's a helluva lot closer this time! What about the artillery, Cap'n?"

The overwhelming fear returned but a sudden, melodious whistle of outgoing artillery played nocturnes in my ear. Captain Anderson's voice came simultaneously over the battalion telephone.

"Hey, Mac, they're firing three rounds for you to adjust. Lemme know what it looks like. On the way!"

I had but a moment to yell "on the way" in the platoon phone before I heard the crunch of the big shells in the distance.

"What d'ya think, Middlebrook?" I asked.

"I couldn't tell too well, Cap'n. I have to adjust by sound, and it sounded over to me."

"This is Long, Cap'n. I can't see too well either, but I'd say it was two hundred over. I couldn't adjust on deflection but it seemed OK."

For a fleeting moment I envied the calmness of their voices, then repeated their decision to Captain Anderson.

"Two hundred over," he repeated. "I'll ask them to give you a battery volley this time. How's that?"

The time seemed much shorter before the whistle of the shells across the pillbox. Three rounds . . . the explosions . . . three rounds . . . three rounds . . . three more explosions . . . three more explosions.

"I can hear it again!" Long shouted over the phone, "but it's running away now! Let 'em raise it a hundred and give it to 'em again."

I repeated the directions. I had a quick-enveloping feeling of elation over our apparent success. I could hear Captain Anderson repeating the sensing at the other end of the wire. Nine more rounds whistled overhead.

The shells hit.

"We must not have gotten it," Middlebrook said, "but we sure scared hell out of whatever it was. He's beatin' hell outa there now. You can hardly hear him he's so far away."

I sighed and glanced at Savage. He had been sitting with his ear practically in the phones. He gave a sly smile. I answered it with a broad beam of pleasure. Willie Hagan, who had surveyed the entire proceedings with a practised eye, turned and joined his companion on guard.

I thanked Captain Anderson. Savage gave the battalion phone a slight ring to indicate that we had finished. The voice of the switchboard operator sounded musical now— "Have you finished, sir? Have you finished?"

Even as I relaxed with relief at the exit of the enemy tank—if, indeed, it had been a tank—I began to think of the carrying detail which had left earlier for L Company's CP.

The crack of mortar shells dropping unheralded from the sky, followed a fraction of a second later by the dull boom of explosions, reached my ears. I exchanged mutual looks of anxiety with Sparky and Savage, but there was nothing we could do but await the return of the detail and hope blindly they had escaped the barrage. I ran to the entrance of the pillbox and watched the orange light of the explosions as the last rounds fell. They seemed centered about two hundred yards to the rear of the CP, directly on the crest of the ridge.

I went back inside to the vigil beside the telephones to await the men's return. Each minute that passed increased my anxiety. The challenge of the guard outside some fifteen minutes later, followed by a mumbled password and the noise of equipment being placed on the ground, was welcome to my ears. They were back.

Sergeant Albin was the first to enter the pillbox. He said, "We just missed it. We had started back and the jeeps had just left when the mortars started popping. There were some L Company men still around and it hit right where they unloaded the equipment, but nobody got it."

I was relieved for the moment but decided I would not risk exposing the carrying detail to the same dangers again. "If the antitank guns make it OK tonight, we'll have Neafach come all the way up with the supplies tomorrow night."

Sergeant Albin told Savage to call the platoons to send carrying parties to take the food and equipment to the platoon areas while he broke it down into platoon sections outside.

"We've got coffee and steak sandwiches out here," he said, "but it's all cold as a witch's tit."

The cold steak sandwiches tasted like food for a king. I knew they must have tasted even better to the cold, hungry riflemen and machine gunners in their rain-drenched foxholes despite the cold and darkness in which they had to eat. The coffee was equally as cold, but the CP group and mortar section could reheat it over K-ration boxes. It was impossible for the riflemen to have fires, even in daylight, so I called battalion for heating tablets, which burn with little smoke, but I was informed that they were a critical item and could not be obtained.

I had asked battalion about the possibility of obtaining a graves-registration unit to remove the bodies from the area, but I was told that no such unit was available. We would have to remove the bodies ourselves. The Colonel finally weakened at my emphasized distaste and agreed to let us bury the German dead in an unoccupied pillbox, removing their identification papers to be sent to the rear, and to let us move the dead Americans to a spot in rear of my CP where the chaplain would pick them up with a jeep and trailer for burial.

The jeeps towing the three 57mm antitank guns arrived around nine o'clock and I was impressed by the apparent lack of noise. The crews placed the guns in camouflaged positions in the brush around the farmhouse, covering both L and I Company fronts. I definitely decided that our own supply jeep could come all the way forward the next night.

Naranjo and Zellin, the messengers from battalion, arrived and brought with them a wire-laying crew from the wire section of Battalion Headquarters Company. The crew laid a new wire from our CP to battalion on the return trip. Another crew from the artillery laid a line to the observer in the farmhouse, thus giving us three separate direct wires to the rear in case any of them should be knocked out by shelling.

The battalion messengers brought copies of the *Stars and Stripes*, Army daily newspaper that most of the men read avidly. I already knew that there were never more than twelve copies for the whole company, and that the papers were usually two days old or more when we received them. *The Spearhead*, a two-page mimeographed information sheet published each day by Division Special Services, with news compiled from radio broadcasts, usually reached us the evening of the day the news was broadcast.

Around eleven o'clock I rose to make a trip to the forward platoons. I was not anxious to go. I could visualize a thousand and one things taking place at the CP while I was gone that should have my attention, not the least of which might be a counterattack. But I wanted to have a closer look at the positions and I felt my visit might make the men feel a bit better. At least it would show them that I was not afraid to visit them. Lieutenant Glasgow also wanted to visit the platoons and check his machine-gun positions, so we decided the two of us would go together.

It was not raining outside but a chill wind blew across the hills and down the valleys to wrap the cold dampness

of the night closely around us. Though the moon was nowhere to be seen, a dull glow of light through the clouds
kept the darkness from being completely black. We made
our way down the forward slope of the shell-pocked rise
that secreted the company command post and crossed a
small stream that trickled down the bottom of the draw I
knew divided the 2d and 3d Platoons and was defended
farther to the left by the two pillboxes occupied by the 2d
Platoon. I saw to our front the outline of the knoll defended by the 3d Platoon and heard the sound of shovels
digging in the rocky earth. A chorus of coughs that I
knew had been aggravated by the weather reached us as
we came closer.

We found the foxhole that the men called the platoon
CP. Lieutenant Antey was around somewhere in the platoon area, but Technical Sergeant John M. Garcia, of
Noble, La., the platoon sergeant, offered to go with us to
find him.

We found him talking with a group of men in his center
squad. His clothes were covered with dry mud and his
hands were equally grimy. Even in the darkness I could
see that a heavy growth of beard covered his face below
his glasses. If I had not known him I could not have
picked him out as the platoon leader, so similar he was
in appearance to the GIs digging in the floors of the foxholes around us.

He escorted us around the platoon area, showing me
the locations of his three squads, his BARs, his bazookas.
Everywhere the men turned to talk with us. I spoke briefly with the three squad leaders: Staff Sergeant Walter N.
Stone, of Athens, Ga.; Sergeant Archie R. Jones, of El
Reno, Okla.; and Sergeant Jack Webster, an Oklahoman
whose adventure in running across an enemy minefield in
France at such a speed that the mines exploded harmless-
ly to his rear was a story told to every replacement upon
arrival in the company.

Any idea that I might have entertained that my visit
would bolster the morale of these men was overshadowed
by the effect the visit had on my own morale. How they
could smile and laugh and joke in their present condition
I could not see, but each man had a cheery word for me
as I approached. If I had possessed any misgivings that
these men would weaken under the hardships of their

cramped position and the adverse weather, they faded away into nothing. Their courage and fortitude made me admiringly envious and brought a lump to my throat.

But Lieutenant Antey was worried.

"I've got some men with terrible colds," he said. "This ass-hole weather. A couple of them have already asked to go back to the aid station and I know they should go, but we're so damned short of men. I told them to try to stick it out until tomorrow night, and if they don't feel any better then I'll send them on back."

I suggested if he had some men he felt were "too sick" then to send them to spend the night in my CP. "They can get a little sleep and come back down just before day in the morning," I said. I didn't really know what degree of sickness I expected him to interpret as "too sick."

As we reached the right flank of the platoon I noticed a man huddled in his foxhole, trembling violently beneath a blanket which covered his head.

Lieutenant Antey grasped him by the shoulder. "I thought I told you to get to digging this hole out deeper," he said sternly.

The blanket came off the soldier's head.

"You're putting me 'way off here by myself so I'll be killed!" he shouted, half-sobbing. "You want to see me killed! There's nobody over here but——."

"Shut up!" Antey said. "You want the whold god-damned German Army to hear you? Get to digging that hole. There're two men right here with you and the next hole's ten feet away. Nobody wants to see you killed."

We turned away. I looked back over my shoulder at the soldier.

"He's been like that ever since he's been with the platoon," Antey said. "Uses every excuse he can to get to the rear. He won't work to get himself warm like I try to get him to do."

"If he doesn't come around tonight, send him back to the CP," I said. "We can keep him there for a night and see how he turns out."

4
SHOOTING WAR

As we moved on toward the 2d Platoon, I decided I would exchange the 1st and 3d Platoons every three days. A variety of underbrush and several tall trees to the front of the 1st Platoon enabled them to move around slightly in daylight, and two pillboxes in the area enabled the men to dry their clothing. The 3d Platoon positions were miserable.

Private First Class Martin W. Carlson, a Pennsylvanian, stood guard at the entrance to the rearmost 2nd Platoon pillbox as we approached. He was a medic, although medics were usually attached to rifle companies from a battalion medical detachment and Carlson was a bona-fide member of Company I. When the company had found itself short a medic once in France, Carlson, who had had some medical training before being transferred to the infantry, took over and was a medic from that time on.

"They let anybody stand guard these days," I joked as we reached the pillbox.

"Yessir," Carlson smiled, "I figured I might as well pull my turn. My red crosses are inside."

We crouched to negotiate the low entrance to the pillbox. The entrance was the fighting aperture from which the Germans had defended the pillbox, since all emplacements in the area were designed for defense to our rear. Our men defended the pillboxes by digging a series of foxholes around the perimeter.

A flickering light from a German canteen with a crude wick maintained a pallid smoke inside the pillbox and cast hesitant shadows on the walls. The room was smaller than my CP but had a number of bunks and space for a table. The men's faces were black from the crude lantern.

"Got the gasoline out of the TD," someone said.

Lieutenant Brock explained that they had moved into the pillbox only a few hours before my arrival and were enjoying its relative comforts. They would bring in a number of men at a time to get some sleep, and during the daytime leave only a skeleton force in the foxholes outside. There seemed to be no fear that the Germans would take and reoccupy the emplacement as had beset the previous unit and caused it to fill in the entrance.

One of the squad leaders, Staff Sergeant John A. Kuziel, of McKees Rock, Pa., was in the pillbox at the time of my visit, along with Lieutenant Brock, Technical Sergeant Middlebrook, and Staff Sergeant Carl Orum, of Lincoln, Nebraska, the platoon guide.

Brock and Middlebrook accompanied us as we left the platoon CP and briefed us on the location of the three squads. We moved up the draw to a second pillbox where members of the squad commanded by Staff Sergeant Sam J. McGonigal, of Haskel, Okla., were digging shallow trenches to connect a defensive network of foxholes. Under a raincoat to protect it from the dampness stood a .50-caliber machine gun.

"We got that off the TD out there in the draw," Sergeant McGonigal said. "Got a lot of C-rations and beaucoup cigarettes."

Thus far I had not noticed any of the bodies of either German or American soldiers in the two platoon areas we had visited. Brock said there was one GI to the right of his CP, however, and two Germans fifty yards in front of McGonigal's squad. I told him of battalion's decision on removing the bodies, but we decided to wait until the next night when I could have a stretcher sent up with our supplies.

We visited the 3d Squad, commanded by Sergeant Robert J. Rouse, of Binghamton, N. Y., and prepared to move on to the 1st Platoon, moving back in the direction of the company CP to come upon the platoon from the rear.

I saw the rearmost pillbox, which the platoon had thus far not occupied. As we approached I could see the bodies of four Americans and six Germans draped in the very positions into which they had fallen in death. They seemed to grope with lifeless arms for the protection of the pillbox. My eyes were drawn irresistibly toward them but I forced myself to turn away.

We pushed through a hedgerow that ran parallel with the company front and came upon a group of men improving their foxholes. They directed us to a pillbox a few yards to their right front where they said we could find Lieutenant Goffigon. The area here was even darker than the surroundings for the tall trees shaded the faint glow of light which did successfully penetrate the clouds from the hidden moon.

Long came out of the pillbox upon the call of the guard, squeezing his way out of the entrance half-blocked by a large slab of concrete that had evidently been blown where it was by some feeble attempt to demolish the pillbox. He was a tall, straight Virginian, young, with square-cut features, and spoke with a Virginia accent.

He showed us about the area, calling attention to the fact that there was a third pillbox fifty yards to his front which he was not occupying, but where he kept an outpost during the day and a listening post nearby at night. He planned to dig open the entrance to the rear pillbox either later that night or the next.

We talked with Sergeant Harry J. Sickmiller, of Wauseon, Ohio, and Staff Sergeant Edward Clark, of Talking Rock, Ga., two of the squad leaders, and prepared to move on to the 3d Squad. Long stopped us to call my attention to a man digging a foxhole to my left.

"What do you think of that, Cap'n?" he asked.

I looked in the direction which he indicated. Five feet from the hole where the soldier dug indifferently lay a dead German, his chest and stomach bare and his stomach a mass of clotted blood and intestines.

"The hogs have been eatin' on him," Long said.

We moved on to the 3d Squad, commanded by Staff Sergeant Raymond Meade, of Centerville, Iowa, and also talked with the machine-gun section leader, Staff Sergeant Alan Diaz, of Laredo, Texas, whose guns were dug in in the squad area.

I told Long my plan for exchanging positions with the 1st and 3d Platoons at three-day intervals. Then Scotty and I turned to go back to the company CP. A soldier concealed in the hedge that followed the trail separating us from L Company challenged us as we passed. I hastily gave the password. An enemy mortar barrage began to fall several hundred yards to the rear of the company CP and we quickened our steps lest the mortarmen shorten their range.

It was one o'clock in the morning when we reentered the pillbox. I tried to settle down to write several letters but I could not concentrate. My thoughts kept returning to the courage and determination of the men in the foxholes. I began to sign my name to the bottom left corner of the envelopes which comprised the day's mail from the men in the company. Except for the official censorship stamp that would be imprinted on the envelope later by the mail orderly, Corporal Robert G. Brodhead, of Chicago, the letters would not be censored further. My thoughts returned again and again to the forward foxholes as I wrote. Cold, hungry, miserable infantrymen, scared as hell inside, but too brave to admit it.

Outside the night was quiet. I stepped outside the pillbox and found that the rain had set in again. An occasional barrage of friendly artillery whistled overhead and I silently thanked heaven that the missiles were not intended for us. Conversations with the platoons over the telephone revealed that quiet prevailed to their front.

It was three o'clock when I suggested to Savage behind a stifled yawn that we awaken Blackburn and Lieutenant Flaim to take our places while we got some sleep.

I awoke shortly after eleven and ate a K-ration, reheating a canteen cup of coffee from the water can which the supply sergeant had brought up the night before. Sparky told me that Scotty had been zeroing his 60mm mortars all morning, firing at selected targets and recording the firing data so that the platoon leaders could call for specific concentrations in the event of trouble. An enemy machine gun had fired from a gate three hundred yards down the draw at men from the 2d Platoon who were investigating the abandoned tank destroyer. Lieutenant Brock had called for mortar fire and the weapon had not fired again.

The first enemy shelling of the day came in shortly after I awoke. It was intended for the 3d Platoon but it fell without damage well to the rear. It was the vanguard

60mm Mortar

of three other barrages that came in during the after-noon but did no damage other than to increase our nervousness.

Night settled down all too quickly. The darkness soon enveloped even the slanting rain that continued to plague the forward platoons. Conversations with the platoon leaders revealed that colds were growing steadily worse. Antey had two men whom he felt obliged to send back to the aid station and Brock had another, an assistant squad leader. Antey said he was sending the man I had seen shaking so violently in his foxhole the night before to spend the night at my CP. He was afraid that after all he might be really ill. He was complaining now of a pain in his side.

I was waiting for the arrival of the supply jeep when an excited whistling came over the sound-powered telephone. I recalled the excitement of the previous night and looked at my watch. It was almost the same time, a few minutes after seven o'clock.

"We hear the tank again, Cap'n." It was Lieutenant Goffigon. "It's a helluva lot closer now than it was last night. Seems to have slipped up on us, and it's headed this way!"

It might have been the calmness of Long's voice or the fact that I was no longer a virgin to the nocturnal visits of the enemy's tracked vehicles, or it might have been the comforting knowledge of the big antitank guns emplaced around the farmhouse, but the overwhelming fear that had engulfed me with the first event was absent now. In its place was a spine-tingling excitement.

It was a matter of minutes before I had an artillery officer on the battalion telephone and had requested the same concentration we had used the night before with the range shortened one hundred yards. He said he would fire three rounds and we could adjust from them.

The time between the call and the overhead whistle of the artillery shells seemed much shorter than it had the previous night.

"I couldn't see those, Cap'n," Middlebrook said, "but they sounded good. Can't tell too much by sound, of course." He paused briefly. "Wait a minute . . . the sonofabitch is taking off to the rear! Tell 'em to increase the range three hundred and let 'em have it!"

I hastily repeated the instructions to the artillery. He said, "Roger," he'd fire for effect. I tapped my fingers on the table until I heard the low boom of the big guns to the rear and knew that the artilleryman's signal would be forthcoming soon.

"On the way!"

"Roger," I said. Then into the other phone: "On the way, Middlebrook."

I waited for Middlebrook's sensing. Then: "We've hit something, Cap'n. There's a fire blazed up bigger'n hell. It's lighting everything up around here as bright as day. Sounds like ammunition popping off."

The artillery officer said he would fire nine more for good measure.

Willie had been on guard again outside the CP. He came in gesticulating wildly with the news that we'd hit a tank and "the sonofabitch is burning like all hell!"

I turned the phone over to Savage and went with Willie to the entrance of the pillbox. Before I stepped out into the open I could see the light from a huge blaze illuminating the countryside. The flames flickered on the walls of the farmhouse. We ran up the sloping walkway to the trail and I looked to the front. The blaze was spectacular, but disappointing. The fire had burned down from its original height and the burning outlines of a haystack were plainly visible. Ears too eagerly pitched for the noise of the destruction of an enemy vehicle must have perceived the sound of exploding ammunition.

I went back inside and explained the situation to the artillery officer. He seemed equally disappointed and asked if that was all.

"We're a bit short of ammunition here," he said. "I think I'll connect you with the big guns and you can zero in a concentration with them. They don't fire too much, and we'd do well to save our ammunition until you definitely locate something."

The fire-direction center of the 15th Field Artillery Battalion, the supporting artillery with 155mm guns, answered. I gave the officer the approximate coordinates from my map of a proposed close-in concentration. From his overlay of my positions he judged that I was firing too close to my lines with the big guns, so he increased the range two hundred yards, saying that we could pull it in closer if the first rounds seemed safe.

Middlebrook was the eyes of the three-way team. I warned all platoons to have everyone keep close in his foxhole, and we soon had a concentration plotted which scattered fragments as far back as my command post. L Company called to see if we didn't think we were hitting a bit close, but Middlebrook and the platoon leaders were overjoyed at the promised protection which the close-in concentration afforded. We pulled in two hundred yards closer than the original safety allowance. The big shells seemed to land almost on top of our forward foxholes, but the riflemen, hiding deep in their holes from the whirring fragments, were delighted. The artilleryman said it would be concentration Queen 163.

Sergeant Neafach arrived with the supplies shortly after eight o'clock, and the three men who were sick with colds climbed aboard. The man from the 3d Platoon whom I had seen shaking so violently in his foxhole had arrived, but I sent him to bed in one of the rear bunks of the CP pillbox. Perhaps he would be over his spell by morning. The supply jeep, driven by Private First Class Earl Hayes, of Perrysville, Ohio, pulled almost noiselessly to the rear.

A check of the supply items revealed that there were cold hamburgers with bread and coffee to supplement the K-ration diet. The stretcher for removing the bodies was also there.

When the battalion messengers arrived I noticed that the man from the 3d Platoon continued to shake violently, as if he were freezing despite the six blankets we had placed over him. He continued to complain of pain in his side, and despite his reputation as a goldbrick, I was worried about him.

I sent him to the rear with the messengers to report to the aid station and called the battalion medical officer to pay particular attention to his case. The aid station returned the call shortly to tell me they had evacuated him. I was relieved that I had not delayed longer in sending him to the rear.

He had acute appendicitis.

The 1st Platoon carrying detail took with them the stretcher for removing the bodies. I apologized to Long for having to order the men to carry out the gruesome task, but the morale effect of the bodies in the area was bad, and it was common decency that the men be given proper burial as soon as possible even though they were not from our own outfit.

I did not ask what the platoons did with the German dead. We had planned to bury them in one of the pillboxes, sending their identification papers to the rear for proper report to the International Red Cross, but now we were occupying all the pillboxes in the area. I presumed that they took them forward of our lines and left them there but I did not question. They brought the papers to my CP.

I knew that the 2d Platoon had no difficulty with the German dead. The only two corpses were fifty yards from their forward foxholes. The morning after my visit with them the bodies were gone. Perhaps even as I had visited them the Germans had sneaked up and taken the bodies away.

The two men from the 1st Platoon who were detailed to carry the dead Americans to the base of a power pole a few yards in rear of my CP made two trips before they stopped in the CP around midnight. Sweat rolled from their faces and the scent of death from their bodies quickly filled the room and was nauseating. The job was too much for two men, they said. The bodies were heavy after more than a week of death.

I disliked ordering two more men to share the distasteful task but I called the 2d Platoon to provide help. I apologized to the men for having to detail them to the job and explained the situation to them.

"Looks like if we got to stay up here and get killed, somebody else could haul our f——g bodies away," one of them said.

The four men stopped back by the CP around two o'clock when their task was completed. I tried to ignore the smell of death that they brought with them, and invited them to have a smoke. They remained for some time talking and heating coffee over a cardboard fire. They said the rain had stopped again but that it seemed to be getting colder.

The night settled down to noises that were becoming routine. A barrage of our own artillery shells whistled overhead on a harassing mission. A telephone call from battalion told me that K Company thought an enemy patrol of six men had slipped through their lines. I warned the platoons to be on the alert and Savage told the guards outside to pay particular attention to the rear. A guard challenged a wire crew from L Company checking the line to their platoon CP in the farmhouse. K Company called to say that they had found what they had thought to be an enemy patrol was actually a few head of cattle. I called the platoons again. Savage notified the guards. The switchboard operator called and said, "Just checking the line, sir." The night wore on.

I awoke the next morning at ten o'clock and stepped outside the pillbox. The sun was shining down with a light so intense that I blinked involuntarily and rubbed my eyes. The effect, after the days of rain and overcast skies, was exhilarating. All seemed right with the world and I wondered why we must be huddling in pillboxes and foxholes shooting at other men a few hundred yards away. It seemed ridiculous and insane.

A glance to the rear of the pillbox brought me sternly back to reality. The bodies of the GIs the men had removed the night before were stacked beside the power pole. The blanket used in covering the stretcher was wrapped around the top body, and only the top of the dead soldier's head protruded, his long blond hair blowing gently in the wind and shining in the sunlight. How peaceful they looked, lying there on the cold, bleak hill, stacked like cordwood, oblivious to the sparkling sunshine. They would be just as oblivious to the cold and the rain to come and bursting mortar and artillery shells and threats of enemy counterattacks.

I turned away and went back inside the pillbox. Hurriedly fashioning a K-ration breakfast. I joined the group of headquarters men sitting around the entrance talking and smoking. I brought out my shaving equipment, and for the first time in a week I shaved and for the first time in four days I washed my face and hands. I felt rejuvenated. I put up my shaving equipment and returned to sit near the pillbox entrance and soak up the invigorating warmth of the sunshine. For the first time since we had moved into the defensive position I was completely warm.

The beautiful day was marred by two enemy artillery barrages but it ended all too soon, nevertheless. Night settled down once again, night with its weary early hours of activity when I would sit nervously by the phones and expect to hear an artillery or mortar barrage fall at any minute with tragic effects to the men of the company as they moved about their early evening tasks—and then its long, dreary hours of quiet in which I waited expectantly for I knew not what. The supply jeep came and was gone. L Company called to complain that my supply jeep was breaking the wires to their platoons. The runners from battalion came and were gone. Two more men from the 3d Platoon, sick with colds, arrived to spend the night in the pillbox in an effort to avoid turning in to the aid station. They would return to their platoon at dawn.

Long and Antey decided to make their shift in platoon positions beginning at midnight. The exchange went slowly. I listened with ears primed with fear for the sounds that would mean an enemy attack while the men were engaged in the shift. Four o'clock came. Lieutenant Antey called to say that the exchange of positions was completed.

Four o'clock and sleep.

I awoke at ten for the start of the fourth day in the pillbox. It was a day of K-rations, of glorious sunshine, of adjusting artillery fire, of testing telephone lines after enemy shelling, of signing one's name to the envelopes of countless letters, of requesting supplies from battalion, of one and a hundred little things that were becoming more and more routine. But always there was the deep, fearful dread of the enemy mortar shell that dropped unheralded from the sky, of the artillery round that screeched a fiendish warning as it approached—and the deep dread too of the darkness that would come tonight just as it had come last night and just as it would come the next night and the next. And any night the darkness might release a horde of fanatical German soldiers eager to kill and drive us from our holes and pillboxes, or perhaps a flame-throwing half-track spouting its flaming oily death into the deepest recesses of the pillboxes.

But the night came and pressed on. Three men were evacuated with high temperatures from colds. The mail orderly brought the first mail we had received since we left France. And the night wore on. It became increasingly difficult to stay awake. I gave up at three o'clock and succumbed to the momentary soothing peace of sleep.

Colonel Tuttle called to talk with me at eight o'clock. Sparky told him I was sleeping, but I heard him and got up, mentally marking off the beginning of the fifth day in the pillboxes. The Colonel apologized for waking me. A number of our planes would be over to strafe and bomb German positions the next day. He wanted coordinates from my map of likely targets for the fighters.

Sparky told me that an alert BAR man in the 2d Platoon had killed two Germans just after dawn. He had picked up a squad of men moving along a dirt road almost a half-mile away. The Germans evidently thought it wasn't light enough to be seen. With another man observing the strike of his tracer bullets with field glasses, the soldier had traversed the length of the squad with his automatic rifle. Two Germans fell. The others made away in a ditch beside the road.

A German machine gunner from high on the ridge to our left flank opened up with long-range fire on the area around the farmhouse before I could get back to sleep. The bullets whined inches above the top of our pillbox. I tried to adjust artillery on his position, but he was evidently firing from a pillbox and my fire proved ineffective. His bursts of fire caused no casualties but kept us more confined than usual. My mortarmen were pinned to their cellar in the rear shed the remainder of the day.

Schmisser MP–40, "Burp Gun"

"The sonso'bitches won't even let a man take a crap," Willie said.

I remembered that the day was more than just October 8. It was Sunday. We would soon have been in the positions for a week. I wondered again how much longer we would be there—if some morning orders would come to assault the high ridge to our front, or it welcome news of relief by another unit would come. But other than the realization that it was Sunday, there was little difference for us in the day. Church services were held in Grofkampkenberg but there was no practicable way our men could attend.

Battalion called shortly before dark. A coded message told me that a patrol from Company L would leave around seven o'clock in an effort to silence an enemy pillbox that had been giving them trouble from their left front. I was to get battalion clearance for all artillery or mortar fires I might call for during the time they were out.

The Germans were nervous when night came. The noise of a burp gun[1] would echo across the hills from far to the right. An answering burst would telegraph its nervous message from our front. Minutes later the same weapon would fire again. Another burst would come from our left front and another from the left flank, emphasizing the horseshoe-like position which we held. The nervousness was like a malignant disease that ate itself up and down the line and back again.

The tracked vehicle that had so alarmed me several nights before returned again shortly after seven o'clock. I discussed it with the platoon leaders and we decided that it must be a supply vehicle that brought up food every night. We would ignore it unless it came closer.

A rapid burst of small-arms fire came from the direction of the L Company patrol. Then three faint explosions. Then quiet. Thirty minutes later another burst of fire sounded from farther to the left; then quiet. The patrol must have met resistance on one route and then tried another, I thought. The second burst of fire must have meant that they were discovered again. I wondered if there were casualties.

The supply jeep came and was gone again, taking with it two more men for the sick list. Temperatures from colds were climbing. Many men who should be in bed were sticking it out in their holes for "just one more day" and then "just one more day." The wracking coughs must have telegraphed the location of our positions to the enemy.

A grenadier from the 3d Platoon heard a noise in the brush to his front. He fired a rifle grenade. The 60mm mortars fired a mission for the 2d Platoon, their muzzle blasts lighting up the back of the farmhouse with an orange flame as they coughed out their projectiles. A few rounds of enemy artillery fell in the draw to our right. We tested our phones.

The night settled down to an ominous silence.

---

[1] A machine-pistol, so called by GIs because of its guttural noise in firing, stemming from a much higher cyclic rate of fire than our weapons have.

5

ONE ROUND AT A TIME

It seemed that I had been asleep only a few minutes when I awoke. The pillbox was a mass of men moving about with apparently no pattern. A deep, dull throbbing filled my head, accentuated by a fierce pounding that pushed relentlessly against my temples.

I jumped from the bunk with a start. The throbbing in my head was a big gun firing; the man seated there by the table was covered with a dull brown dust; blood was streaming from a gash on his forehead!

"A tank's firing right at us, Cap'n," Sparky said excitedly. "They hit the shed with the mortarmen in it. Sergeant Patterson got a cut on the head."

I tried to shake the cobwebs of sleep from my brain. I had been asleep for hours. It was daylight. It was eight o'clock in the morning.

I moved over to the wounded man. He was Sergeant Lee Patterson, a North Carolinian and one of the squad leaders from the mortar section. The wound was bleeding profusely. Another man held a handkerchief immediately below it to prevent the blood from running into the sergeant's eyes.

"It's not bad," the sergeant said. "Just a cut from some loose brick. It was flying all around the cellar when the shells hit. Looks worse than it really is, I guess."

One of the men from the CP group yelled to us from the entrance, "They've hit the house! They've hit the f——g house! It's burning like all hell!"

For one awful moment realization of what it would mean if the farmhouse burned swept over me. There was no other place for all those men inside to go . . . those that escaped. They could never crowd into this one pillbox. And now the entire hill would be completely exposed.

I pushed my way through the crowd of men and reached the entrance. The heat of flames struck me as I reached the outside. Another soldier ran across from the rear shed to the pillbox. The tank fired again and a shell swished close overhead.

I realized with relief that the roaring mass of flame was not the farmhouse but the big shed that had served as our latrine in the rear. It was half full of straw that evidently quickly fed the hungry flame. The smaller shed whose basement had housed two squads of my mortar section was a shambles of broken timbers. Just past the shed the abandoned tank destroyer was being greedily consumed by flame.

The tank or SP gun was firing from the left flank from the same vicinity as the machine-gunner who had harassed us the preceding day. The armor-piercing shells whirred inches above the top of the pillbox.

The flames from the shed leaped higher and higher, fanned by a steady breeze from the rear that pushed them closer and closer to the farmhouse. The men inside the house must have been watching it even more anxiously than I. I felt relieved when I heard the crackle of the farmhouse roof and realized that it was a slate roof and would not burn.

"How'd it start?" I asked of no one in particular.

Sergeant Tom Castro, of San Antonio, Texas, one of the mortar squad leaders, answered. "We were all asleep in the cellar of the shed. I guess it was the first shell that hit square through the door above us. It ricocheted down into the cellar and bounced around the walls. Knocked brick everywhere. The second one hit right after. Then they hit the TD. We took off over here."

I noticed that all the men from the mortar squads were covered with brown dust from the shattered brick.

"I don't see how that f——g shell missed getting one of us," another man said. "There were ten of us in that one little cellar."

The enemy gun continued to fire. I went back into the pillbox and called the artillery observer in the farmhouse to ask if he could spot the enemy weapon but he had been unable to pick it up.

Lieutenant John B. Fudickar, of Pendleton, Ore., the antitank platoon leader, spoke over the phone before I put it down. He had a man who was hit pretty badly and wanted to bring him over to my CP. They might hit the house. The Kraut gun had already knocked out one of his 57mm antitank guns.

I called for litter bearers from the aid station to come to the L Company CP, and Lieutenant Fudickar and three men brought the casualty over on a makeshift stretcher made from two rifles and a blanket. The aid man from the L Company platoon across the trail gave him a shot of morphine.

"He was out taking a crap when the shootin' started," someone said. "Helluva thing to shoot a man with his britches down."

The soldier had a deep gash in his stomach from a piece of sharpnel.

The aid man dressed Sergeant Patterson's wound. Two men got the litter we had used to remove the bodies from our area, and they started back towards L Company's CP with the casualty. Sergeant Patterson could walk.

The tank stopped firing, and the excitement was over almost as quickly as it had begun. The mortarmen made running trips to the cellar of the wrecked shed and brought their dusty equipment to the CP.

There seemed to be no other spot for emplacing the mortars. The two sheds had provided the only conceal- ment the weapons had enjoyed. I called the L Company commander, Captain Walter J. Eisler, of Butler, Pa., and explained the situation. He said he thought he could dou- ble up his men in the pillboxes to our rear and give us the use of the emplacement seventy-five yards from my CP. That seemed to be the only solution. Scotty made a hur- ried reconnaissance and returned in a matter of minutes. He could put two of the mortars in the entrance of the rear pillbox, but that left one weapon still exposed behind the farmhouse.

But Sergeant Castro's squad was soon digging away at the sloping forward side of the entrance to our CP. We were to have a 60mm mortar embedded in our front door.

Captain Anderson telephoned that the fighter planes should be over shortly and that we should display our

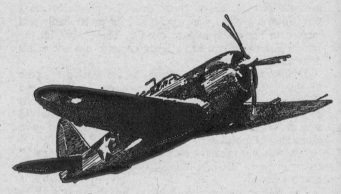

P–47

identification panels in front of our forward foxholes. We
were excited at the prospect of seeing the fighters in action
and chattered like excited school children, but we had no
sooner displayed the bright orange and rose panels than
we were ordered to pull them in. The planes would not
be over until shortly after noon and they had decided not to
use panels. I reluctantly ordered the platoons to pull them in.

The sun came out. I was seated at the table inside the
pillbox when the first drone of the fighter planes reached
my ears. Battalion had warned us against rubbernecking,
and I in turn had cautioned the platoons. But not a man
would miss seeing the demonstration for any amount of
pillbox safety. My company headquarters and Sergeant
Castro's mortar squad formed an impromptu cheering
section at the mouth of the pillbox.

Five sleek P-47s, their wings shimmering in the sunlight, droned high above us in the blue and crossed our
position. Three of the planes seemed to stand guard above
the German-held ridge to our front while the other two
peeled off into graceful dives down, down, down toward
the German pillboxes. Not a shot was fired at them. Every
German in the area must have been hugging the bottom
of his hole for dear life.

The two planes seemed to be on reconnaissance; they
did not fire their cannon nor drop their bombs but

climbed gracefully back into the sky for a rendezvous with their companions. Then they appeared to decide that now was the time. Each plane circled high into the air and came down with the skill and grace of a pirouetting dancer upon its target, the bullets from its cannon beating a staccato chant of death as it dived on the Germans below.

Someone behind me said, "Oh, them goddamned beautiful birds."

We watched in silent admiration as the planes climbed once again. They appeared to be working individually now upon previously assigned targets. Three of the P-47s dived again, their cannon fire beating a path on the ground before them. The other two came in on their targets in gliding dives. Someone cried "Look!" and we saw two single bombs dropping toward their targets. One crushing explosion followed the other. A third plane headed in on a bomb run. Its missile found its mark—the pillbox which had housed the machine-gunner who had harassed us the preceding day. Slabs of concrete cascaded into the air. We cheered.

"That was one of the targets we gave 'em," I said, proud somehow like a school kid who has his theme chosen for reading to the class.

Three of the planes climbed high into the sky and soared off to the rear. The others made a final strafing run and droned off into the distance to join their companions. Our cheering section began to break up as the men filed back into the pillbox. The Germans had not fired a single shot at any of the planes.

"Well, their work's all done for the day," someone said.

"Yeah," a mortarman answered, reaching for a shovel, "they'll go home now and have a short Scotch and a hot bath and shack up with some *mademoiselle* or some Limey wench. What a life!"

"Yeah, and draw a double salary for it," a headquarters man put in.

"That's the life for me."

Willie Hagan said, "Oh, dry up. You never had it so good."

The burning of the shed across the trail had destroyed our only latrine. The barn portion of the farmhouse made a satisfactory substitute, but continued shellings and harassing small-arms fire made us wary of crossing the open space to the house. As a solution we began to dig a latrine on the sloping back side of the pillbox entrance. A group of men was working on the latrine when the first big shell came in.

The whirring, screaming approach of the shell preceded it, louder than any we had experienced before, as if a boxcar were hurtling through the air. When it hit, there was a resounding explosion that seemed to rock the very foundations of the pillbox. Flying shrapnel sprayed the trees around the farmhouse. Someone said, "My God! What was that?" The men who had been working outside more dived than ran into the pillbox. There was an excited exchange of words as each man gave his opinion of what the Nazis were throwing at us now. This must be the kitchen sink.

Silence fell over the group. A faint explosion from far behind the German lines came to our ears. A few seconds later came the whirr of the approaching shell, then the explosion. It was close. Little metal concussion taps on the walls of the pillbox reverberated with a metallic tinkle, announcing to us for the first time that they were there.

The face of each man bore a querulous expression, asking with his eyes for the explanation from the faces of his neighbors. Someone said the concussion would blow us apart if one of those babies should hit in the entrance. Another agreed. In the distance we heard the sound of the big gun firing again. Someone cautioned quiet. We waited expectantly. There followed the scream of the shell, the explosion, the shrapnel spraying the trees around the farmhouse.

"Might as well let battalion in on the fun," I said. "They want shelling reports[1], so we'll give them one while it's going on."

Another shell exploded while I was getting headquarters on the phone. Captain Anderson answered.

"They're hitting us with a big baby this time, Andy," I said. Someone stepped to the door to take a compass

---

[1] By comparing shelling reports from areas all along the front, the artillery might, by resection of azimuth readings taken on the sound of the enemy gun, determine the approximate location of the enemy weapon.

azimuth on the sound of the gun firing. "I'm getting you an azimuth."

"We hear it back here," Captain Anderson said. "How long does it take to reach you?"

I looked at my watch. "Hold on," I said, "here comes one now."

The big gun boomed in the distance. The seconds ticked away. Thirteen seconds—fourteen seconds—the scream of the shell—I ducked unconsciously—fifteen seconds—sixteen seconds—seventeen sec—BOOM!

"That one was right on top of you, wasn't it?"

"Yeah. Damned close. Seventeen seconds. They seem to be trying for the farmhouse."

The soldier returned with the azimuth.

"One hundred and sixty-six degrees," I repeated into the phone.

A minute of silence. Then, again, the distant boom of the gun. The elapse of endless seconds. The crash of the shell. The spray of shrapnel.

"It's a railroad gun," Willie announced, authoritatively. "They had some of those bastards at Brest. They gave us hell 'till the air corps came over and knocked 'em out."

"I wish to hell the air corps would come over now."

"I take back everything I ever said about the air corps."

The shelling continued, one round at a time. They exploded to the right of us, to the left of us, to the rear of us, and to the front of us, but never, as we feared, in the entrance of the pillbox. And through it all, the target—if, indeed, the house was the target—stood unscathed.

We counted the rounds. We reached number thirteen and waited again for the distant report of the gun but it did not come.

The battalion adjutant, Captain James T. Noton, of Austin, Texas, telephoned around six o'clock. Division had set up a rest camp at Vielsalm, Belgium, and Company I must send fourteen men and one officer for a forty-eight-hour rest. They would leave from battalion headquarters at eight o'clock in the morning of October 11.

I begged to have the quota reduced since we were so short of men, but the answer was no. Sergeant Albin broke down the quota equally among the platoons, allowing one man from company headquarters. I designated Lieutenant Brock, over his protests, as the officer to go.

The Germans were nervous again when night came. Burp guns echoed up and down the line in the early part of the evening. They tossed in an artillery barrage around ten o'clock that fell to the rear of the CP but caused no damage. The 1st and 3d Platoons began their exchange of positions at eleven o'clock and were through shortly after one.

The night settled down to its routine noises. An outgoing artillery barrage whistled a goodbye message above the pillbox. Snores from the sleepers filled the room. Sometimes a sleeper would snore so loudly that I thought surely the enemy would hear, and I would awaken him and tell him to turn over. I didn't know what I expected the Germans to do if they heard it.

Savage sealed envelopes for me as I signed my name as censoring officer. I wondered how soldiers could write so much mail. One man had written his wife five different letters in the one day and enclosed them in as many different envelopes.

Two o'clock. I had had only four hours' sleep the preceding night and it began to tell on me now. I could hardly keep my eyes open. Two-thirty *Stay awake! Stay awake!*

"We'll have to turn in earlier tonight," I said to Savage. "I just can't seem to stay awake. Let's call it quits at three."

Savage sleepily mumbled his agreement.

I was nodding often as the hands of my watch neared three o'clock, awakening each time with a start and shaking my head in an effort to clear the sleep from my brain.

A shot rang out.

It seemed to come from the very entrance of the pillbox and was the cue that set off a fusilade of small-arms fire that reverberated back and forth among the hills. I could discern the slow chatter of one of our heavy machineguns, then the intermingling of the guttural tone of a burp gun. All the sounds seemed to emanate from the area around the farmhouse, as if every conceivable type of small arms vied to be heard above the accompanying noises.

The explosion of a German-type concussion grenade

joined the uproar. An American grenade exploded and its fragments whined through the air. A few rounds of mortar fire exploded above the din. I heard the guards scuffle and curse as they tripped on the entrance to the pillbox.

I was suddenly more afraid than I had ever been before. My body seemed weak all over, and I wondered if I had the strength to stand up. I opened my mouth to sound the alarm, and I wondered if anything would come out.

"Wake everybody up!" I shouted, surprised that words actually came forth. "I don't want anybody caught asleep in this damn pillbox."

We had waited long enough. The Germans had come.

6

"IT'S TOO DAMNED SERIOUS . . ."

The sound of the small-arms fire continued, heightened
by the explosions of dozens of light mortar shells.

The paroxysm of fear that gripped me left my body
trembling. I was not so much afraid of what was happening as I was of the horrible visions my mind had dreamed
up of what would happen should we fail to repulse the
attack. I visualized the mad dash to reach the entrance to
the pillbox to escape entrapment within, only to be met by
a hail of enemy fire or the hellish blast of a flame thrower.
My imagination ran a gantlet of evil.

*So this is a counterattack. Well, this is what you have
been waiting for. Now the company of veterans will find
out what it has in this youthful, inexperienced CO. Quit
shaking, dammit. Stop trembling all over. Get control of
yourself. Act like a soldier, goddammit! At least you can
impersonate an officer!*

Savage tried the battalion phone. The handle which
should have produced a ring made an unnatural grating
sound.

"The line's out," he cried. "I'll try the other line. Blackburn, get your radio set up outside."

The sound of the battle rose to a crescendo of crackling small-arms fire and booming mortars. The explosion
of fragmentation hand grenades sent pieces of steel whining into space in all directions. The mortarmen from
Sergeant Castro's squad stood poised near the door waiting for my word to begin dropping shells into the metal
tube outside. Men from my headquarters group lay half-
reclining on their elbows on their bunks, the dazed expression of sleep still on their faces.

Sparky tried the phone to the platoons. The line was

still in! The 1st Platoon wanted artillery fire to their left front and around the yellow farmhouse that stood between them and the town of Kesfeld to their front. The Krauts were hitting their left flank, and they could hear movement and shouting in German in the underbrush to their front. Technical Sergeant Eli Smith, of Baltimore, Md., the platoon sergeant, was on the phone. Long was outside the pillbox.

"I can't get through on the other wire either, Captain," Savage said. "I talked to the artillery observer in the house. His line's dead, too."

"That leaves the radio," I said and turned to Sparky. "Tell Scotty to fire his 60s for Goffigon. I don't want Castro to fire his. He's too close."

I hurried through the dark winding passageway from the pillbox. Blackburn was adjusting the longer of the two antennae for his 300 radio. The cord to which the speaker and receiver were attached enabled him to leave the box of the radio on the outside and pull the telephone-type receiver inside the entrance.

Overhead the tracer bullets from countless weapons etched a fantastic, fleeting pattern against the night sky. The firing seemed to come mainly from the front of L Company's right flank platoon seventy-five yards from us in front of the farmhouse, but I could occasionally discern the characteristic sound of our light machine guns firing and I knew that the first platoon was engaged. The German guns said, "Brrrrrrrrrrp." Our machine-guns answered, "Put-put-put-put-put."

The firing stopped abruptly. The mystery-laden silence was for a moment even more terrifying than the noise of the gunfire. Had the Germans broken through? Were they even now rushing toward the entrance to the pillbox?

It seemed like minutes that must have been only seconds before another single shot rang out and again set off the blaze of fireworks. The curtain of fire formed itself above us again.

Blackburn's efforts to get battalion on the radio rose above the din of the fire fight.

"Hello, Able One; hello, Able One"—the noise of the butterfly switch turning as he waited for an answer—but no answer—"Hello, Able One; hello, Able One; come in, Able One." The amplification of the radio lent an eerie quality to his voice, increasing its volume so that I thought it must surely direct the attacking Germans to the very spot.

The sudden cough of the 60mm mortars to my rear told me that Scotty had been ready and waiting the moment we called for fire. The dry, rasping cough of the weapons was like music. Behind me Sergeant Castro and his squad fretted because I did not let them fire.

"I can't get 'em, Cap'n," Blackburn said. His voice was half-frantic. "Battalion's sitting on their fat asses and haven't thought once of setting up their radio."

"Keep trying," I said, my voice shaking. "Maybe they'll get the lead out. We've got to get through." It sounded trite after I had said it.

I went back into the pillbox. "What does the 1st Platoon say now?" I asked. It was a stupid question but it gave me an excuse to go back inside the pillbox and I thought perhaps getting away from the damp night air at the entrance would lessen the shaking of my body. It didn't.

"The mortars are coming in fine," Sparky said, "but he still wants artillery. L Company must not be firing any mortars or artillery."

"Maybe their platoon line is out," I said. "I haven't heard anything but our 60s. Tell Scotty to shift left to L Company's front."

I checked my map in the light to know the concentration to call for should we succeed in getting battalion on the radio and stepped back to the entrance.

"Hello, Able One; hello, Able One; get Andy on. Get Andy on." It was Blackburn. He had gotten through.

I waited impatiently while the operator called Captain Anderson to the radio. I wondered if I could control the quiver in my voice when I talked with him. The sound of firing sputtered and died to only a few rifle shots. But then it increased once again to its rapid tempo, enlivened now by the sound of our mortar shells exploding close in to the front of the L Company platoon.

"Hello, Able One; this is Andy. Send your message. Over."

I took the receiver from Blackburn.

"Hello, Able One; this is Mac. Attack is hitting my left

flank and right flank of Love Company. Their lines must be out too. Fire us concentration 221. Over."

I shivered from a combination of the chill and the fear within me, and I knew I had failed to keep my voice from quivering.

"Roger. Wait."

The small-arms fire stopped almost as suddenly as it had begun. We waited expectantly in the pregnant silence for it to begin, but except for the sounds of the men in the pillbox behind me all was quiet. A hand grenade exploded and its fragments whined through the air. One of Scotty's mortars coughed rapidly three times. Then, silence.

"Hello, Able One; hello, Able One. Over."

"Hello, Able One. Over."

"Hello, Able One. Two-two-one on the way. Over."

"Hello, Able One. Roger. Wait."

A second later I heard the sound of the artillery pieces firing in rear of us, followed quickly by the whine of three outgoing shells. Even before they had exploded to our front three more explosions came from the rear and three more shells whistled overhead to explode in the draw to our front. I heard the last three shells of the concentration begin their outward journey.

"Maybe we can catch 'em on their way home," Blackburn said.

The concentration was perfect. I called for concentration 223, which would place fire to the front of the L Company platoon, and for a repeat on 221 to our front. I told Scotty to hold up on his mortar fire now that we were getting artillery. We would need the ammunition.

The threat had passed.

We signed off temporarily on the radio, leaving it open until just before dawn when a wire crew from battalion would repair our telephone lines. I went back into the pillbox. Almost half the men were already sound asleep again.

Bit by bit the story of the German attack materialized. A heavy machine gunner on the right flank of Company L had heard a noise to his front shortly before three o'clock. A figure loomed up before him only five feet away. For some reason the gunner had challenged instead of firing.

Browning HMG

The German fired his rifle in answer to the challenge, wounding the machine gunner in the shoulder and setting off the fireworks of the attack. But the machine gunner had killed the German who had wounded him.

The rest of the night was a nightmare of whining grenade fragments as the nervous GIs around the farmhouse tossed hand grenades at anything that moved. A wire-repair crew from L Company was almost hit by a grenade from one of the antitank men, and my guards feared for their lives as they stood in the open in front of the pillbox. I called Lieutenant Fudickar and asked that he stop his men from promiscuously throwing grenades. The situation improved but not before they had neatly killed two roving hogs.

It was five o'clock when I finally climbed into my bunk. I wondered what the men of my headquarters group thought of me as a company commander now. Had I been a complete failure? Had I done anything correctly? Was my fear as noticeable as I imagined it must have been? But perhaps they thought of me as one of them now that we had experienced our first action.

That was how I wanted it to be.

A man from L Company, moving about his foxhole the following morning, found a wounded German soldier a few feet away. He was taken prisoner and evacuated to battalion where he talked freely to interrogators. His story was telephoned to me, revealing that the prisoner was a member of a company of forty men who had been specially trained for retaking pillboxes and had moved into our area the preceding day. There were two such companies in the area. He had understood that tanks equipped with flamethrowers were to have been used in the assault, but he did not know what had happened to change the plans. They had been told that the pillboxes occupied by the Americans would be heavily stocked with K-rations and cigarettes, and that all they took would be divided among the men of the company. Their objectives were the farmhouse, the pillbox occupied by my command post, and the three pillboxes to the rear of my CP.

To reach the vicinity of their objectives they had guided on the glowing embers left from the early morning fire when the large shed to the rear of the house had burned. He had been only slightly wounded in the arm and could have escaped after the fight, but he wished to be taken prisoner by the Americans. It seemed to him that a large number of his comrades had been killed or wounded in the attack, but, yes, he thought they would make another attempt to recapture the pillboxes.

An enemy tank that fired on the forward platoons and avoided all efforts to silence it with artillery by moving around to different positions awoke me at nine o'clock. It caused no damage except harassment and finally ceased firing after an hour.

Private Zellin, one of the battalion messengers, arrived midway the afternoon with a stranger whom he introduced as Fred Bankers, a war correspondent with the Associated Press. I expressed surprise that Zellin had brought him over the exposed route in daylight; except for my reconnaissance on the day we moved into the position, we had avoided going across the crest of the hill except at night.

Mr. Bankers was writing a feature story on life inside the Siegfried Line. He took the names and addresses of most of the company headquarters men and Sergeant Castro's mortar squad and asked questions about the life we were living.

"Well, if you're from Boston," he said to Butare, the 2d Platoon runner, "I suppose what you'd like best about now is a dish of good old Boston baked beans. Right?"

"That's right," Butare smiled. "Nothing better."

The correspondent turned to Private Croteau. "And how about you?" he asked. "What would you like best from the States about now?"

Croteau was sullen and seemed to object to the correspondent's questions.

"I've got nothing to say," he said morosely.

The other men in the pillbox looked up with a sudden interest in what was being said. The correspondent seemed to miss the tenseness which his question and the answer had developed.

"Oh, come now," he said. "Surely there's something we could say you're missing for the folks back home."

"I've got nothing to say," Croteau said with an inflection in his voice.

I looked at his eyes. There was a curious flame kindling there that caused his eyes to sparkle in the flickering candlelight of the pillbox. The correspondent started to speak again.

"OK," Croteau interrupted. "I've got something to say. Tell them it's too damned serious over here to be talking about hot dogs and baked beans and things we're missing. Tell them it's hell, and tell them there're men getting killed and wounded every minute, and they're miserable and they're suffering. Tell them it's a matter more serious than they'll ever be able to understand. Spread it on thick, and leave off the sweet syrup that all the others write about" . . . there was a choking sob in his voice . . . "tell 'em it's rough as hell. Tell 'em it's rough. Tell 'em it's rough, serious business. That's all. That's all."

A tense silence followed his outburst. I was slightly embarrassed by the happening and attempted to cover up.

"Croteau's right," I said. "Try to bring out what a wonderful job these riflemen are doing over here, a little of the hell they're going through. And when they do get home, those of them that do, that there's nothing on this earth the people at home can do for them in return that would be half what they deserve."

Zellin left with the correspondent at dusk to return to battalion. A few minutes after their departure an enemy

light artillery barrage centered to the rear of the farmhouse but there was no damage. I figured that the two
men had had sufficient time to leave the area before the
barrage came.

Sergeant Albin spoke to me about Croteau.

"I'm sending him in to the aid station tonight, if that's
all right with the Cap'n," he said. "He's been running a
temperature with a cold for three days, but he's tried not
to say anything about it. And you heard him this afternoon. His nerves are shot. He's been coming to this ever
since he got pretty badly shaken up in that pillbox explosion at Brest."

Croteau left us that evening.

Night, with its nerve-wracking ordeal of darkness, settled down around us again. The supply vehicle arrived and
Sergeant Albin called the platoon to send carrying details for their supplies. The platoons did not want to send
carrying details at the moment. The darkness seemed
"just too quiet right now . . . something must be up." It
must be only nervousness, I told myself, but I agreed for
them to wait. The 1st and 2d Platoons would send men
as soon as "things look clear." The 3d Platoon had everything they needed for the night and would like to wait
until shortly before dawn. Something might happen while
their carrying party was gone, and they were so damned
short of men.

The nervousness of the rifle platoons brought the company's low strength to my attention. Croteau had been
the thirteenth man to be evacuated since our arrival in
the pillbox positions. The strength of the company on the
night we had moved in was fifty-six below normal. The
thirteen evacuations had reduced the total to 123. Only
eighty of these were in the actual forward fighting positions . . . eighty men to defend a five-hundred-yard front
with a two-hundred-yard gap on the right flank.

Then I remembered that fourteen men and one officer
must leave before dawn the next morning for forty-eight
hours in the division rest camp. Two of these men would
come from the mortar section and company headquarters, leaving only sixty-eight men and two officers in the
forward foxholes. The thought staggered me.

An enemy artillery barrage swished into the area

around ten o'clock and brought the guards scurrying to the protection of the pillbox. I was grateful for the barrage at the moment the shells were falling; it seemed to break the mystery of the silence around us. But when it was over the atmosphere seemed more tense than before.

The 1st and 2d Platoons sent their carrying parties for ammunition and supplies at eleven o'clock. The atmosphere was as tense as ever, they said, but they knew they had to send for the supplies eventually.

I stepped outside the pillbox to urinate. The night was gripped again in a death-like stillness. The mysteries to the front were cloaked in an all-enveloping veil of dense darkness. Someone near the farmhouse threw a hand grenade. A squeal of terror told me that the local pig population was having difficulty with the antitank gun crews again.

I went back inside and continued my lonely vigil beside the telephones, stifling yawn after yawn as I tried to write a letter, turning instead to censoring the stack of outgoing mail.

The hands of my watch showed that it was approaching one o'clock. I stared at the watch with half-seeing eyes and thought of the time pattern of the past German attacks. They had struck the company on our right at one o'clock in the morning three days before we relieved the 28th Division company. Last night's attack against L Company and my left flank was set at three o'clock. The time neared the hour, and the love of consistency which history and fable have given the Germans preyed upon my mind. If they attacked tonight it would most likely be on the hour.

I strained my ears in an effort to hear through the pillbox door and into the murky blackness beyond for some sound—I knew not what. My fear and nervousness increased with each passing minute until I thought I would surely scream.

The loud jangle of the telephone bell made me jump with a start. Savage was dozing (*how do you do it?*); I would take it.

"I Company, Captain MacDonald speaking."

"Just checking your line, sir." It was the operator.

The door of the pillbox seemed to me a megaphone in the stillness. I asked the operator if he could not leave our switch open and whistle for us instead of ringing.

"Yessir. We'll whistle for you, sir."

"And check the line every fifteen minutes or so. Something might happen."

I checked the lines to the platoons. Everything was quiet but the quietness was loaded with suspense.

"It's too goddamned quiet, Cap'n," Middlebrook said.

Lieutenant Antey and Sergeant Webster had left the 3d Platoon area to investigate two pillboxes several hundred yards to their right rear with the possibility of using them for the men of the platoon to rest in the daytime.

The rapid chatter of an automatic rifle somewhere along the company front broke the stillness.

"What was that?" I asked.

Long said, "It was from my platoon. I'll check and call you back."

I told the platoons to send the men to go to the division rest camp to the CP at three o'clock. That would allow time for them to get to battalion before daylight.

Long said he had a report on the BAR that fired in his area. Someone or something had set off one of the grenade "booby traps" his men had set to the front of their position and a soldier had fired toward the noise. But now all was quiet.

I looked at my watch. Five minutes until two.

Maybe it will be two o'clock tonight. They haven't used that time before. Yes, tonight it will be two o'clock.

I prepared myself for the sound of the first shot or the first round of artillery fire that would be designed to soften up our position before they would move in for the kill. The KILL! I shuddered. But two o'clock came and two o'clock went, and all was quiet. I tried to laugh at my fears.

Savage and I talked again. I was getting sleepy. Savage was yawning. Somewhere a hand grenade exploded. I held my breath. Everybody's nervous, I thought.

Five minutes until three. Four minutes until three. Three minutes. Two minutes. One minute. *Now, now, now!* But not a sound. Perhaps my watch was a few minutes fast. Perhaps they had been delayed in the jump-off. Perhaps my nervousness was kindling my imagination.

You're frightening yourself for nothing. They took a beating last night. They won't be back tonight.

Three-fifteen. *God, but I'm sleepy.* Three-twenty. *I*

can't keep my eyes open for another minute. Three twenty-five.

"Savage, what d'you think? I'm so sleepy I can't hold my eyes open."

"Go on and get some sleep, Captain. You've been up almost all the time we've been in this goddamned place. Colonel Tuttle called this morning and wanted to know when the hell you did any sleeping."

"Oh, I get as much as anybody else. The Colonel just sleeps when I do."

"You're gonna get yourself sick, Captain."

"OK. We'll wake Sparky and Blackburn in a few minutes. I hate to be asleep when anything happens. It scares the hell out of me, and I can't think like I want to."

Three-thirty. *Maybe they'll try the half-hour tonight.* Three thirty-five. *Oh, hell, what am I worrying about? If they didn't hit us at three, they're not coming. I'll get some sleep.*

I woke Sparky. He and Blackburn changed places with Savage and me and began to heat themselves cups of coffee. I called the platoons to make sure the men for the division rest area were on the way. They were starting out now. I cautioned Sparky to wake me if the slightest disturbance occurred but I knew they wouldn't wake me unless it seemed absolutely necessary.

I climbed into the bunk. It was warm where Sparky had been lying. I must have fallen asleep before I even pulled the covers over me. All was quiet.

It seemed that I had been asleep for hours when I awoke suddenly with a start. Sparky's voice came to me from somewhere in the distance. "I'm trying to get artillery! I'm trying to get artillery!" Blackburn's voice was somewhere there beside it. "Get me Captain Anderson! Get me Captain Anderson!" But what was that noise in the background? What was that pounding? Someone must be beating on the pillbox with a sledgehammer. What was that deafening noise?

I jumped from my bunk. My feet stung from the rough contact with the concrete floor. That was artillery and mortars exploding in my head. I couldn't think. I shook my head sharply to clear the sleep from my brain. The Germans had come again. And what mortars and artillery!

Good God, they must be firing every weapon for miles around.

There was a wild look in Sparky's eyes.

"They've hit all three platoons, Cap'n," he cried. "Head on. They're pounding the hell out of 'em. Worst barrage I ever heard. Worst barrage I ever heard, Cap'n."

7

NINE LONG DAYS

The artillery bombardment continued. Through the maze of explosions I could discern the crushing sound of the big railroad gun which had bombarded us two days before. The center of the shelling passed from the CP pillbox to the pillbox which housed the two mortar squads and on to the L Company pillboxes and back again like a pianist running a scale, with a few rounds exploding directly above us always like accompanying chords. The barrage was deafening.

The old fear swelled up again within me and left my body cold and clammy. Would I never learn to stop trembling? Would I never learn to be calm like the others? Or just how calm *were* the others?

I reached for the platoon phone. Thank God it was still in. Middlebrook was on.

"For God's sake, get us some artillery, Cap'n," he cried. "They're knocking the hell out of us. Small arms and burp guns and this goddamned mortar and artillery fire. I never saw such a barrage. We've got to get some help or we'll never stop them."

Blackburn had Captain Anderson on the battalion phone and I wondered how the line had survived the shelling. I took the phone from his outstretched hand.

The men in the pillbox were all awake now. The mortar squad stood ready to move to their weapon the moment the artillery should lift. I told Sergeant Albin to get everybody ready to move outside on the double. We might have to fight from the slit trenches on top of the pillbox if they broke through the rifle platoons. I lived in horror that someone would be trapped inside the pillbox.

"This is Mac. Andy," I said into the phone. "They're

knocking the hell out of us. Damnedest artillery I ever saw. Give us some artillery all across our front. They've hit all three platoons."

"Give me the concentration numbers," Captain Anderson said. "There'll be a delay. They're hitting K Company too, and they've got a priority mission[1] on the artillery. I can give it to you as soon as they've——"

The phone sputtered and was dead.

"Oh, Christ! Get the radio, Blackburn!"

Blackburn dived for the entrance. Savage worked with the battalion phone but it was no use. The line was out. Middlebrook continued to call frantically for supporting fire. I wondered how much longer it would be before the platoon lines would go out.

"For God's sake, hurry, Cap'n," Middlebrook said. His voice was half-frantic. "I've got two wounded men here in my pillbox now. God knows how many more are out there."

I called for the 1st and 3d Platoons. Long said he was catching hell from the barrage, but the main attack seemed to be across the open ground against the other two platoons. Sergeant Garcia with the 3d Platoon said he had one man hit already that he knew of. They were saturating his position with fire. SP fire seemed to be coming from somewhere. Lieutenant Antey and Sergeant Webster had not returned from the check of the pillboxes to the rear.

I turned the phone over to Sparky. For the first time I noticed that Lieutenant Brock and three men from the 2d Platoon were at the rear of the pillbox, their faces drawn and black from the crude lights they had used in their platoon's pillbox CP. They had arrived to go back to the division rest area.

"Quite a send-off we're giving you," I said, suddenly afraid for the other men scheduled to go to the rest area. They should have already left their platoons and might have been caught in the enemy barrage.

Brock smiled.

I hurried out the L-shaped entranceway. Blackburn had set up his radio outside and was huddled in the entrance

---

[1] All artillery in direct support of the regiment assigned to one mission.

with the receiver and speaker. It was after midnight and the call sign for the day had changed.

"Hello, Tare One; hello, Tare One," he called.

The radio was strangely silent. My heart jumped the remainder of the distance to my throat. Suppose we couldn't reach battalion?

"What about the artillery phone?" I asked, half to myself.

Blackburn said, "Savage tried it. It's out too. Maybe those sonofabitches at battalion will turn on their radio sometime tonight. Hello, Tare One; hello, Tare One."

There was the sound of a butterfly switch being pressed somewhere on another radio. We waited expectantly.

"Hello, Tare Three to Tare One. Tare Three to Tare One. I hear you and can relay to Tare. I hear you and can relay to Tare. Send your message. Over."

It was L Company. For some reason our radio wasn't reaching battalion, but L Company could hear us and would relay our message.

Now that we could reach battalion I hardly knew what to call for. K Company had a priority mission on the artillery. The enemy barrage kept us from using our own 60mm mortars. That left the 81mm mortars with Company M, but that would mean precious minutes of delay in reaching them through our roundabout communications. But that seemed our only chance, except—I suddenly remembered—the 155s! That close-in concentration we had zeroed to our front. What was it called? Queen 163. Queen 163. *Oh, God, let us get the 155s!*

"Hello, Tare One to Tare Three. Roger. Tell Tare to give us the 155s. Concentration Queen 163. And fast. Over."

L Company said "Roger" and repeated my message. I told them that was correct. They said, "Roger. Wait." The formality of radio conversations angered me. Why the hell couldn't they get along without so many "hellos" and "Rogers" and "repeats" and "outs?" My watch was ticking away minutes that might mean life or death to the men in the foxholes, and to ourselves.

The enemy artillery barrage lifted suddenly. The pounding increased with a new fury upon the forward platoon positions, or perhaps it was that I could hear the shelling they were getting now that our own had ended. Before I had time to realize what was happening, Sergeant Castro's

155mm Long Tom

mortar squad had whisked past me, shouted a few fire
direction orders and fed shell after shell into the mortar
tube. The blast from the firing almost knocked me from
my standing position at the doorway. The sound of Scotty's two mortars to our rear coughed an answer. Now we
could start giving them something in return.

Small-arms fire from the front joined in the mêlée.
That would mean the Germans were closing in for the
assault. Our 60s couldn't stop them. *Please, please, please,
fire the 155s!*

"Hello, Tare Three to Tare One. Over."

"Hello, Tare One to Tare Three. Send your message.
Over." I rattled the words off in my impatience. Perhaps
this was the news that the heavy artillery was on the way.

"Hello, Tare Three to Tare One. Tare says 'Roger' on
Queen. Mac, this is 'Chief.' I have a concentration to your
front with my 60s. I'll fire it if you want. Over." It was
Captain Eisler, the L Company commander.

"Hello, Tare One to Tare Three. Thanks, Chief. Give us all you can. Over."

Savage came to the door. He said, "Middlebrook says the mortars are coming in fine. He wants another two hundred yards to the right." He turned to me. "He says he needs a litter, Captain. He's got one man that's hurt pretty badly, and there may be others."

"Hello, Tare One; hello, Tare One. Over."

Blackburn looked at me in surprise. That was battalion calling us on the radio. He took the speaker from my hand and answered.

"Hello, Tare One," battalion came back. "We hear you can check five. We changed our batteries. Andy says Queen 163 is 'on the way'!"

My heart seemed to skip a beat. Savage ran back inside to relay the news to the platoons, and the big artillery shells whispered their messages of outgoing death. The deafening explosions to our front were followed by the noise of shrapnel spraying the trees around the farmhouse, and small pieces of spent shrapnel fell around us. I called for a repeat on the barrage, and when battalion said "Roger," I knew we had won.

No attacking force could withstand a barrage like that.

I checked casualties with the platoon leaders over the platoon phone when all was quiet, marveling that the light wire had stayed in.

Lieutenant Antey had returned to his platoon when I called. He and Webster had started back to their position when the enemy barrage began, but except for being badly shaken up they were unharmed. He had two men wounded; one had been hit in the shoulder, another in the left forearm, but both were walking wounded.

The 2d Platoon was hardest hit. One man was hit in the left hand, another in the left shoulder, and the man whom they thought initially was badly wounded had only a small piece of shrapnel in his side and could walk back to the aid station with a little assistance.

The 1st Platoon and the weapons platoon had no casualties although a light mortar shell had burst within the sandbag enclosure of one of the rear mortars. By some freak stroke of luck even the mortar was undamaged.

It was broad daylight when Lieutenant Brock left with

the last of the men for the aid station and the division rest area. The rest area men from the other platoons had not started out when the attack came. The 3d Platoon carrying detail came for their rations and returned, and a wire-repair crew came from battalion and left again.

The German attack was over. The death-like stillness that prevailed on both sides of the valley seemed to mock at the foolish little men who had made such hell for themselves a few minutes before.

It was another day. The newspapers at home would write of offensive action and say bluntly that "extensive patrolling persisted on other sectors of the front." That would mean us.

I was awakened when Colonel Tuttle called at noon to discuss the attack. He said that we had evidently repulsed a large-scale assault. K Company had discovered the enemy's approach over the open area to their front a few minutes before four o'clock and had gone to work immediately with artillery and mortars. A prisoner taken by K Company said there were tanks in the assault, and I remembered Sergeant Garcia having said that SP fire was hitting his platoon. K Company could count at least thirty enemy dead to their front. Figured on the usual ratio, that would mean that approximately two hundred Germans had participated in the attack.

The afternoon was quiet until five o'clock when the big enemy railroad gun opened up again on the area around the farmhouse. It was evidently in the same position as before; the azimuth to the sound of the gun checked, and it took seventeen seconds for the huge shell to reach us. We sat stone-faced and rigid in the dubious protection of the pillbox as the enemy fired, round by round, for thirty minutes.

Someone called from the 3d Platoon to check the telephone line.

"They're giving you rear-echelon people hell up there today, aren't they, Cap'n?" he said.

"Yeah," I answered, "but the Blue Star Commandos[2] can take it. Maybe you people don't know there's a war on?"

---

[2] The Infantry's nickname for the Army Service forces, having its basis in the blue star shoulder patch insignia of the Services of Supply.

Salberg closed one of the iron doors in the entrance to the pillbox. The effect was almost unbelievable. The explosion of the next shell scarcely disturbed us except for the merry tinkle of the concussion caps in the sides of the pillbox.

Night fell and was ominously quiet again. Some soldier who must have been as nervous as I was tossed an occasional hand grenade. It was "too goddamned quiet" again. I was increasingly sleepy, but even after Sparky awoke at four and insisted that I take his place, I did not go to bed. I was determined that I was not going to allow myself to be fogged with sleep if another attack should come, and I was more concerned than ever now with the reduced number of men in the forward platoons. But the ominous stillness of the night was misleading, and the enemy did not come.

I went to sleep at five o'clock.

The enemy began to make up for any peace he had given us during the night with an intense mortar barrage that began at eight o'clock and continued at intervals through the day. A 20mm antiaircraft gun opened up on the forward platoon areas shortly after ten o'clock, firing from a pillbox. The railroad gun paid us another visit at 3:30 P.M. and stayed for twenty-five nerve-wracking rounds. We closed the pillbox doors and waited, half expecting to find the farmhouse burned to the ground or knocked from its foundations when we opened the doors again.

I wondered just how much longer we would be forced to endure this ungodly position. I felt I would be a nervous wreck if we had to remain here even one more night, but there was no indication that relief was in sight. This was our ninth day in the pillboxes. How much longer—a week, a month, six months? If only there were some date we could set to work toward that would give us an incentive for survival!

The line to the platoons was knocked out in the shelling by the railroad gun. I told myself that I should not worry about the line going out during daylight hours, but my nerves were more the ruler of my brain than any sense of reason. I insisted that we must have communications, and after the 536 radios failed to function, Sergeant Savage reluctantly volunteered to repair the line.

As soon as Savage disappeared from the mouth of the pillbox, I realized the absurdity of allowing him to go out alone on the exposed slope in daylight. The need of the telephone line seemed trivial in comparison to the possibility that he might be wounded, or even killed. With my new sense of reasoning, I longed for some way to call him back, but there was nothing I could do except sit and wait.

I listened expectantly for the sound of the 20mm anti-aircraft gun or the crack of a mortar shell, but no sound came. It seemed like hours before he finally returned. The line was in, and I breathed a sigh of relief. He had found the huge crater from one of the shells of the railroad gun astride the phone line. Ten feet of the line were missing. He had curled himself into the crater and used its scant protection while splicing the wire.

As darkness approached, I began to adjust myself for another night of suspense in the confines of the pillbox. A telephone call came from battalion. It was Colonel Tuttle. I was totally unprepared for the news he had for me.

I tried to keep my voice at a normal pitch through the conversation, but I wanted to jump and kick and scream with joy. Tears came to my eyes, and I thought I would choke with happiness. It was almost too wonderful to be true. My battalion runners would arrive around midnight leading the men of Company B. We were getting out of the pillboxes . . . and *tonight!*

Company I was to be relieved!

Five minutes passed after the battalion commander had hung up before I could say a word, and then I merely mumbled ineffectively, "We're getting out . . . tonight." The way I said it the speech could not have been in the least impressive, but the faces of the men around me lit up as if I had casually mentioned that the war was over and they were going home.

We did not know what was in store for us after we were relieved—it might be even worse or more hazardous than the pillbox positions—but we could anticipate at least one night's rest, and it was difficult to imagine any instance that could be as uncomfortable or as nerve-wracking as our present location. Any change would have to be for the better. We were moving back!

The B Company commander, Captain Kay K. Cowan, of Austin, Texas, telephoned a few minutes later. His time was too short to get forward on reconnaissance, so I gave him what information I could over the phone. My two battalion runners would lead his company forward, and I would provide platoon guides to meet him at my command post. The runners would guide my men to the position now occupied by Company B, an assembly area in a patch of woods near the small town of Heckhuscheid, two miles to the rear. I would leave my heavier weapons and any excess equipment to be picked up by my supply jeep at dawn.

I dreaded the passing of the hours until midnight, fearing some catastrophe that might happen in our last few hours in this dreaded spot, but the duties of preparing for the relief kept me busy, and the time passed much more quickly than I had expected.

Our relief arrived shortly after midnight. I dispatched the platoon guides with their respective reliefs as quickly as possible in order to clear the nose of the hill of as many men as possible. B Company's headquarters group quickly overran our CP, and I sent my own men, with the exception of Savage, Blackburn, and Sergeant Albin, to the company rendezvous point at the fir forest in our rear to relieve the congestion in the pillbox. My nine days in the cramped quarters had given me an acute case of claustrophobia.

Captain Cowan and I sat at the table, and I began to relate our experiences in the position and various details with which he might be concerned. Savage worked similarly with the communications sergeant, and First Sergeant Albin worked with his counterpart from Company B.

I became conscious of pains in my stomach, and a wave of nausea came over me. Putting my hand to my forehead, I realized for the first time that I had a burning fever. I excused myself and walked outside to climb the incline to the latrine. An intense cold had combined with the K-ration diet to give me a violent case of dysentery.

Later a supply vehicle from Company B arrived. My own men appeared with the heavier weapons to be stacked at the CP to await Sergeant Neafach's arrival at dawn. Sergeant Albin completed his work and left with

Blackburn and the men who had brought the weapons for the meeting place in the rear. Savage volunteered to remain with me, and we planned to wait for our supply vehicle at dawn and return with it.

Word came by telephone that my forward platoons were moving out. The last to leave was the 3d Platoon.

A few minutes later a call came for Captain Cowan over the platoon phone. A tenseness came over his face as he answered. He handed the phone back to the soldier sitting at the table.

"They just killed one of our own men," he said to me. "One of my squad leaders was moving around to the front and was going back to his hole. One of the BAR men let him have it . . . thought he was a German."

I wondered how it would feel to have one of your own men killed by an accident. Having a man killed by the enemy would be bad enough, although I had been mercifully spared even that thus far. I shuddered.

"My men are nervous as all hell," Captain Cowan said. "They've heard all sorts of rumors and stories about these positions. Makes them trigger-happy."

I decided to try to get a few hours' sleep before dawn. Savage was already snoring in one of the bunks. The night was quiet now, the stillness accentuated by the past activity of the relief.

I tried to sleep, but the pains returned again to my stomach, and I got up and went to the latrine. The upset stomach and the burning temperature seemed to make me more nervous than ever.

Returning to the bunk, I tried again to sleep. Savage continued to snore blandly, and I envied him. The battalion telephone rang, and I thought the noise would send me to the ceiling of the pillbox. One of the B Company platoons called. They heard a noise to their front and would like some mortar fire. Captain Cowan calmly called the rear mortar squads. They fired two rounds. I wanted to scream at him, asking why in the almighty hell he didn't fire enough to do some good. I tried again to relax, but it was no use. My responsibility was gone now, and I wanted to go with it. I felt I could not bear to stay in this nasty, rotten, stinking, cluttered pillbox one moment longer.

The battalion telephone rang, and Captain Cowan repeated its message over the platoon phone. L Company reported a thirty-man German patrol behind their lines. They had thrown hand grenades, but the patrol had continued to the rear. Be on the alert.

I jumped from my bunk. My God! It was all too clear. They were throwing grenades at my 3d Platoon. Just enough time had elapsed for them to have reached the draw in rear of the L Company pillboxes. I grabbed the battalion phone and called L Company. Yes, it could have been one of my platoons. They hadn't thought of that.

I went back to my bunk more miserable than ever. I wondered why I had ever decided to wait here for the supply jeep. I had no business here now . . . my men were gone.

Technical Sergeant Frederick Weber, of Altoona, Pa., my weapons platoon sergeant, came into the pillbox with Private First Class Jesse L. Ramsey, of Jerusalem, Ark., the platoon radio operator. They had been on the tail of the company after it pulled out from the patch of fir trees, and with eight other men, including Lieutenant Glasgow, had lost the main column in the darkness. They didn't know the route back. Was there someone here who could guide them back?

I heard the sound of a B Company man outside opening the large wooden boxes which contain K-ration cartons, and my tortured nerves magnified the sound until it seemed that someone was demolishing a frame building. The Germans would surely toss in a heavy barrage at that sound.

I jumped from my bunk. I was getting out. I would guide them back. *Wake up, Savage! Wake up! We're getting the hell out of this miserable place! Wake up, goddammit! We're leaving! Wake up!*

The four of us made our way across the crest of the ridge, past the bodies of the American dead which my men had stacked there, and I imagined I saw the blond hair blowing again in the wind. A misty rain had begun to fall, and a chilling wind was picking up strength. In the blackness I could make out the vague outline of the bodies stacked against the power pole . . . a harvest for the devil.

Time and historians have a way of dispelling some of the fog of war which inevitably envelops those on the actual fighting line at the time of the fighting.

In these pillbox positions, for example, I know now that we were facing the German 91st Infantry Division, commanded by General der Artillerie Walter Lucht. Like almost all German units at this stage of the war, the 91st Division had been severely crippled in Normandy and in the race across France as the Germans fell back on the Siegfried Line.

During the second week of September, the American 28th Division, a part of the V Corps under Lt. Gen. Leonard T. Gerow, had attacked near Kesfeld and had penetrated the first belt of Seigfried Line pillboxes. General Gerow was getting ready to commit an armored division to exploit the success when shortly after midnight on September 15th, a German counterattack hit the tip of the penetration. In the counterattack, the Germans used two self-propelled flame-throwing vehicles. These were Schuetzenpanzerwagen (armored halftracks) with portable flamethrowers mounted on them. Thus the later concern of me and my men of Company I about a flame-throwing halftrack was fully justified.

The counterattack took back some of the pillboxes from the men of the 28th Division, but another battalion of the 28th recaptured them the next day. Nevertheless, the counterattack, when coupled with other minor reverses in the general area, was enough to discourage committing American armor. This region along the Belgian-German border has few good roads, and the terrain is rugged and inhospitable. Thus the American First Army commander, Lt. Gen. Courtney H. Hodges, decided to halt the attack around Kesfeld and concentrate his strength farther north, near the city of Aachen.

When Company I and the other units of the 2d Division arrived in early October, both sides were content to defend without resort to major offensive action. General Lucht and the 91st Infantry Division, nevertheless, were under orders to retake all the pillboxes by small-scale local counterattacks. They made their most earnest effort near Kesfeld because here was the deepest American penetration of their line.

That explains why Company I had a rough time.

8

RAIN AND SHOWERS

I found it difficult to realize where I was when I awoke the next morning on the floor of the house in Grofkampkenberg that served as the 3d Battalion CP. My stomach felt much better, and my fever had almost disappeared. The events of the night before and the days before that already were vague in my memory. I felt like I had slept off a drunk. The battalion commander and his staff were eating a breakfast of hot cakes and syrup and steaming hot coffee that seemed too wonderful to be true.

My clouded brain began to clear, and I remembered how we had become lost in the black space between the pillboxes and Grofkampkenberg during the night and had followed the telephone wire into battalion. I had not known the route to our new assembly area. Scotty had slept in the haybarn outside with the men, and I had bedded down for the night on the floor of the CP.

The clean-shaven faces and well pressed uniforms of the battalion staff officers made me conscious of my own bedraggled condition. I had neither washed nor shaved for days, and my face and hands were black with smoke from the cardboard fires in the pillbox. The United States Army would have hesitated to claim my grimy clothes as items of issue.

After breakfast a driver arrived to transport us by truck to the assembly area near Heckhuschied, and Colonel Tuttle told me that we would relieve Company C in their defensive position after dark. The position was much more tenable than the one we had left, he added.

As I was leaving Colonel Tuttle received a telephone call from Captain Joe Stephenson, of Shreveport, La., the K Company commander, and I waited to hear the message. Two German medics had come up to his forward platoons and had been brought back to his command post. They wanted to arrange a four-hour truce along the battalion front to allow removal of the dead from the attack against I and K Companies, and wished to return to their lines to give the American decision. Colonel Tuttle agreed to a two-hour truce but stipulated that the medics must call the information across the lines. They would then be taken prisoner and repatriated later through the Geneva Red Cross to be assigned to another sector of the front.

The drive to Heckhuscheid necessitated a roundabout trip through the woods to the rear even though the town was only slightly over a mile to the northeast from Grof-kampkenberg. The highway between the two towns was under enemy observation.

Heckuscheid was situated along a high ridge. Three unimproved streets, clustered on either side with sturdy stone houses complete with manure piles, eventually curved and connected with the paved highway from Grofkampkenberg that ran along the south edge of the town and on to the east to the C Company positions which we would occupy. The highway made a junction there with a north-south highway that ran generally parallel to the Siegfried Line and entered the German town of Kesfeld in the valley in front of the pillbox positions we had left.

My company was in an assembly area in the woods a few hundred yards to the south of Heckhuscheid. My command post was in a five-room rose-colored house beside the highway. Parts of the town were under enemy observation.

A number of men had gone for showers when we arrived. There had been no transportation available, but they had walked the two miles to the regimental CP town of Heckhalenfeld, eager at the prospect of getting a bath. The men who had been to the division rest area would return in the afternoon. The company had had a hot breakfast brought up by our own kitchen, and there would be a hot meal for lunch. A single shell from an enemy 88mm high-velocity gun had screamed into the area around eight o'clock, exploding on the highway near the CP and injuring one of the buck sergeants from the 3d Platoon.

Lieutenant Antey had been suffering from concussion since the night of the last German attack in the pillbox positions. He was having dizzy spells and his head ached constantly. At my insistence he reported to the aid station and was evacuated. Technical Sergeant Garçia, the platoon sergeant, took over the platoon.

Our kitchen jeep was leaving to obtain rations at Service Company and would pass by the regimental shower point, so I took advantage of the ride. Savage went with me.

The firing batteries of the 37th Field Artillery Battalion overlooked the town of Heckhalenfeld, the noise of the big guns almost deafening us. An engineer unit had set up a water-purification system and shower point beside a small, swiftly-running stream that curved its way along the north edge of the deep valley in which the town was located. We went inside a large squad tent beside the stream and selected approximate sizes from neat piles of clean clothes.

The shower room in a half-demolished barn across the stream was crowded with laughing, joking GIs in various stages of nudity. Clouds of steam rose from the end of the barn containing the showers, half-hiding the muscular naked bodies of the soldiers. A large metal oil can had been fitted with pipe to serve as a glowing red stove.

Undressed, we waited our turn in the line for the showers. The water was exhilarating, although it was so hot at times that I thought it would surely take off my skin, and then so cold that my teeth chattered. It had never occurred to me that I could derive so much pleasure from a bath. It was my first, other than from a helmet, for two and a half months.

After lunch I left with Captain Howard C. Alphson, of Grand Forks, N.D., the C Company commander, and my platoon leaders to reconnoiter the new positions. We walked in the shallow ditch along the highway toward the east, running as we reached a road junction at the eastern edge of town, since, as Captain Alphson explained, we were under observation and "the Kraut shell the hell out of it all the time." Two partially destroyed houses and a burned hulk of a jeep at the road junction attested to the fact.

We passed two other houses on the left of the road.

The ground on our right was open but rose slightly now to screen our movements from the right front. The area to our left was a series of rolling hills with deep wooded draws.

We came to a third house approximately a half-mile from Heckhuscheid, and Captain Alphson explained that it was used as a CP by his 3d Platoon. Sergeant Garcia stayed to reconnoiter his platoon area, and we continued to a spot where two houses a few yards apart formed an L-shaped courtyard in their rear. A thin hedge of fir trees formed the other two sides of the courtyard. The house on the left was occupied by the 2d Platoon, whose positions were on a knoll two hundred yards to the northeast. The house on the right faced broadside to the enemy and housed the company CP with the 1st platoon CP in the barn section on the right. The ground in front dropped off sharply, and the north-south highway ran a few yards in front of the building.

From an upstairs window Captain Alphson pointed out the light machine guns on a knoll with the 2d Platoon. A half-mile to the right front were pillboxes within the Siegfried Line occupied by the 2d Battalion. Almost two miles to the left lay the town of Winterspelt atop a hill held by Cannon Company of our regiment, acting as a rifle company. Both the wide gaps between our position and the friendly elements were completely undefended.

Six hundred yards to the front I saw the dragon's-teeth of the Siegfried Line, backed up by a series of enemy-held hills and a high ridge topped by three gutted buildings on the horizon.

We gained entrance to the company CP by climbing a ladder to a second floor rear window. I decided that the architect must have been a German sympathizer and had constructed the doors on the side of the house facing the enemy. The room on the second floor was a shambles of broken furniture but the lower floor was neatly arranged. The windows were sandbagged to protect against shrapnel.

Company C had suffered no casualties since taking over the position. There had been a few mortar barrages when the men became too brazen in moving about the buildings, but generally the area had been quiet. Since the exposed highway to the rear prevented the transportation of supplies by day, the men had set up one burner from their kitchen in the barn of the house occupied by the 2d Platoon and there cooked "10-in-1" rations for the company.

We returned to our wooded assembly area in time for a hot supper and began the relief immediately after dark, exchanging positions one platoon at a time. I found myself much calmer than when we first occupied the pillbox positions. The last units of C Company left shortly after one o'clock, and I settled down to sleep. I had insisted that either Sparky or myself should be awake at all times, but consented to Sparky taking the larger part of the night watch until I could catch up on my sleep.

The succeeding days were like Utopia in comparison to the gruelling days and nights in the pillboxes. The men improved their foxholes, putting log and plank covers on them and enlarging them so that one man could sleep while another pulled guard. We set out antitank mines on the highway and booby traps and barbed wire to the front of the foxholes. Contact patrols ran nightly to Cannon Company but experienced no difficulties. Although all men from the rifle platoons occupied their foxholes at night, we kept only a skeleton force on position in daytime, allowing the men to come back to the warmth of the houses to rest. A cold, beating rain set in the first morning, but the men complained little since they were able to dry their clothes in the daytime. We slept on an assortment of mattresses and pillows and hay. The venturesome 2d Platoon killed a heifer the second day, claiming she had stepped on a mine, and I was invited for a delicious steak. Another group left for the division rest area.

The enemy harassed us little, except for the ominous knowledge of his presence. Though we received a few rounds of 20mm fire the first morning, October 14, it was high and caused no damage. Three fanatical Germans crawled through the underbrush to within a few feet of the foxholes of a forward outpost of the 2d Platoon around ten o'clock the first morning, but one was killed and the men thought they wounded the other two. The papers from the dead German were brought to my CP, and I forwarded them to battalion. The Germans always seemed obligingly to carry unit identification papers with them on patrol. Artillery continued to shell the road junction to our rear and the town of Heckhuscheid, but only one barrage fell near our positions.

On the night of October 15 Lieutenant Fudickar's antitank platoon from the farmhouse in the pillbox positions arrived to exchange positions with another platoon in our area. They brought us the news that the Germans had finally scored a direct hit on the farmhouse with the big railroad gun, setting fire to the barn section of the house, but the men had prevented the fire from spreading. In general, however, the area had become much less active since our departure.

On Monday afternoon, October 16, Colonel Tuttle telephoned that I was to leave one rifle platoon, plus my light machine gun section and one mortar squad, to defend the area around the houses, pulling the remainder of my company back into the assembly area on the edge of Heckhuscheid. That would enable us to feed hot meals to all except the platoon outposts, and would give the battalion a larger reserve force in the event of an enemy penetration of the undefended sectors.

We disliked the proposal, since we were becoming acclimated to our new positions, but as so often happens with Army orders, we obeyed them. We left slightly before dawn the next day, leaving the 2d Platoon, the light machine-gun section and Sergeant Castro's mortar squad in the readjusted positions. I planned to relieve them every two days.

Our CP group moved again into the rose-colored house beside the highway, and the platoons moved into the woods. The men constructed squad bunkers dug several feet into the ground and built of logs from fir trees. They were not elaborate, but they proved more comfortable than individual foxholes and slit trenches.

Enemy shelling of Heckhuscheid increased. My CP was under observation and the enemy seemed determined to blast it away. As we lay flat upon the floor during the barrages, it often seemed that they would succeed. There were numerous near misses and the outside walls were sprayed with shrapnel. It was here that I was introduced to the German Nebelwerfer, a multi-barreled affair fired electrically, whose terrifying moaning shells gave them the GI nickname of "Screaming Meemies."

Nebelwerfer

Just after dark on October 19 Staff Sergeant Threadgill, the mess sergeant, and Corporal Woodrow W. Lloyd, of Jacksonville, Texas, the transportation corporal, were returning to Service Company after bringing up the supper meal by jeep. An incoming artillery barrage caught them between the CP and Heckhuscheid. A shell landed a few feet behind the jeep, wounding Lloyd slightly in the shoulder and severing an important nerve in Threadgill's right arm. Both men were evacuated. Staff Sergeant William F. Elliott, of Mt. Pleasant, Texas, took over as mess sergeant, but Lloyd's position was held open in anticipation of his early return.

Sparky was evacuated temporarily with a light case of intestinal flu. We received twenty-five replacements, some of them former members of the company who had been wounded and were returning to duty, among them Staff Sergeant John T. Winegardner, of Altoona, Pa., who became platoon sergeant of the 3d Platoon. Private First Class Abraham Rojetnik, of Bronx, N. Y., a replacement who spoke German fluently, joined company headquarters as an interpreter. Men came and went to the division rest area, bringing back tales of warm brick barracks and tiled showers and Red Cross girls and *beaucoup* wine and cognac. Sometimes they brought back the wine and cognac.

The 3d Platoon relieved the 2d on the outpost, and the following night the Germans set up a loudspeaker near the position and treated the riflemen to a round of jive music and a plea to come over and surrender, that "Communist, Jew-loving Roosevelt" had involved them in a hopeless war. The platoon was hardly impressed. They called for a heavy artillery barrage on the location of the sound.

The weather was abominable. It either rained or the skies were heavily overcast, and the ground became soggy with mud. The dirt roads became almost impassable. Day by day the weather grew colder, and the daylight hours grew shorter.

Cigarettes became difficult to obtain. Each man was ordinarily issued one package per day, but we considered ourselves lucky now to get three packages for an entire week. The *Stars and Stripes* told us of a growing cigarette famine at home due to shipments to soldiers overseas, and we wondered if they were being dumped into the ocean.

Everyone got showers at regiment and clean clothes of a sort. Socks were issued along with the food occasionally. We received two issues of month-old magazines from Special Service and two issues of Armed Services editions of popular books. My mother wrote that she had thought of sending me a home recording of the family's voices for Christmas but had reconsidered. I wrote her that she showed amazing foresight—there was not a radio or phonograph available anywhere.

Church services were held on Sunday in a barn near battalion headquarters. I was preparing to attend when I was called to a meeting of company commanders at battalion. There Colonel Tuttle told us that permission had been granted by higher headquarters for the regiment to withdraw from the defenses now held within the Siegfried Line to a new line on higher ground running north-south, generally along the line now held by my platoon outpost. We were to construct log dugouts on the reverse slopes of the ridges and "dig in for the winter." The pillboxes we had formerly occupied would be blown up and the troops would withdraw to defenses to be prepared prior to D-day, November 1.

I went with Captain Anderson in the afternoon on a reconnaissance of the sector which Company I would occupy. We would defend the hill now held by my platoon outpost and occupy the reverse slope of the ridge running north along the highway toward Cannon Company's positions. Company L would tie in with us at the houses occupied by the outpost and would extend west along the Heckhuscheid highway and into town. My company would be defending almost three-fourths of a mile with a gap of over a mile on the left flank. This sector alone would ordinarily have been defended by a regiment, and I was told that the same situation existed along the entire division front of twenty-seven miles.

We began work on the new positions the next day with the assistance of a platoon of engineers from the 2d Engineer Battalion.

My 1st Platoon would defend the area around the houses at the old C Company positions. A deep draw and a gap of six hundred yards would separate them from the 2d Platoon positions, which were half-hidden, on the reverse slope of a steep hill to the left of the draw, by a forest of trees which had already shed their leaves for winter. A clump of trees and bushes beside the highway and between the two platoons would house a daylight outpost.

My company CP would be near the bottom of the reverse slope behind the 2d Platoon, ten yards above a deep draw that followed the rear contour of the forward platoon positions. Another hill, covered with fir trees, rose to the rear of the draw and would be occupied by the 3d Platoon in support. The company kitchen would be partially dug in on the reverse slope of the hill occupied by the 3d Platoon, and a 60mm mortar squad would be placed with each rifle platoon.

The deep draw behind the forward platoons joined five other draws at a densely-wooded point three hundred yards to the left rear of the positions. Here a squad of men from Company K would maintain an outpost position covering the junction of the draws. The remainder of the distance to the Cannon Company defenses in Winterspelt would be undefended.

During the initial days of construction, we continued to occupy the assembly area near Heckhuscheid, going to and from work each day like a labor gang. The engineers usually met us at the area, and one day found two Germans near the embryonic positions waiting to surrender with a white flag.

A reconnaissance patrol came in on the 1st Platoon at the outpost position on October 25 during the early morning hours of darkness, but none of my men was wounded.

The next morning at four o'clock, Sergeant Meade, one of the squad leaders, was standing guard in his foxhole on the knoll to the left front of the houses when he saw the glint of a bayonet in the darkness a few feet in front of him. Firing his sub-machine gun quickly, he killed the intruder and set off a maze of rifle and machine-gun fire from the other defenders that repulsed the German attack. Two other Germans were killed. The men estimated there were forty Germans in the surprise bayonet assault.

The German attack did not frighten me, because it was over before I received the news, but I could not avoid joining the other men in thinking that the enemy was following Company I around. We had endured a veritable hell in the pillbox positions, only to find that the area quieted considerably after our departure, and now we had moved into a supposedly quiet sector only to have the enemy hit us with a savage bayonet assault.

The veterans with the company were even more of this opinion than I. They had seen the company cut to ribbons by a German counterattack on Hill 192 near St. Lô, France, and blown to bits by the German pillbox explosions on the outskirts of Brest.

Evidently, I had inherited quite an outfit.

The advantage of post-war study makes it obvious now that Company I was not being singled out for special treatment. We had been counterattacked near Kesfeld because there was the deepest penetration of the German

91st Division's *line*. *At the farmhouse near Heckhuschied we got similar treatment simply because we had just moved in. It was common practice to make small counterattacks when new units were observed coming into position. This way the enemy might take prisoners or otherwise identify the new unit in hope of determining what his adversary intended to do: was he going to continue to defend, or was he getting set to launch a big attack?*

But like many another soldier in many another company, we could not have been convinced of that at the time. Clearly, it seemed to us, "the enemy was following Company I around."

9

QUIET AREA

On the day of the bayonet assault I left for the division rest area in company with Sergeant Savage and our quota of other enlisted men. All my officers had already been there, and Sparky had returned from the medical clearing station where he was treated for influenza.

We made the thirty-mile trip to Vielsalm by truck convoy. The town was sprawled among a series of high, surrounding hills, and seemed undamaged outwardly from the war. The rest camp had been established in a former Belgian Army barracks, neat brick buildings facing on a concrete quadrangle. The camp was complete with an indoor weapons range, a Red Cross club presided over by three attractive American girls in trim blue uniforms, a mess hall with tables and dishes, an auditorium-gymnasium where USO shows were held, a movie theater, and showers, whose tiled individual compartments and steaming hot water were beyond the fondest dream of any infantryman. The streets were named after American cities. The gymnasium was "Madison Square Garden" and the movie theater had been christened the "Paramount."

First Lieutenant John R. Glenn, of Waycross, Ga., was director of the camp. He met our convoy and gave us a brief orientation. The men were assigned to bunks and told when they could use the showers, but there were few rules and regulations. The only roll-call formation would be held at ten o'clock in the morning, two days later. That would be our day of departure.

I made my way to the showers after lunch. I had turned off the water in my compartment when I heard my name mentioned in the dressing room. I stopped instinctively to listen. It was Private First Class Robert J. Beach, of Fairview Village, Ohio, whose nickname of "Brooklyn" belied his midwestern nativity but not his definite Brooklyn accent. He was talking with an acquaintance from another company.

". . . and it looks like we've finally got the company commander we've been looking for. He came in about a month ago. A replacement."

"What's he like?"

"He's damn young," Brooklyn went on, "but he doesn't seem scared to come around and see you once and a while, no matter where the hell you are. He seems to care what happens to you."

My hand was raised to open the door of the compartment, but I halted abruptly. It would embarrass Brooklyn for me to step out into the dressing room now. I turned on the water again to wait until the two men had gone.

Perhaps here was the answer to the querulous thoughts that had plagued me persistently since I had first joined the company. Would I be accepted despite my youth and inexperience? If this was the answer, it was even more than I could have hoped for. If only Brooklyn's words mirrored the thoughts of the entire company!

I tried to believe that they did.

I attended a movie with Savage that night and a USO show featuring Joe Twerp and Herb Shreiner. We went down to the village the next morning and bought wine and souvenirs. A group of GIs told us about a shop near the edge of town which sold ice cream. We found it and a bakery nearby, and after standing in an olive drab line, had apple pie à la mode. We were like kids, excited with the slightest luxury.

When I returned to the company at Heckhuscheid, I found that little had happened during my absence except for continued enemy shelling. A self-propelled gun had blasted away at the house on the outpost position that had formerly housed my CP and had almost demolished the forward wall, but no one was injured.

The 2d Platoon received my permission to move into their new positions in the afternoon, and I followed two days later with the entire company.

We began to cover our front with a maze of double-apron barbed-wire entanglements. The regimental anti-tank platoon laid antipersonnel mines for us by night. Initially, each rifle squad, the machine-gun section, each mortar squad and each section of an attached machine-gun platoon from Company M constructed one log dugout each from fir trees. Six bunks, arranged in tiers of three and made by stretching potato sacks over timber frames, were the principal furnishings, but the men supplemented these with tables, table covers, mirrors and stoves from the houses in the 1st Platoon area and Heckhuscheid. Doors, and sometimes windows, were brought from Heckhuscheid. The town was denuded.

As the days passed more bunkers were constructed, providing two per rifle squad, two for each machine-gun section, and one for each platoon CP. The fighting fox-holes were elaborately constructed with covers and floors. Men ate from mess kits in a chow line usually reserved for rear areas, except for men of the 1st Platoon who carried their chow to the platoon area in large marmite cans, since they were at such a distance from the kitchen.

My company CP was larger than the squad huts. Its furnishings included a large table and a sofa which the men transported from Heckhuscheid to serve as my bunk. The back of the sofa was detachable and doubled for another bunk at night. Our stove was an abortive German masterpiece that was always either too hot or too cold and filled the room with smoke. The company headquarters messengers constructed a supplementary bunker near the CP.

Battalion headquarters was slightly over a mile to our rear. Our supply route rambled over and around a series of high hills in an effort to avoid enemy observation, and the engineers constructed a long corduroy bridge over the junction of the draws on our left. Despite the bridge, however, vehicles were continually getting stuck in the soft mud of the valley.

We established an elaborate intra-company communication system with nineteen sound-powered telephones and six German phones which enabled any squad or outpost to communicate directly with me in the event of trouble.

105mm Howitzer

Life became routine in the relative comfort and quiet of our new location. The weather was rough—freezing rain, sleet and snow combinations—but we sat in our log dugouts and read in the *Stars and Stripes* of offensive operations of other American soldiers on more active sections of the front and were grateful.

Only the 1st Platoon positions suffered from enemy action. They were shelled at least once daily, and the right squad in positions on the forward slope around the houses was unable to move about in daylight except behind the houses. The mortar squad with the platoon was kept busy oftentimes at night throwing shells at suspected patrol movements to their front, but there were no more assaults upon the position.

Two rounds of artillery fire from our own 105mm guns fell short in the 1st Platoon area one night but caused no damage. The next morning a single round of 155mm artillery fire crashed into the trees above the 2d Platoon positions, wounding one man slightly on the forehead. Supporting corps artillery finally admitted that one of their gunners had made an error in adjustment.

The big guns echoed up and down the deep draws at night, sounding as if they were fired from just outside the CP door. Enemy robot bombs began to buzz over our positions at frequent intervals, but they were merely curious sights to see. We were amazed at the stories of fear of the bombs in the rear areas.

Sending out patrols became a mental hazard with me. Our nightly contact patrols to Cannon Company were not particularly dangerous, but I shuddered each time the battalion intelligence officer called for me to send out a patrol into the enemy lines. I would spend long weary hours awaiting their return, all the while cursing higher intelligence officers who seemed to have nothing more to do than send out patrols. I knew that a certain amount of patrolling was essential to determine enemy activity to our front, but oftentimes men were sent out with ridiculous missions to get information we already knew from daylight observations, and had reported. I knew that some of the patrols accomplished little more than providing a neat, typewritten report to go to the next higher headquarters. I considered my company extremely fortunate to have no one killed in the dangerous patrolling, particularly after three men from Cannon Company were killed in an ambush in front of our position.

It seemed that since we were now in a "quiet" position every officer in the division with the rank of major or above wanted to inspect the company area. They condemned the men for not having shaved or for wearing knit wool caps without their helmets, evidently an unpardonable misdemeanor, or for untidy areas around the dugouts. The officers did not inspect my 1st Platoon area, however, usually passing it over with the excuse that it was a bit far to walk, but we laughed inwardly, knowing that it was the threat of enemy shelling that kept most of them away.

I finally protested the inspections to Captain Anderson, and a captain from regiment was sent up a few days later with the primary mission of inspecting my 1st Platoon area. That was the virtual end of the inspections, however; either from my protest or the fact that all the inspection-minded "brass" had satisfied their egos with visits to "the front." We wondered how many Silver Stars and Distinguished Service Crosses came from the visits.

The days were not monotonous. I visited each platoon at least every other day and either adjusted artillery and mortar fire or assisted the headquarters men in improving the CP at other times. The men were busy improving their dugouts or foxholes, and at night held long sessions of poker or general discussions by the light of kerosene lanterns purchased in Vielsalm.

Church services were held at battalion on Sundays, and many men walked the distance through rain and mud and sleet and snow to attend. A quota for showers at regiment was allowed each day and men continued to go to the division rest area.

Three men were included in the regiment's quota for passes to Paris. When they returned, they were a never-ending source of information on the conduct of the remarkable *femmes* in the gay city. Each returning soldier had virtually the same remark: "Damned good-looking girls come right up to you on the street and say, 'you zig-zig me, babee?' Of course, they want to be paid, but what the hell? They'll stay with you all night for a thousand francs." *Couchez avec* became a part of our colorful, if not so grammatically correct, vocabularies.

Only a few men were wounded. The 1st Platoon medic was hit by shrapnel minutes after I had paid a visit to the platoon area. Sergeant Sickmiller, one of the 1st Platoon squad leaders, wandered into one of the squad's hand grenade booby traps in the darkness and caught a fragment in his leg. Staff Sergeant Raymond Meade contracted pneumonia, and his temperature rose alarmingly high during the night before we could evacuate him.

Replacements and hospital returnees continued to arrive until the company was overstrength. They included

First Sergeant Steve Neubert, of San Antonio, Texas, former company first sergeant who had been wounded in Normandy; Technical Sergeant Bernard Sieland, of St. Paul, Minn., former platoon sergeant of the 2d Platoon; Private First Class Jacob R. Charles of Washington, Pa., and Private First Class Clovis P. Robinson, of Lexington, Ky., both former SCR-300 operators with the company; and First Lieutenant Delos Wilson, formerly an officer with an antiaircraft unit, only recently reassigned to the infantry. I assigned him as 3d Platoon leader. Private First Class Charles Purdue, of Little Rock, Ark., formerly company commander's personal runner, rejoined company headquarters, and Private First Class Joseph Wright, of Denver, Colo., a replacement, was assigned to headquarters as a radio repairman. Salberg, the headquarters "bazooka" man, had become my runner after Croteau was evacuated.

The officers received a monthly whiskey ration consisting of one quart of Scotch, one pint of gin, one or two bottles of cognac, a bottle of champagne and a bottle of Cointreau. Though the officers paid for the rations, they were for the most part far from personal items. The bottles were passed among all the men of the platoons until they were exhausted, which was accomplished rather rapidly, and we wondered at letters to the editor in the *Stars and Stripes* complaining about officers getting whiskey rations when enlisted men did not.

On November 10 Middlebrook was called to division headquarters where he was commissioned a second lieutenant. He was reassigned to the company, and I held him temporarily in company headquarters as an excess officer.

Enemy patrol action was confined to noises to the front of the 1st Platoon and one four-man reconnaissance patrol which worked its way close in on the left flank of the 2d Platoon at eleven o'clock one night before we opened fire with mortars. Occasionally, we fired the 60mm mortars at curious blue and red lights that appeared several times along the highway to our front. We decided that the Germans were signalling with a small flashlight equipped with blue and red shields. One lone German surrendered to the M Company machine gunners attached to the 1st Platoon, claiming that he had been accused of stealing an overcoat from a fellow soldier and that he would rather face the American PW cages than a German court-martial.

On Tuesday, November 21, a reconnaissance detail from Company F arrived preparatory to relieving us for seven days while we reverted to regimental reserve for a rest and reorganization period. We did not like the idea of moving. Except for the shelling of the 1st Platoon area and the patrolling called for my higher headquarters, there was little to cause us to desire the move.

We were relieved shortly after noon the next day, and the men hiked to the rear by platoons, assembling at battalion where they loaded on trucks and moved ten miles to the northwest to Lommersweiler, Belgium, located on the banks of a tributary of the Our River, which separated Belgium from Germany, four miles from St. Vith, Belgium. I remained with Sergeant Albin for orientation of the incoming company commander, Captain George H. Duckworth, of Shelburn, Ind., and his first sergeant.

We arrived by jeep in Lommersweiler at dusk, half-frozen from a driving cold wind and rain. The town was a typical small farming town. We shared its occupancy with Company L and apathetic German-speaking civilians and smelly manure piles. The men had several rooms in each house equipped with bunks similar to the bunks in our log dugouts. The town was equipped with electric lights which worked at various times during the day but went off with amazing alacrity with the approach of darkness.

The company mess hall was a converted community entertainment hall, a small wooden building with a rostrum at one end. Movies were shown twice nightly in the hall, once for Company L and once for Company I. Arrangements were made for the division orchestra to play for our noon meal the next day, Thanksgiving.

Entering the mess hall as usual for the noon meal, I took my customary place in the chow line, but Sergeant Neubert met me and insisted that I go up to the front table. I went forward reluctantly. The cooks had already prepared a plate for me. It was sitting on the table, weighted down with turkey and dressing. I began to eat, and the mess hall was practically full when the orchestra stopped playing and swung into "Happy Birthday."

It was only then that I remembered that this was something special; this was my birthday.

Sergeant Neubert came out on the rostrum bearing a large cake decorated with twenty-two candles of assorted sizes. The men took up the "Happy Birthday" song with lusty voices. I could not repress a choking sensation in my throat, and it was all I could do to keep back the tears of gratitude. The cake was crude, for the materials had been limited and the Army provides no candles, but there was no denying the looks on the men's faces and the lusty singing of the song.

My fears were happily over. These veterans of Company I had accepted me as their company commander.

The seven days began to roll by swiftly. A Red Cross doughnut wagon visited the town on Friday. On Saturday we traveled by truck to a town across the river where we practiced for a battalion parade in the morning, had lunch brought to us by the company kitchen, and paraded in the afternoon. None of us favored the parade, and the rain that fell intermittently all day added not at all to our pleasure. It was hard to appreciate the regiment's desire to claim that ours was the first formal parade on German soil since the occuption troops left after World War I.

On Sunday there were Protestant church services in the mess hall with Chaplain Isaac M. Anderson, of Chicago, officiating. Catholic services were held at regiment and transportation was provided.

We relieved Company F beginning at 6:30 on the morning of November 30. Despite our reluctance at leaving our former area, we were now reluctant to return. The relief was accomplished without incident, however, and we settled down once again to a routine existence in the defensive position.

We received post-exchange rations of candy, cigars and one cigarette lighter for a company of two hundred men. First Lieutenant Robert J. Roftis, of Toledo, Ohio, a battalion medical officer, came to my CP to administer typhus shots to the entire company. There were more calls from battalion to send out patrols and more sleepless

hours awaiting their return. Mortar and artillery fire fell
sporadically on the 1st Platoon. The weather alternated
between rain, sleet and snow with only an occasional
glimpse of the sun. I was pinned to the ground for fifteen
minutes by enemy machine-gun fire while visiting the
right squad of the 1st Platoon. An enemy tank and armored car were sighted far to our front driving to
the door of a pillbox and then churning again to the
rear.

Four lucky men were named for ninety-day rotation
furloughs to the US, the outfit's first experience with anything to compare even slightly with the Air Corps' rotation system. Most men who took the time to figure, however, found that unless drastic changes in the system took
place, it would be at least 1999 before they would see the
States again—barring serious wounds, the only salva-
tion.

Rumors spread persistently that our division was pulling
out of the defensive positions to go into the attack. A
reconnaissance party from a company of a division that
had debarked at Le Havre, France, only three days before
arrived on December 10 to give meat to the rumors. They
were overjoyed at the prospect of seeing their first combat
in such ideal defensive positions, and they showed little
fear of the thinly-spread lines.

I was called to battalion headquarters to get the information on the relief. Our division was pulling out to move
to the vicinity of Elsenborn, Belgium, farther north on the
German border, to launch an attack against the vital dams
of the upper Roer River. We had to remove our division
shoulder patches. It was to be a highly secret offensive
operation.

It had begun to snow when our relief appeared the
next afternoon. My men were amazed at the appearance
of the men from the incoming unit. They were equipped
with the maze of equipment that only replacements fresh
from the States would have dared to call their own. And
horror of horrors, they were wearing neckties! Shades of
General Patton!

The date was five days before December 16, 1944. The
location was near St. Vith, Belgium, on the southern half
of the First Army front.

The relieving unit was the 106th Infantry Division.

This division—these green, inexperienced men—was destined to go down in history as one of the hardest-hit American units of World War II. A large German force would roll through the 106th Division in the Ardennes winter counteroffensive, the so-called "Battle of the Bulge."

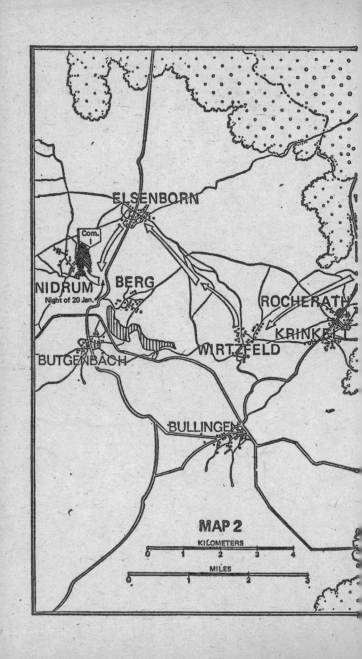

ELSENBORN

Com.
I

NIDRUM
Night of 20 Jan.

BERG

ROCHERATH

KRINKELT

WIRTZFELD

BUTGENBACH

BULLINGEN

MAP 2

KILOMETERS

0   1   2   3   4

MILES

0   1   2   3

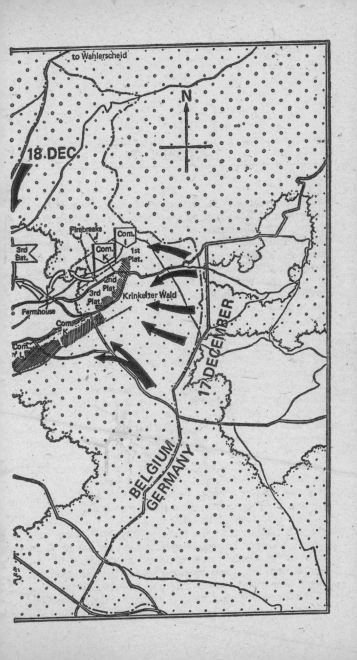

10
DIGGING IN

We finally reached our destination, a giant fir forest three miles west of Elsenborn, at nine o'clock, half-frozen from a five-hour nightmare of cold, snow and hazardous blackout driving. The men half jumped and half fell from the open two-and-one-half-ton trucks to the ice-covered road, cursing the misfortune which had subjected them to such an ordeal. We had plowed along the snow-covered roads at break-neck speeds, the drivers endeavoring to keep the tail light of the preceding vehicle in view, only to experience a period of freezing waiting while the convoy was held up by an obstruction ahead about which we knew nothing. The snow had grown steadily deeper as we went farther north until now there was a foot of frozen whiteness covering the ground.

We hiked for a mile along the icy highway through the forest, slipping and sliding in the darkness, until we met our guide, Staff Sergeant Howard Wolfgang, of Taylor, Pa., who had preceded us on the battalion billeting detail. We crossed a bridge over a small icy stream and turned right on a one-way trail leading up a hill into the dense forest, the reflection from the snow alleviating somewhat the darkness of the night. A hundred yards up the trail Sergeant Wolfgang stopped and pointed to the thick snow-covered forest on either side of the narrow trail.

"This is it, Cap'n," he said.

I felt like crying. My feet and my body were half-frozen, and the prospect of spending the remainder of the night in the frozen forest made me miserable. I directed the platoons into areas on either side of the trail, and they began to search the woods for some semblance of shelter.

The forest, deathly silent a moment before, was soon

filled with the tramping of many men, punctuated by sharp curse words and the sound of shovels scraping against the frozen earth. Blackburn said that the CP group had found several old slit trenches covered with logs. I joined him, and the platoons reported one by one that they were getting set up in old foxholes and slit trenches that would be satisfactory for the night and could be improved the next day.

Our kitchen truck arrived and parked on the one-way trail, only to be routed out with the arrival of other trucks that needed to move farther up the trail. Gradually, the battalion settled down for the night.

I shared a hole with Savage and Blackburn. Logs had been placed over the top, giving a four-foot clearance underneath. We scraped off the snow from the sieve-like roof and placed a canvas shelter-half over it, but drops of icy water from the remnants of melting snow dripped upon us the remainder of the night.

The next morning we had eaten a breakfast of hot cakes and syrup, prepared by a kitchen crew that had found no time for sleep, when I was called to battalion. We were to go to regimental headquarters for a meeting of company commanders.

Colonel Jay B. Lovless, the regimental CO, greeted us with the startling information that our Division, the 2d, had moved out at seven o'clock for an attack against the Siegfried Line stronghold of Wahlerscheid in the Monschau forest.

The division's ultimate objective was to gain control of the dams on the upper Roer River or force the enemy to blow them to eliminate the threat of floodwaters wrecking river crossings planned farther north. Our regiment was in division reserve. Already another division had almost reached the dams over another route only to be routed and suffer heavy losses by German counterattacks.

We followed the description of the offensive avidly. In one day, or two, or perhaps three—in any event, before the fight would be completed—we would probably be engaged in the action.

Each subsequent day we searched eagerly for news about the progress of the attacking units. Were they meeting much resistance? Were casualties heavy?

My personal fear of being committed in the attack

grew day by day. I had seen action now, but I had seen only defensive action along a sector that was listed as "quiet." I had yet to experience the death of one of my men, and I knew that casualties would be much higher in the attack. Would I be as paralyzingly afraid on the offense? Or more so? There would be no pillboxes or foxholes for shelter when the enemy fire began. Would I, personally, come out alive?

The reports of the fierce fighting filtered back to us, and we lived on borrowed time. Some men went for showers at Camp Elsenborn, a former Belgian Army garrison occupied by rear elements of the division. Robot bombs buzzed steadily overhead, increasing each day in number until by Saturday, December 16, they roared across every few minutes. We could hear the deep rumble of far-off artillery even better at night than in daytime, and the portentous rumble increased in intensity with each night like deep drums setting the scene for the main act.

Colonel Tuttle returned from regiment at noon on Saturday. Having seen the Colonel return, I knew even before I picked up the telephone that the call was the one we had been dreading. It was Captain Morris B. Montgomery, of River Forest, Ill., who had become battalion operations officer when Captain Anderson was transferred to regiment.

"Have your exec get your company ready to move on a moment's notice. You report to battalion right away."

The expressions on the faces of the headquarters men around me mirrored my thoughts. They silently began to gather their equipment. I tried to act gay as I walked across the trail to battalion. Perhaps this wasn't the call we had been expecting. It could be only an administrative move. But I knew within me that it wasn't. We were headed for trouble.

There was a serious expression on the Colonel's face as he pointed to his map.

"There has been a Kraut penetration in the 99th Division's sector near Rocherath," he said. "We are to move as soon as possible to a forward assembly area in the woods near this road junction about a mile beyond Rocherath. That's about all the information I can give you, except that we're not going to participate in our division's attack. I don't know whether we attack or defend. Montgomery and I are leaving now to contact the regimental commander from the 99th."

There would be no time to send a billeting detail. We would take blanket rolls, three meals of K-rations and packs, but the bulk of our heavy equipment would be transported later by our kitchen trucks, including my type-writer and an article I had written entitled "Nine Days in a Pillbox." There was no need to issue more than a basic load of ammunition. We would be in a forward assembly area initially whether we attacked or defended.

The company was almost ready to leave when I returned. The headquarters men had gathered up my equipment. The trucks were lined up on the main road through the forest, and we climbed aboard. I Company would leave, preceded by Major Vern L. Joseph of Fond du Lac, Wis., the battalion executive officer, in a jeep. I climbed into the cab of the lead truck.

Our route took us to the southeast through the town of Elsenborn, past a large dam and a lake, beneath the ruins of a demolished railroad underpass and up a hill into the town of Bütgenbach and down the hill again into Büllingen. Everywhere there were code signs pointing to rear area installations—"Victor," "Index Rear," "Ivanhoe Forward." Our trucks turned to the north toward the twin farming towns of Krinkelt and Rocherath, so close together atop a hill that we did not know when we left the one and entered the other. An ambulance met us with its siren screaming and its red signal light flashing on and off. The skies were overcast with the approach of dusk, and we could hear the heavy rumble of artillery in the distance. Fresh shell marks with dirt sprayed in ugly little patches on the snow told us that Krinkelt and Rocherath had undergone intense shellings, and recently. The GIs we passed did not give us the usual happy smiles and shouted well-wishes and insults to which we had became accustomed in rear areas. The rumble of the artillery lent a deep undertone to a dread and fear that communicated itself to us as we traveled.

"They shelled the hell out of us when we brought some other troops in here today," my driver said.

To make conversation I asked, "How far are we from the front?"

"I dunno," he answered, pointing to a long thick fir forest to the east. "It's over thataway."

We turned right toward the east at a crossroads six hundred yards beyond Rocherath. Two dirty stone farmhouses guarded the crossroads. I knew that straight ahead led to Wahlerscheid and the attack the other regiments of the division were making. Our route was taking us directly toward the long line of woods which had been on our right.

Buzz bombs roared overhead and unseen antiaircraft guns and .50-caliber machine guns blazed flaming arcs of fiery steel through the overcast, dusk-heavy skies in their wake. We had not been accustomed to firing at buzz bombs in the area we had left, and the din of the guns provided a tingling thrill like the opening kickoff at a football game.

The long convoy of trucks pulled to a halt on the highway at a road junction on the edge of the fir forest. I could see the highway extending to the left through the woods toward the east where my map showed it entered the Siegfried Line at a point a mile and a half distant. The road to the right ran south along the edge of the woods back toward Büllingen. The snow around the road junction had been churned into a yellowish mixture of snow and dirt from recent heavy shellings. I tried to ignore the tenseness that came over me as I thought that at any minute a hail of screaming shells might descend upon us.

I jumped from the cab of the truck the moment the convoy pulled to a halt and motioned for the men to dismount. They lined up quickly in single columns along either side of the road, and I signalled "Forward." Captain Montgomery was standing with Colonel Tuttle a few feet beyond the junction. I began asking directions as we approached to avoid halting the column. I definitely did not like the appearance of the ugly shell marks in the snow.

"Take your company down the road to the left," Captain Montgomery said, catching step with me and pointing to his map. "You'll find a slight bend in the road about six hundred yards down. Beyond that is a draw running perpendicular to the highway. Place one platoon astride the road as a roadblock. Swing your other two platoons to the right rear to defend parallel with the highway. You'll tie in with K Company's left flank at a firebreak."

"What's up, Monty?" I asked. "We attack?"

"There's a battalion from the 99th somewhere between us and the Krauts," he said, "but they've had the hell knocked out of them, and nobody knows exactly where they are. The old man's got orders to attack right away— tonight—to reestablish their positions, but I think he's going to stall some way until morning."

I tried to deny the portent of his words, and I looked at him incredulously. We had only a basic load of ammunition. It was practically dark already. We knew virtually nothing about our present location, our objective or the enemy situation. Even if we did not attack until dawn, our knowledge would be almost as limited then as now.

"Which way's the enemy?" I asked, half making light of the assignment.

"I dunno. Nobody seems to know a goddamned thing. They say it's that way," and he motioned with one arm to the east.

He dropped out of the column, and we continued down the road. The sight of the fresh shell marks in the snow around the road junction continued to haunt me. Shelling in the tall fir woods would be even more disastrous than in the open. Tree bursts would triple the casualty effect of the bursting shells.

The sound of small-arms fire came from somewhere far down the road. In the gathering darkness I saw a soldier run toward us from the woods on the right. I could make out an Army truck parked beneath the trees behind him and other soldiers gathered in a group about the truck.

"Hey!" the soldier called, motioning to us. "Don't go down there! That's where the fightin's goin' on."

His words astonished me. I wondered why he thought we had come this far if we did not know there was fighting going on. I accepted it as one of war's crazy incidents.

"I know it, buddy," I said. "That's why we're going. But thanks."

I looked at Savage. He raised his eyebrows and shrugged his shoulders.

The slow mournful scream of Nebelwerfer shells pierced the air. The men began to scatter to the sides of the road. I signalled for the company to follow, and we plunged into the woods to the left of the road, our packs and equipment rattling loosely as we ran. It was only a moment before the big shells began to expode to our rear.

"My God!" I thought. "They've hit the road junction!"

Some of the men dropped instinctively to the snow-covered ground. Someone said to stand up beside a tree—there would be more protection against the tree bursts standing than in a prone position.

A moment of silence followed the explosions, and I wondered how much damage the shelling had done. I was deeply thankful that I had succeeded in getting my company away from the road junction, and now I wanted to put as much distance as possible between us and the target area.

I motioned the company forward and continued through the woods, tracing a course along the bottom of a shallow draw, deep with snow, that ran parallel to the left of the highway. When I saw the bend in the highway, I signalled the company to halt and told Long to follow me with the 1st Platoon.

I broke into a half-run, anxious to get the company set up before it should become completely dark. Beyond the bend in the road, I could tell by the slope of the ground that the draw was several hundred yards farther. Already the area we had traversed from the point designated for my right flank was too large for one company to defend adequately in wooded terrain, so I told Long to establish his roadblock at the bend in the highway.

Another barrage of Nebelwerfer fire screamed toward the road junction. A robot bomb roared overhead, erupting another blaze of antiaircraft fire from guns to our rear.

Moving back to the company, I led the 2d Platoon across the highway, telling Lieutenant Brock to tie in his defense with Long's right flank, extending as far as possible to the right. Then I directed Lieutenant Wilson and the 3d Platoon into position beyond the highway on Brock's right. Our frontage was too wide to hold out a support platoon.

I looked around for a group of abandoned foxholes to use for a command post, but there were none. I chose a spot a few yards beyond the bottom of the draw where the trees were not so dense.

When a platoon of heavy machine guns arrived from Company M, I directed one section into position on the highway with Long's platoon and the other with the 3d. I told Scotty to place his light guns in the draw on the 1st Platoon's left flank. They would need a concentration of fire there since the entire left flank would be undefended. Since there was only one spot from which the 60mm mortars could possibly get overhead clearance to fire, the mortar section began to set up along the near side of the highway.

The Nebelwerfer barrage against the road junction was over, and I heard the other companies moving down the highway. Enemy artillery shells whistled so close overhead that the tall fir trees swayed gently from the breeze. We ducked involuntarily, but the big shells were intended for targets well to our rear. An answering barrage from the 99th Division artillery whistled over us, headed in the opposite direction. There seemed always to be a curtain of heavy shells racing above us.

My CP (command post) group dropped their equipment and began to scrape off the top of the snow with small GI entrenching shovels. A soldier came over to me in the darkness.

"I'm Lieutenant Jackson," he said. "I'm to be your observer from the 99th artillery."

He indicated two men who were with him, and I made out one man with the box-type radio which forward observers used. I told them to join my headquarters. They knew as much about what we were going to do as I.

I told Savage to begin laying telephone wire to the platoons. I did not believe that Colonel Tuttle would attack until dawn, and we would need communications during the night.

I made another round of the platoons. The lieutenants shared my hope that the orders would be changed and we would defend, although they were more than dissatisfied with the present positions. There was no field of fire for the weapons in the thick forest, and a completely undefended flank and rear in a dense woods were certainly not to be desired.

We tried to tell ourselves that the German action to our front could be only a local German attack. The battalion ahead of us was evidently inexperienced and was holding a lengthy line similar to the one we had recently left with the 106th Division. *We* would have little trouble.

I moved back to the CP location where the men were engaged in futile efforts to dig slit trenches in the frozen earth with the little entrenching shovels. Zellin and Naranjo, the battalion runners, had arrived. The Colonel wanted to see me. I should bring my map.

We found battalion headquarters in a group of old foxholes immediately beyond the firebreak which separated us from K Company. A dense growth of young firs touched the ground with their branches. Faint streaks of light came from the interior of the Colonel's foxhole. He was inside giving the order to one of the other company commanders.

I waited my turn and then crawled into the wet hole. There was room inside for one man to sit half comfortably. Both Colonel Tuttle and Captain Montgomery were crouched inside, and my presence made it almost impossible to breathe. Someone threw a shelter-half over the entrance after me.

The Colonel began to give me the details of the situation. A battalion from the 393d Regiment of the 99th Division, defending a high ridge to the east and facing the Siegfried Line, had been attacked early that morning by superior enemy forces who took advantage of the battalion's open flanks to knock them off position. That battalion, or remnants of it, continued to fight somewhere between us and the enemy, partially surrounded and all communications gone except through the artillery liaison officer. Our battalion had been attached to the 393d, since they had no reserve force. Our mission was to counterattack to reestablish the original positions.

Get set. It's coming now . . . the attack order. At last you're going to attack. There's no chance now for a reprieve.

The CO of the 393d had insisted that we attack immediately to relieve the besieged unit, the Colonel continued, but he had succeeded in putting off the attack until morning. We would jump off slightly before dawn, at seven o'clock, attacking astride the east-west highway. Company I would attack on the left. Additional ammunition would be available later at battalion.

The platoon leaders were assembled when I returned to the company. I had only one map of the area, and there was no place where we could have a light to examine the map with the lieutenants. Sergeant Albin's slit trench was deeper than the others, but at that it amounted to little more than the snow scraped from the ground and a few inches of frozen earth removed. The men hastily threw dead branches across the makeshift hole, and I wriggled underneath with my map and a book of matches. One by one the platoon leaders crawled in to receive the order. I would strike a match and give them a brief glance at the map, now wet and sodden from the melting snow. I wondered if I could have drawn any worse conditions under which to issue my first attack order.

The last of the platoon leaders was underneath the rubble with me receiving the order when a call came over the 300 radio from battalion. It was Colonel Tuttle.

He said, "Mac, this is Paul. There's been a change in the orders I just gave you. Tell your platoons to dig in where they are. You report back to me. We'll hold where we are."

The men around me through some sixth sense knew that the attack was off. I thought they were going to do an impromptu dance in and out the trees.

I returned to battalion. The Colonel said the regiment had finally decided that the German attack was on too large a scale for one battalion to counterattack successfully. Our mission now was to "hold at all costs" in our present positions. A limited number of large shovels, picks and axes was available. We had been able to get a limited amount of ammunition, but thus far there were no bazooka rockets or antitank mines. Two US Sherman medium tanks would be sent to my left flank to cover the highway leading into the area, however. They would arrive around seven o'clock the next morning.

"You should know," Colonel Tuttle concluded, "that your supply sergeant was wounded slightly in the Nebelwerfer barrage. Altogether there were seven killed and twenty wounded."

Sherman Medium Tank

The night wore on. Enemy and friendly artillery continued to whistle overhead, the big guns pounding in a continuous sonoric chant. Buzz bombs roared overhead on constant schedules, setting off a blaze of fireworks from the antiaircraft guns in our rear. Small-arms fire punctuated the night noises far to our front. Around two o'clock a German burp gun erupted several hundred yards to our right. An American machine gun gave a slow, studied answer, like a Model-T Ford in contrast to the "Brrrrrrp" of the enemy gun. Rifles fired. An enemy reconnaissance patrol had hit L Company.

Lieutenant Jackson set up his artillery radio, and the voices from its speaker broke above the sound of scraping shovels in the CP area. Fire direction talked back and forth with the artillery liaison officer in the lost battalion of the 393d to our front. There were calls for fire and a relation of the battalion's seemingly hopeless plight. Their casualties were overwhelming. The regimental commander relayed a message for them to hold out as long as possible, but there would be no relief.

I kept only one shovel with the CP group, and by continual digging, alternating with the large shovel, we were able to construct a semblance of slit trenches in the frozen earth. Savage, Blackburn and I dug together. It was two o'clock before we had a hole which would completely hide our bodies below the surface of the snow when we lay on either side.

Most of the men had one or two blankets, or a GI sleeping bag. Neither Savage nor Blackburn had blankets— they had left them on the kitchen truck, expecting the truck to reach us in the assembly area. We spread my sleeping bag over the inch of cold mud that accumulated in the bottom of our hole and took turns hunching inside the hole to catch a few minutes sleep. It was not large enough for the three of us.

We lit cigarettes underneath shelter-halves and cupped them carefully in the palms of our hands lest the light show to some enemy patrol. When I lay down to sleep, my overcoat clutched tightly around me and my head resting inside my helmet, I would drift off for a few minutes, only to awaken sharply with the realization that I was shaking violently from the cold. I would get up, walk in a small circle, stamp my feet, and return to try once again to sleep.

As dawn approached I heard the clatter of the tanks on the highway. Calling Long on the sound-powered telephone, I told him to intercept them and show them his positions. They had been directed to take defilade positions on our left flank to protect the highway against enemy tanks. The highway was the only possible tank approach into the area.

I ate a K-ration as soon as it was light enough to make a fire from its cardboard container, and we tried to improve our slit trenches by putting dead logs across them to protect against shell bursts in the trees above us. The artillery's radio kept up its sonorous chant of messages from fire direction to the liaison officer in the lost battalion. The big guns barked to the rear of us. Buzz bombs roared overhead. Enemy shells whistled close above the tops of the fir trees and crashed into the open fields and the towns behind us.

Around ten o'clock, stray bullets from the small-arms fight up ahead began to zing through the woods. That was enough to tell us that the attacking Germans were not far away. Lieutenant Jackson called me to his radio. An important message was going through to the lost battalion.

"Do you think you can fight your way out?" the sender asked.

"I don't know," the liaison officer answered. His voice sounded tense and tired. "We're completely surrounded, but we'll try. We'll try to fight our way out."

There was a minute of silence. Then came a series of "overs" and "Rogers," and the liaison officer spoke again: "We're leaving our aid station to care for the wounded. We're coming out!"

A fury of small-arms fire sounded to the front. Stray bullets whined through the trees around us.

I called the platoon leaders and told them the message we had overheard, then notified battalion. I told the platoon leaders to be alert for the men of the 99th. The Germans would not be far behind.

The CP group began feverish attempts to finish covering their slit trenches. I thought how pitifully inadequate this little group would be should the Germans discover our exposed left flank and avoid the main force of the company in their attack. There was Savage, the phone to the platoons cupped to one ear; Blackburn, Charles and Robinson, the radio operators; Salberg, my runner; Butare, Willie Hagan, Burger and Lampton, the platoon runners; Wright, the man we had retained in headquarters to repair radios; Albin and Neubert, my two first sergeants; Lieutenant Flaim and Lieutenant Middlebrook; Lieutenant Jackson and his two artillerymen; Lieutenant Donald Y. Salder, of Brownwood, Texas, 81mm mortar observer from Company M and his one assistant—hardly a formidable obstacle should the enemy come the undefended route in force.

I took stock of our defensive situation. We were one rifle battalion thrust into a densely wooded area, with no terrain features that favored the defender, with orders to "hold at all costs." We were hastily dug in along a highway facing the direction from which we hoped the enemy would come, if he had to come. No company had been able to withhold a support platoon . . . there was no support company . . . thus the defense was a thin single line of riflemen.

A shallow draw lay to the front of my rifle platoons, with a higher ridge rising beyond it over which the enemy would soon be coming. Another draw led up my left flank, protected by two light machine guns and a few riflemen in a position in which no man in his right mind would place machine guns—unless he had no other method of defending the probable enemy approach. Our right flank lacked fifty yards of tying in with K Company along a firebreak which bisected the highway. We had no anti-tank defense except the two Sherman tanks and a bazooka with three rounds of ammunition. We were being supported by 99th Division artillery, an outfit about which we knew nothing, except that this was their first action except for holding a "quiet" defensive sector for a month. But there was nothing that could be done now but wait.

At 10:30 a jeep loaded with men clipped down the highway toward the rear at breakneck speed. That would be the vanguard of the retreating battalion from the 99th. The Germans would be here soon.

11

WE RUN LIKE HELL

A ragged column of troops appeared over the wooded ridge to the front of the 2d and 3d Platoons. There were not over two hundred men, the remnants of nine hundred who had fought gallantly to our front since they were hit by the German attack the preceding day. Another group the size of a platoon withdrew along the highway, donating the few hand grenades and clips of ammunition which they possessed to my 1st Platoon. Two men stayed to fight with my company. Two enlisted men, carrying a badly wounded lieutenant, stopped exhausted with my 3d Platoon. They could carry him no farther. I called for a litter squad.

The riflemen could not be sure if the next troops that appeared over the ridge were friendly or enemy. I alerted the artillerymen to call for fire in the event the approaching troops were Germans. Lieutenant Brock's call came a few minutes later, scarcely preceding a hail of small-arms fire which sounded like the crack of thousands of rifles echoing through the forest. There was no doubt now. My men could see the billed caps of the approaching troops. They were Germans.

Since the presence of friendly troops to our front had prevented Lieutenant Jackson from zeroing any artillery concentrations, I had to depend on an overlay of concentrations which the lieutenant had plotted by map. Three rounds whistled over the treetops and crashed in the draw to our front. Was that all of the concentration? Brock called for more. I relayed his request to the artillerymen, demanding a battery volley. Three rounds whistled overhead in answer. I called again for a volley, but only three rounds came. Lieutenant Jackson said the artillery was short of ammunition. I felt a sinking feeling growing in the pit of my stomach.

Long was on the sound-powered phone. Had I given an order for the two tanks to withdraw? I had not? Well, they *were* withdrawing. They were moving up the highway toward the rear!

I got Colonel Tuttle on the battalion radio. There had been no orders for the tankers to withdraw. He checked with the tank commanders and reported back that the tankers were merely moving to my 3d Platoon area to "improve their positions." I would have preferred their presence on the left flank, but I accepted the explanation. After all, they knew their job, and there was only the one tank approach. I was satisfied as long as they were in the company area.

Enemy bullets whistled through the trees around us. I jumped into the slit trench with Savage and Blackburn. Request after request for artillery and mortar support came from the platoon leaders. I called for every concentration listed on my overlay and for variations of each. The inevitable, maddening three rounds fell each time. The platoon leaders begged frantically for more. I began on one side of the company area and called for concentrations all across our front and back again. Lieutenant Sawyer called for barrage after barrage of 81mm mortar fire. The crack of small-arms fire reached an ear-splitting crescendo like static on a forgotten radio during an electrical storm.

The conversations over the battalion radio told me that the enemy was hitting K and L Companies as well, but the main force of the attack seemed directed against us.

The 3d Platoon called again for artillery in the draw to their front. The enemy had withdrawn to the bottom of the draw and was regrouping for another assault. The small-arms fire stopped. A tense silence settled over the forest, broken now and then by the crack of a single shot.

Long suddenly called for artillery fire on a ridge which rose high above the other terrain features a quarter of a mile to his front. He had spotted a mass of assembled enemy infantry and at least ten enemy tanks! We fired two of the three-round salvos. Long said there were no hits on the tanks, but they had dispersed. I quickly forgot about the tank threat in the excitement of the situation.

Another hail of small-arms fire told me the attackers had reorganized for a second assault. Frantic cries for artillery and mortar support came from the platoons. Lieutenant Wilson wanted two litter squads. He had two men badly wounded. Couldn't I get the litter to remove the lieutenant from the 99th?

I lay flat on my back in the slit trench, the platoon phone to one ear, the receiver of the battalion radio to the other. The chill from the frozen earth seeped through my clothes and I shivered, but I was surprised at my own calmness. The long nights of shaking terror in the pill-boxes had convinced me that I could never be calm in combat. I did not know what had possessed me to keep calm. Surely, this was the most serious situation in which I had ever found myself.

The small-arms fire reached another crackling crescendo. Long had several men wounded. He didn't know how many or how badly. The enemy bullets were too thick to move around. I called again for litter squads.

Wave after wave of fanatically screaming German infantry stormed the slight tree-covered rise held by the three platoons. A continuous hail of fire exuded from their weapons, answered by volley after volley from the defenders. Germans fell right and left. The few rounds of artillery we did succeed in bringing down caught the attackers in the draw to our front, and we could hear their screams of pain when the small-arms fire would slacken. But still they came!

Artillery and Nebelwerfers, with their accompanying terrifying screams, played a deep accompaniment in the background. The shells exploded to our rear and around the road junction to our right. We ignored their crushing explosions, thinking only how thankful we were that their effects were reserved for others than ourselves.

The small-arms fire rose and fell again and then again, indicating that the attacking troops had withdrawn momentarily to the bottom of the draw to regroup before launching another suicidal assault. Reinforcements streamed over the ridge behind them to join the assaults. The draw and the highway were littered with their dead and wounded, but there seemed to be no end to their fanatical attacks.

I heard no more about the tanks that Long had spotted

earlier. The knowledge of their presence was less fore-boding since I knew that the two Shermans were present to defend the lone tank approach. The open left flank con-tinued to plague me, and I kept in constant touch with Long, asking if he could observe enemy troops moving around to the left. The woods prevented him from seeing, but he knew from the firing in the draw on the left that the light machine-gunners were having a stiff fight.

All three platoons and the 60mm mortars began to beg for more ammunition. I sent three men from company headquarters to the firebreak opposite battalion to see if there was any ammunition left there. There was none. Re-peated calls to battalion brought assurances from Captain Montgomery that they were "doing all we can." Battalion had moved from the firebreak farther to the right rear.

The 2d Platoon reported a company soldier killed. It was the first death in Company I since I had taken com-mand three months before, but the news was not so stag-gering as I had expected it would be. There was too much other excitement.

The dead soldier was Technician Fifth Grade Martin W. Carlson, the Pennsylvania aid man whom the riflemen idolized, who had jumped from his foxhole to aid a wounded soldier nearby. A bullet pierced his helmet, and he fell face forward in the hole of the wounded riflemen he had sought to aid. He was a "noncombatant" accord-ing to the rules of warfare and was denied the privilege of wearing the Combat Infantryman Badge and the ten dol-lars per month pittance for dangers and hardships en-dured, but death had made no distinction.[1]

Message after message came over the platoon phone. Lieutenant Wilson was badly wounded. He could not walk and must have a litter. Ammunition was running lower and lower. The M Company machine-gunners with the 1st Platoon were out of ammunition except enough to keep one gun firing a few minutes longer. The 60mm mortars found their ammunition supply so low that they fired only when the enemy was actually assaulting. Germans were being killed as close as ten yards to forward foxholes. Hand grenades were practically all gone.

There was no solace from battalion. Each call for litter-

---

[1] A badge was later designed for combat medics.

bearers or additional ammunition was met with the maddening words: "We're doing all we can." I told them we could not hold out much longer unless we got additional ammunition. Captain Montgomery said we *must* hold. "Our orders are to hold at all costs," he said. I wondered if he could possibly realize the meaning of those words. We must hold until every last man was killed or captured. *Company I's last stand! And what is to be gained? Nothing but time. Time born of the bodies of dead men. Time.*

Seven times the enemy infantry assaulted, and seven times they were greeted by a hail of small-arms fire and hand grenades that sent them reeling down the hill, leaving behind a growing pile of dead and wounded. But withal the attacks seemed poorly organized. There was no supporting artillery or mortar fire upon our positions, and I wondered why they had not yet found the open flank on our left. There was only the suicidal wave of fanatical infantrymen, whooping and yelling and brandishing their rifles like men possessed.

I looked at my watch. It was 3:30 in the afternoon. Time was passing amazingly fast.

Long said he saw the enemy tanks! There were five of them, giant Tigers lumbering down the road three hundred yards away, surrounded by over a hundred enemy infantrymen.

Get those Shermans into action. It's your only hope. You might hold off the infantry, even with your ammunition practically exhausted, but riflemen can't fight Tiger tanks. The 1st Platoon has your only three rounds of bazooka ammo. Unless the Shermans can stop them, three rockets are all there is between you and Company I and Kingdom Come.

I called Sergeant Garcia to send a man to contact the tankers and tell them to move immediately to their former positions on the left flank. This business of "improved positions" was so much bosh. Garcia's answer was stunning:

"They're gone, Cap'n. They pulled back to K Company fifteen minutes ago."

I did not take time for the full meaning of his words to sink in. Giving our call sign over the radio, I asked for Colonel Tuttle and told him my plight. Either I got those

Tiger Tank

tanks back to my left flank or I could not possibly hold the positions.

While waiting for the Colonel's answer, I tried barrage after barrage to destroy the big Tigers with artillery and mortars, but we made not a single hit and the near misses only stopped the infantry temporarily, not fazing the great steel monsters in the least. They waddled effortlessly on toward the hapless riflemen.

A round of 88mm fire snapped the top from a fir tree above our heads and fragments sprayed in all directions. There could be no doubt now. The Tigers had arrived.

Round after round crashed into the area . . . a momentary shrill whistle followed by a deafening explosion and the sharp thud of the round being fired, the latter reaching us after we heard the shell explode.

"For God's sake, Cap'n," Long screamed over the phone, his voice half-sobbing. "Get those tanks down here. Do something, for God's sake. These bastards are sitting seventy-five yards away and pumping 88s into our foxholes like we were sitting ducks! For God's sake, Cap'n!"

"What about your bazooka?" He said a bullet had gone in one end and bent the tube so the rocket would not pass through it.

Colonel Tuttle was on the battalion radio. The tankers said it would be suicide for them to face the Tiger tanks. They would not move unless he gave them a direct order, and then he was afraid they would disobey it. And he was inclined to agree that they stood no chance against the more heavily-armored Tigers and their 88s.

I burned with anger, and I must have been insubordinate. If my men could fight the armor-plated monsters with nothing but rifles and die in the attempt, the tankers could afford to try it with medium tanks.

"If we don't get the tanks, we can't hold another five minutes," I said slowly and finally. "Thank you, sir. Roger. Out."

Shades of General Custer. Company I's last stand. Hell, what does it matter? You never expected to get out of this war alive anyway. Not really.

I gave Long the news. He was frantic. There was absolutely nothing he and his men could do. A direct hit had landed on one of the heavy machine guns. Another had hit in Technical Sergeant Smith's foxhole. Smith was the platoon sergeant. Long didn't know if he was dead or not. The other machine-gun crew was out of ammunition and was withdrawing. He was powerless to stop them. He was afraid his left flank in the draw was falling back, but he couldn't see to make sure.

"Hold, Long!" I cried. "For God's sake, hold! We've got to hold!"

I wondered how I made my voice so convincing. I wanted to throw away the platoon phone and the battalion radio and everything connected with war and bury my head in my hands and cry, cry, cry.

The infantry assault upon the other platoons continued.

The sound of battle reached a height which I had never thought possible before. The burst of the 88mm shells in the woods vied with the sound of hundreds of lesser weapons. It couldn't last forever, I thought. It must stop sometime. It *must* stop! But when? And how?

I looked toward the draw between me and the highway. About twenty men were walking down the draw toward the rear. I recognized several men from the light machine-gun section and a machine-gun crew from M Company. The others were riflemen from the 1st Platoon.

I did not know where they were going. All I knew was that somehow I must stop them. I jumped from the slit trench and ran toward them, ignoring the crack of bullets through the trees, waving my arms and shouting for them to stop. They turned to look at me with vague, blank expressions. They seemed to wonder who was this crazy man who wanted them to do this foolish thing. I saw that it was the entire left flank of the 1st Platoon. The thin lines of the remainder of the platoons would soon be cut off from the rear. The 60mm mortarmen, a few yards away, were dismantling their weapons.

I managed to get the men to move to my CP, but I could not stop them there. They walked slowly on toward the rear, half-dazed expressions on their faces.

I jumped into the slit trench and grasped the radio handpiece. I sat on the edge of the trench, ignoring the whistle of bullets and the crash of 88mm shells around us as everyone seemed now to be doing. "Get the platoon leaders on the phone," I called to Savage.

"Hello, Roger One," I said into the radio, not waiting for acknowledgment that they were receiving my message. "This is Mac. My left flank has fallen back. I can't stop them. The Germans are overrunning my left platoon. I'll try to build up another line along the firebreak. We can't hold here."

There. I had said it. This was I Company turning tail and running. This was I Company retreating. This was I Company hauling ass. This was I Company running like a sonofabitch. Strangely, I didn't give a damn. I was utterly void of feeling.

Savage held the platoon phone toward me. "I can't get Long," he said, "and Scotty's here with us now."

Don't sound afraid. You've got to sound like you mean business.

"Hello, Brock," I said calmly. "They've overrun Long's position. Swing your platoon back to the left rear and we'll build up another line along the firebreak. Did you get that, Garcia? Pull back and we'll tie in with K Company. My CP's pulling out now. We've *got* to hold at the firebreak. Do you understand that? We've *got* to hold at the firebreak."

The men in my CP group were already moving toward the rear. I grabbed my musette bag and my carbine. Savage took the phone. Blackburn grabbed the radio. We ran toward the rear.

We reached the north–south firebreak and crossed it. The foxholes which battalion had occupied were along the far edge of the clearing in a patch of small firs whose interwoven branches formed a dense green barrier. I knew that any fight here would be at close quarters, because the Germans would be able to advance unseen to the edge of the firebreak fifteen yards from the foxholes we would occupy, but it was the only spot where there would be any possibility of holding.

I ran up and down the line, shouting, "We've got to hold 'em here! We've got to hold 'em here!"

The men stared back at me unbelievingly. I was asking headquarters men armed with carbines and pistols to hold off hordes of attacking Germans that had already broken through all our rifle platoons could offer. There was only one machine gun, a light gun manned by Private First Class Richard Cowan, of Wichita, Kansas, set up five feet from the foxhole which I occupied.

The Germans were upon us almost before we knew what was happening. We could not see them for the low-hanging branches of the fir trees across the firebreak, but we could hear their shouts and shrill whistle signals which evidently came from their leaders. I decided they were a flanking group that was on its way unseen around our left flank even as we left our former CP. The attackers who had dislodged the 1st Platoon could not have reached us so quickly.

Cowan began to spit machine-gun fire across the narrow firebreak, and I heard a German scream with pain. The headquarters men fired their carbines and pistols into the low-hanging branches. The fir trees to the right were too thick to see the area where the rifle platoons were supposed to be going into position. I wondered if they had been able to build up any semblance of a line.

A round from an enemy tank broke the top from the small fir above Cowan's head, sending him reeling from his gun, but he jumped back and continued to fire. I knew that the big Tigers had reached the junction of the firebreak with the highway. Hails of enemy bullets thrashed the snow and the fir trees around us.

I ducked beneath the cover of my foxhole to try to get battalion on the radio, but without success. Then I stood up and looked out of the hole. Great God! There was no one left but Cowan. The others had fallen back!

I jumped from the foxhole and yelled to Cowan to withdraw. Savage and Blackburn followed me. I left my musette bag lying on the ground, but my carbine was over my shoulder. Absentmindedly, I screamed to "get the radios." Savage jumped back into the foxhole, and Blackburn and I turned and plunged through the thickly interlaced branches of the little firs. Bullets followed us, lashing the firs on all sides of us, and I wondered if maybe I had been hit. I felt no pain, but I could not see how any human being could endure those hails of bullets and not be wounded.

I stumbled blindly through the brush, unheedful of the branches scratching my hands and face. My overshoes were slick, and I tripped and fell face downward in the snow. I rose again and stumbled blindly on.

As we plunged through the firs I was separated from Blackburn and the group that had held briefly at the firebreak. I did not worry that Savage or the others were not with me. They were some place else in the fir thicket. I came across Sergeant Albin and Sergeant Walter L. Dieterich, of Cincinnati, Ohio, a machine-gun squad leader. We plowed through the firs together until we came unexpectedly upon K Company's CP, a series of half-completed foxholes dug in the frozen red earth.

Captain Howard C. Wilson, of Houston, Texas, the K Company commander, was talking frantically over his 300 radio. He turned as I approached.

"Damn, but I'm glad to see you," he said. "Battalion lost contact with you, and I haven't heard a thing about how your company's coming."

He seemed more relieved than perturbed at seeing me, and I wondered what he thought brought me to his CP. Perhaps it was the way I stood looking at him blankly. There must have been nothing in my face to tell him that my company was no more, and that even now hordes of Germans were rushing toward us unchecked.

Through my mind raced only one thought—I had failed and failed miserably. My orders had been to "hold at all costs," and I, personally, had failed, and because of my failure the entire battalion would be routed or annihilated. And all from a local German counterattack. I Company had fallen back, but I could not blame the men. They had given in because in some way I had not led them correctly. It was I who was responsible. I would turn in my captain's bars if I ever reached the rear, or perhaps they would court-martial me. I did not care.

"There's nobody on your left flank," I told Captain Wilson in a matter-of-fact voice that I hardly recognized as my own. "They just knocked the hell out of us, and the whole company's fallen back. I couldn't tell you where any of I Company is right now except these two sergeants and myself."

"Good God! What can I do, Mac?"

"I don't know," I said. "You can't hold here. There's nothing on your left."

Bullets whistled through the trees. Shells from the enemy tanks crushed gaping holes in the green growth of the firs. Men looked at each other with blank expressions on their faces. A lieutenant kneeling in a foxhole beside an artillery radio spoke to me:

"You might as well get in away from the bullets, Captain."

As if in a daze, I moved to his foxhole, and Albin and Dieterich sought cover. The lieutenant proffered his hand.

"I'm Lieutenant Michelson,"[2] he said.

I took his hand and mumbled my name.

"Helluva spot to meet," he replied, "but I'm glad to meet you. Maybe we'll get together under a little better circumstances some day."

Now isn't this silly? You're about to die, and here you are shaking hands like you might be at a charming little tea.

"Yeah," I said. "Maybe."

The bullets whined around us, and the 88mm shells exploded with crushing explosions that made me jump. Captain Wilson stood in his foxhole with his platoon phone glued to his ear.

---

[2] Soldier's name in this instance is fictitious.

"My left platoon has fallen back," he cried. "It's those goddamned tanks."

"Yeah," I said. "I had three rounds of bazooka ammo, and they knocked the bazooka out."

"I've got six rounds," Captain Wilson said.

Two men grabbed a bazooka and disappeared into the underbrush in the direction of the enemy. I thought how foolish it was to think of stopping ten Tiger tanks with one bazooka. The two soldiers returned a moment later, panting for breath.

"Good God, Cap'n," one of them said, "the woods just a few yards from here are full of the bastards. We'd better get the hell out."

"That settles it. Tell the other two platoons to withdraw into Krinkelt and Rocherath. Notify battalion. Tell them we're gettin' the hell out!"

We plunged again through the thick fir trees toward the rear. I heard battalion on Captain Wilson's radio telling L Company to withdraw into Rocherath before the full force of the enemy's flanking drive should hit them.

We reached the edge of the patch of small firs. To our left lay the exposed highway leading up the hill into Rocherath. To our right the corner of the fir thicket joined the corner of a patch of larger trees which extended two hundred yards up the hill. We chose the latter route without hesitation.

We ran halfway through the patch of woods before we came to a group of abandoned foxholes. Captain Wilson yelled to the group to halt.

"We'll hold up here," he shouted. "We may be able to hold them up while some of the others get out."

I could not see what good we could do from this position, but I was taking the commands now, and I took cover alone in a foxhole on the edge of the woods facing the highway. It was good to let someone else do the thinking for a while, even if I disagreed with the decision. I was not afraid—instead, I was strangely apathetic to the whole affair. The Germans were hot on our tails. So what? They had been hot on my tail for almost as long as I could remember now, and they had cut my company to ribbons. They might as well get me too.

German infantrymen emerged from the fir thicket we had left such a short time before and milled around two abandoned US tanks parked in the open beside the forest.[3] A Company M machine gunner, Private First Class José M. Lopez, of Brownsville, Texas, set up his gun beside a hole five feet to my rear. He opened up on the German infantry, the blast of the muzzle forcing me to sink to the bottom of my hole for cover.

The Germans wasted no time in returning the fire, riddling the area around the machine gun and my foxhole with burp-gun and rifle fire. A Tiger tank appeared at the road junction where the battalion had been shelled the night before and fired point-blank at Lopez' exposed position. The long barrel of the 88 on the tank seemed to reach half the distance from the hull to my foxhole. Lopez continued to fire.

An American jeep with two aid men, their red Geneva crosses pointed on their helmets, tore down the highway from the direction of Rocherath toward the road junction. I held my breath. The Tiger tank would surely blast them from the road. Couldn't they see that the Germans were here now? They did. With the jeep spinning on two wheels they turned around and tore back up the road. The tank did not fire.

Over the noise of Lopez' machine-gun firing I could hear Captain Wilson shouting to withdraw into Rocherath. I wanted to obey, but I was caught in the cross-fire of the heavy machine gun and the attackers. I gritted my teeth and waited for a lull in the firing. None came. I jumped from the hole and ran blindly toward the rear. Bullets snipped at my heels. The tank saw that we were running again and opened with renewed vigor, the big shells snapping the tops from the trees around us as if they were matchsticks, but I saw no one fall.

Dusk was approaching, and it was difficult to see for any great distance. I could not make out the town of Rocherath that I knew was high on the hill to our left front, but we plunged blindly up the hill, following a thin hedgerow that would be scant protection should the Germans elect to follow us with fire.

---

[3] These were, I have since determined, the two tanks which had been assigned to support my company. In a gallant action, they had stood against the Tigers at the road junction on the edge of the woods. Both were knocked out, and the officer in charge, 1st Lt. Jack L. Miller, was killed.

I slipped and fell face down in the snow. I cursed my slick overshoes. I rose and fell again. I found myself not caring if the Germans did fire. Snow had gotten inside my shoes and my feet were soaked. My clothes were drenched. Perspiration covered my body, and my mouth was dry. I wanted a cigarette.

I felt like we were helpless little bugs scurrying blindly about now that some man monster had lifted the log under which we had been hiding. I wondered if it would not be better to be killed, and perhaps that would be an end to everything.

12
"NICE WORK, MAC"

High on the hill to my left I could see L Company withdrawing. Enemy artillery pounded in the middle of the ragged retreating column, the fiery glow of the explosions shining brilliantly in the gathering darkness. *Isn't artillery fire pretty at night?* Other barrages exploded over a wide expanse of snow-covered ground to the front. I wondered why there was no answer from our own artillery.

We came upon a group of dirty infantrymen digging in along a hedgerow. *What people are these? There was supposed to be nothing between the Germans and Paris but our thin line of riflemen in the woods.* I did not know who they were or what had brought them here, but they looked to me like dirty, bedraggled gods who had suddenly descended from the heavens to set this ridiculous situation right.

"What outfit?" I asked.

"Ninth Infantry," a GI answered, his face covered with beard and dirt. "It ain't enough we attack for five f——g days. We gotta turn around and take up somebody else's defense."

"It's that goddamned 23d," another said. "They let a Kraut patrol knock the hell outa 'em."

Captain Wilson and the other men were gone. Only Albin, Dieterich and I were left. I saw a major and two captains on reconnaissance. They asked my outfit.

"I saw your battalion commander a few minutes ago," the major said and directed me to a farmhouse beside the highway.

We changed directions and made for the farmhouse. Infantrymen were digging in to the front of the house. I stepped inside a stone barn on the right. Captain Montgomery was there.

"Hello, Mac," he said simply, shaking my hand.

The thought that I had been a miserable failure came back with a force that brought tears to my eyes, and words would not come from my throat. Monty tried to comfort me. The Colonel was in the basement of the house. I would feel better after I talked with him.

We walked across the courtyard and down the dark steps of the house into the basement. A group of enlisted men were eating K-rations. Colonel Tuttle was talking quietly with a group of officers. A dim candle lit the room.

"Nice work, Mac," Colonel Tuttle said.

I could control myself no longer. The choking sensation in my throat became wracking sobs that I could not hold back. The Colonel tried to comfort me, and I felt foolish and childish, but I could not stop. Someone gave me a cigarette. I held it with trembling fingers.

I was suddenly conscious that Colonel Tuttle was saying something to me, but at first I could not make any sense of what he was saying. This had been no local German attack. The enemy had already broken through and taken Büllingen, catching the Division quartermaster and engineer troops unaware in the undefended town. The main supply route from Krinkelt to the rear through Büllingen had thus been severed. The other two battalions of our regiment had been thrown into the battle, and the division was abandoning all its gains in the Wahlerscheid offensive to hold this critical area. Our battalion had held long enough for the 9th and 38th regiments to withdraw past the vital crossroads guarded by two stone farmhouses that I remembered from the trip forward. The 9th was setting up a line along our present location, and the 38th had taken over the defense of Krinkelt. There were unconfirmed rumors that this was a big German push all along the First Army front.

The news stunned me.

I stammered, "You mean——you mean——"

"I mean you did a good job, Mac," the Colonel said. "The Germans are throwing everything they've got. You held out much longer than I expected after I learned the true situation."

So I had not failed! And I Company had not failed! I was almost happy that the German offensive *was* on a large scale. My men had done an excellent job against heavy odds, and those who had died were not dead because of some personal failing of mine. The realization made me want to cry again.

"They got our kitchens, too, Mac," the Colonel continued. "They were evacuating Krinkelt when they ran smack into a column of German tanks. Got all five of them. Büllingen had already been taken."

I thought of my typewriter and the article I had written, "Nine Days in a Pillbox," that were stored on our kitchen truck, and then dismissed the thought as being ridiculous when there were probably lives lost on that same kitchen truck.

I went with Captain Montgomery back to the barn outside. It was dark now. War was all around me still, but I felt much better. There would be courage to go on. I still did not know what had happened to my company, but I could believe now that they might have made their way out of the forest along the route taken by Company L.

Sparky, Lieutenant Middlebrook, Wright and Butare were in the barn. The two men and two officers and Albin, Dieterich and myself made a total of seven men from Company I. They seemed as glad to see me as I was to see them.

"We heard you were killed, Cap'n," Sparky said.

The idea seemed remote and far away, and I laughed.

"We know a lot of your men ended up in Krinkelt and Rocherath," Captain Montgomery said. "The Colonel and I are going there now to contact L Company. They got out pretty light except for an artillery barrage after they left the woods. We'll send them and any of your men we find to meet you here. You dig in with L Company to defend the right flank of the 9th. There's no one between them and Rocherath."

We found a pile of fresh hay in the end of the barn facing the enemy. I dug out an armful and spread it in a rear corner of the barn. I was cold. My clothes were soaked and my feet were drenched, but I pulled a portion of the hay over me and drifted off into a sleep of utter exhaustion.

It was neither the sound of the tanks firing nor the artillery exploding nor the staccato chant of automatic weapons that woke me. I seemed to hear them somewhere in the background, but my fatigued body did not respond. Someone was shaking me.

"Wake up, Cap'n! Wake up! The sonofabitches have hit us again. They're all over the goddamned place!"

I jumped to my feet. The sound of battle in my ears was real now, and I could see the flash of tracer bullets as they passed the open door.

"Where's L Company?" I asked.

"They didn't get here," the soldier answered, and I could not make out who he was in the darkness. "The others are gone. We'd better get the hell out."

With that he was gone from the barn. I did not think to pick up my carbine. I looked toward the forward end of the barn where the hay had been stored. A tank was firing point-blank into the barn. The dry hay was a mass of flame.

I ran from the barn. The surrounding area was lit up from the flames and the paths of thousands of fiery tracer bullets. I saw a soldier, silhouetted against the tracers, throw a can of gasoline at a tank. The tank burst into flame.

There seemed to be no lull coming in the firing. I ran toward the rear of the farmhouse, snagging my trousers on a fence post and tearing at them madly. I flattened myself against the back wall of the stone building just as a shell from an enemy tank crashed into the front. The house rocked precariously, trembling from the impact of the explosion.

The snow-covered area to the rear of the house became the beaten zone for countless tracer bullets. Tank fire crashed around the building. Artillery fell without pattern in the snow. The night was ablaze with more noise and flame than I had thought possible for men to create. Here was a "movie war." Here was Armageddon.

I could see the outlines of a bomb crater halfway between the house and the first hedgerow behind it. I waited for a lull in the firing before leaving the momentary safety of the back of the house. I ran as fast as I could run across the open field and dived headfirst into the bomb crater. My body hit two other men huddling in the hole. They were Wright and Butare.

"Where're the others?" I asked.

"They all got out, I think," Butare said. "I saw them all but Algin and Dieterich. They were sleeping in the front of the barn."

"Well, we can't stay here," I said, thinking of the completely open flank. "We'll find battalion headquarters and stick with them."

We climbed from the crater and ran across the remaining portion of the open field. A hedgerow loomed ahead of me, and I dived headfirst across it. My head burrowed into a deep snowdrift, and I lay there for a moment panting from the exertion. I found Wright and Butare again and we followed the course of the hedgerow on hands and knees toward the north. I knew that we should reach the highway again after it passed the farmhouse and curved left to lead to the crossroads and then into Rocherath. We crawled on, paying no attention to the wet snow which chafed our hands and knees.

A burst of tank fire on the hedgerow before us brought us to a stop. We lay flat against the snow. A voice came from the other side of the hedge.

"Who's there?"

"Some men from Company I, 23d," I said.

"That you, Cap'n?" It was Middlebrook. He crawled through the hedgerow to join us.

"I left the barn with Sparky," he said, "but we got separated."

The four of us moved on behind the hedgerow until we reached an area where the firing was less intense. I looked back. The barn beside the farmhouse was enveloped in flame. Two objects to the front were burning. They must be German tanks. Beyond the barn near the woods the radar set of an antiaircraft battery still smoldered. It must have been destroyed by its crew when our battalion had been knocked from position, I thought.

We reached a road running east-west, but it was covered with snow, and I could not tell in the darkness if it was the highway. A company of soldiers was digging in on the north side of the road. They didn't know where they were, but they were from the 9th Infantry. They had been told to dig in here. Maybe I could find their lieutenant. He might know their location.

I found a lieutenant. He said he didn't know how to get to Rocherath, but his battalion CP was at a crossroads to the northwest. If I'd take the road on our right, we couldn't miss it. There were two farmhouses at the crossroads.

Troops were moving up the road, one shivering unevenly spaced column on either side. A misty rain set in to add to the cold. The troops would sink slowly and silently to the ground as an artillery shell or a round from a tank whistled dangerously close to the road. The center of the battle continued to emanate from the vicinity of the barn and farmhouse we had just left, the fiery glow of the burning barn diminishing rapidly now. Our own artillery was firing, and I could tell from the lusty, unsparing number of rounds that 2d Division artillery had gone into action.

Two gaunt grey buildings loomed against the dark sky at the crossroads. A major cursed beneath his breath as he tried to turn a column of trucks around in the muddy road. I asked if he knew where I might find headquarters of the 3d Battalion, 23d Infantry. He directed me to the nearer farmhouse.

I found Colonel Tuttle in the cellar. He was waiting there for orders with the few remaining men of his battalion headquarters. He had been unable to get through to Krinkelt and Rocherath when he left me at dusk. Enemy tanks and infantry had infiltrated into both towns, and fierce fights were raging back and forth. Major Joseph, Captain Montgomery and fifteen enlisted men were with him. They had heard from Lieutenant Robert M. Green, of Bevery Hills, Cal., the battalion intelligence officer. He had collected a sizable force from the battalion, including a number of my men, and was fighting along with elements of the 38th Infantry in Krinkelt.

The Colonel and Major Joseph had one supper K-ration between them. They prepared to eat it, and I realized for the first time how hungry I was. It was midnight, and I had not eaten since breakfast, and then it had been only a K-ration. I refused politely, but they insisted, and I had a bite of the hash. I had never consumed a more delectable morsel.

Colonel Tuttle told me to spend the night with them. In the morning he would send me out to try to round up more men from the battalion. The cellar was damp and my soggy clothing made me shiver violently, but I sat down on a mattress in a corner and tried to sleep. I slept for a few minutes, woke up shaking, walked around the room several times and sat down again.

The noise of the battle filtered through the cellar walls for the remainder of the night, and did not lessen in intensity with the coming of dawn. Captain Montgomery came back from the CP of a unit of the 9th Infantry across the road with the news that the enemy had struck anew at K Company of the 9th, the company defending the farmhouse where we had waited to go in with Company L. The company commander, First Lieutenant Stephen E. Truppner, of Baltimore, Md., had called for artillery fire on his own position around the farmhouse when the enemy overran the area. Only twelve men from the company escaped.[1]

I set out at seven o'clock with Middlebrook, Wright and Butare in an effort to locate other men from the battalion. We had gone only six hundred yards when I realized that it was impossible to traverse the route which the Colonel had pointed out on his map. The area was an inferno of small-arms and artillery fire as the Germans continued their efforts to dislodge the dogged doughboys who prevented them from reaching the vital crossroads. We returned to the farmhouse.

The day passed slowly. The din of the battle did not slacken. Someone discovered a case of K-rations on the second floor of the farmhouse, and we each ate several with child-like enthusiasm.

Captain Montgomery brought in various reports from the CP across the road. Thirteen enemy tanks had infiltrated an American column during the night, hiding in barns in Krinkelt and giving the defenders of the town

---

[1] A letter received from Sergeant Albin after publication of the first edition of this book told me how Albin and Dieterich, only seconds behind me in escaping from the burning barn, had found their path blocked by the short rounds of American artillery fire. They had taken refuge in the cellar of the farmhouse with the men of Company K, 9th Infantry, and were captured with Lieutenant Truppner and his men after a German tank stuck its gun full in the door of the farmhouse and opened fire.

57mm Antitank Gun

several hours of veritable hell with the coming of morning. Seven had been knocked out with bazookas and tank destroyers. The 1st Battalion of the 9th, the unit defending the vital crossroads, was holding successfully, but their casualties had been tremendously heavy. There were numerous gaps in the line, and the entire left flank of the division, which included the road to Wahlerscheid to our left over which the 9th and 38th regiments had withdrawn from the attack against the Roer River dam, was completely undefended. A platoon of antitank guns had been placed around the two farmhouses, and a platoon of tank destroyers operated from the crossroads answering calls from various units in distress.

I tried not to think of the men from I Company, but I could not help myself. My thoughts ran continuously to Sergeant Savage and the others, and I wondered how many had survived the fierce fight in the forest and the fierce fighting which followed. Several of the men at the battalion CP had seen one or two of my men since the fight in the woods, but there was no news of Savage. I tried to think where I had seen him last, and the revelation that the last time had been when we pulled away from the firebreak frightened me.

An emergency call from the 1st Battalion of the 9th for men to fill a gap in their line caused Colonel Tuttle to round up all available riflemen, including Wright and Butare, and place them under the command of Lieutenant Middlebrook. I told them goodbye at the door upstairs, thinking how miserable they must feel at the prospect of going out into that blazing no-man's land to meet the Germans again. I thanked heaven that I was an officer whom the Colonel considered he must save to command Company I again when we should get back together, but I felt little and selfish with the feeling.

Middlebrook returned at three o'clock. They had been engaged in a fight even before they reached the area designated for them to defend. He had come back for more men. They could not hold the spot alone. Colonel Tuttle said there were no more men.

A burst of machine-gun fire zinged over the crossroads. From the cellar the fire sounded as if it came from an extremely long range. No one seemed perturbed until a soldier came running down from upstairs.

"We'd better get the hell out, Colonel!" he shouted. "Those bastards are closing in from the left . . . not more'n two hundred yards away!"

The Colonel's coolness communicated itself to me, but I could not rid myself of the feeling of dejection that came with the realization that now I must run from Germans and death again. It seemed to me that I had been running from Germans for as long as I could remember. Was there no stopping place?

The Colonel told everyone to get his equipment ready. He went upstairs and returned a moment later to announce that we were leaving. Enemy troops were approaching along the undefended Wahlerscheid road.

I left my slick overshoes in the cellar. Maybe some German would get them, and then *he* could fall face down in the snow.

We dashed across the crossroads toward the southwest, machine-gun bullets whining over our heads. Our objective was the town of Wirtzfeld. It was next to impossible to get into Krinkelt and Rocherath. I could see the tank destroyers backing from the sheds around the farmhouses to meet the new threat.

Wirtzfeld was a little farming town surrounded by hills.

We went to the house used as a command post by the 2d Battalion of our regiment. Their troops were dug in on the hill to the southeast of the town, facing Büllingen, but they held the commanding ground and had been able to organize it before the enemy hit them.

Middlebrook came in. He had tried to reach the men whom he had left in position when the CP pulled out, but he was unable to make it. A fierce fight was going on now at the crossroads. The 1st Battalion of the 9th had sent remants of a rifle company to help the TDs stop the threat in order to hold open their escape route until dark.

I learned at the 2d Battalion CP that a number of my men were fighting with 2d Battalion companies, and others had assembled at the battalion CP.

Among them was Scotty, who told me that almost all his weapons platoon had made their way back to Elsenborn and now were driving ammunition vehicles back and forth to the front. All the men who had been with me in the brief defense of the firebreak were safe, he said, to the best of his knowledge, except those who had gone with me, Sergeant Savage, and Private First Class Lampton, the weapons-platoon runner. One of the men had seen Lampton get hit and fall as they pulled back from the firebreak. He had thought Savage was with me.

We billeted for the night with the headquarters group of the 2d Battalion. I slept on the second floor of a thatched-roof house, taking off my wet clothes and drying them by a roaring fire in the kitchen downstairs. I lay awake for what seemed like hours thinking of the men of the company who still had not been heard from—including Savage. I was too exhausted to stay awake long, and I drifted off into a sleep that was interrupted many times during the night by heavy shelling. I was on the forward side of the house and on the second floor with the scant protection one could expect from a straw roof, but I was so tired that I made no effort to go downstairs when the shellings began.

The next morning Colonel Tuttle called for a volunteer from among the lieutenants to take the remaining men to strengthen the line between the 1st and 2d Battalions. Scotty and Middlebrook both insisted on going, but the Colonel finally designated Scotty.

It was eleven o'clock when Colonel Tuttle told me to assemble the remaining men, mostly specialists. He had talked with regiment by radio, and we were to move to the vicinity of Elsenborn where approximately two hundred men from the battalion had been assembled and were digging in a second line of defense for protection should the enemy make another penetration. Cooks and clerks from rear headquarters units had already assisted these men in digging positions a mile to the rear of Wirtzfeld where the division would withdraw its defenses as soon as the situation was stabilized sufficiently to effect a withdrawal.

We assembled at a barn across the street from the 2d Battalion CP. Major Joseph told me there would be a three-quarter-ton truck arriving in a few minutes to take us to the rear. I also might be interested in seeing the driver, he said. I wondered why he was talking in riddles.

I saw the truck come around a bend in the muddy street. There were bullet holes in the shattered, dirty windshield, and I could not see the driver until he pulled up alongside. Then there was no mistaking the slow grin, the drawling, surprised, "Hello, Captain."

No one else ever pronounced the two syllables of the word "captain" quite like that.

13

WE ALMOST HAVE A BABY

Savage and I ran for each other like two college girls suddenly reunited. Smiles wreathed our faces. We both tried to talk at once. He had heard that I had been killed. I had not known what had become of him.

"I jumped back into the foxhole after you said 'get the radios,'" he explained at length. "First thing I knew, there were Germans all over the place. They made me come out and took my watch and moved me over to the highway where they had two other GIs. Then one of our artillery barrages started falling. The Krauts hit the dirt. I grabbed one of their burp guns and started spraying, and we ran like hell. All three of us got away."

Since his escape, he had been hauling ammunition with a truck he had found abandoned in Krinkelt. He had a few close ones, as the bullet holes in the windshield testified, but he had come through without a scratch. He had brought a load of ammunition to the crossroads where I had been around noon the day before and had seen Major Joseph, but the major had not mentioned that I was there.

When no one was looking, he lifted a shelter-half in the front seat to show me his proudest possession. He had found it in Krinkelt.

"That's why I wouldn't ever give up this truck, even when the going got pretty hot," he said.

There was a half case of gin and a half case of Scotch.

We moved on to the rear and set up for the night in Elsenborn. My shattered nerves were coming under control, but the enemy shelled the town fiercely during the night, and I discovered that we were as close to the actual fighting in Elsenborn as we had been in Wirtzfeld. The Wirtzfeld–Rocherath–Krinkelt positions stuck out into enemy territory in a salient.

Colonel Tuttle had visited regimental headquarters and I learned details of the "big picture" from him. The 9th and 38th regiments, with scattered elements of the 99th Division, were defending Krinkelt and Rocherath. The remaining two battalions of the 23d were defending the supply route into Krinkelt and the town of Wirtzfeld. The 1st Infantry Division had been moved into line and now defended Bütgenbach, thus halting the thrust from Büllingen on the most direct route to Elsenborn. The action was the north flank of a major German effort. Several divisions to our south, including our old positions near Heckhuscheid, had been completely overrun, and Nazi spearheads were gaining daily. The holding of the Elsenborn corner protected routes to Verviers and Eupen and subsequently the First Army supply base of Liège and the vital port of Antwerp. The German general's name was Von Rundstedt.

We had engaged in the opening blows of what soon became known as the Battle of the Bulge. But we could not know at the time the full extent of the contribution made by the men of the 2d and 99th Divisions. The fact is, we had dealt a stunning blow to the main effort of the German counteroffensive. In the words of Hugh M. Cole, the U.S. Army's official historian, we "had knocked part of Hitler's personal operations plan into a cocked hat."

The basic German plan was to strike the thin American positions in the Ardennes with three armies, cross the Meuse River, and drive to Antwerp. This would cut off four Allied armies in northern Belgium and Holland. In staging this massive attack, the Germans made their main effort on their right wing around Elsenborn in order to gain vital roads leading toward Antwerp. The initial objective was Elsenborn itself because this little farming village sits astride the first high ridgeline inside the Belgian border.

General Josef "Sepp" Dietrich and his Sixth Panzer Army drew the assignment. Dietrich in turn directed his strongest thrust by the I SS Panzer Corps against Elsenborn itself. The corps assigned to three infantry divisions the mission of opening a hole in the 99th Division's thin lines so that two SS panzer divisions, and later two more SS panzer divisions under a different corps command, could plunge through. According to the timetable, the infantry was to penetrate the 99th Division's positions on the first day, the tanks were to get over and beyond the Elsenborn Ridge on the next, and the armor was to cross the Meuse on the third.

It did not work out that way—partly because of a determined stand by the 99th Division, partly because of the unexpected presence near Elsenborn of the 2d Division.

A German task force did get through a gap in the line on the first day and capture the town of Büllingen, where, among other accomplishments, German tanks shot up my battalion's kitchen trucks. This was the notorious Task Force Peiper under Col. Joachim Peiper, which was later to murder more than a hundred defenseless American prisoners in what became known as the "Malmedy Massacre." Continuing forward in the darkness, Peiper by-passed the Elsenborn Ridge to the south, only to wither eventually on the vine. Without Krinkelt and Rocherath, the Germans could not get onto the Elsenborn Ridge, and when daylight came American guns on the ridge were able to knock out everything that tried to move through Büllingen. Unable to get reinforcements or supplies, Peiper eventually was cut up and destroyed.

Meanwhile, in the woods east of Krinkelt and Rocherath, the German infantry was having such a difficult time on the first day against the 99th Division that Dietrich threw in the two SS Panzer divisions to help. The tanks which hit Company I the next day, December 17, were from Dietrich's 12th SS Panzer Division. According to their timetable, they were to be over and beyond the Elsenborn Ridge that night, but as darkness fell, all they had accomplished was to knock over Company I and the rest of the 3d Battalion, 23d Infantry, in the woods.

By this time, American commanders had recognized that something big was taking place, something out of the ordinary. The First Army commander, General Hodges, had authorized the 2d Division's General Robertson to withdraw his 9th and 38th Regiments from the Wahlerscheid attack in order to hold Krinkelt and Rocherath. The men we met at the farmhouse—where I first saw my battalion commander, Colonel Tuttle—had been sent there by General Robertson himself when he heard what had happened to my company and the whole 3d Battalion in the woods.

For two more days and nights the 2d and 9th Divisions fought to hold the twin villages. It was touch and go. German tanks got into the villages more than once, but courageous men armed with bazookas hunted them down. The Germans could not get through.

Sepp Dietrich's telephone rang constantly with messages from the German high command. What was wrong at Krinkelt–Rocherath? they demanded. But the question, as well as exhortation, was fruitless. Late on December 18th, Dietrich left the job at the twin villages to his infantry and sent his tanks to try to get to Elsenborn by a different road, by way of Büllingen. But by this time the 1st U.S. Infantry Division had moved into position to block this thrust.

During the night of December 19th, as the surviving Americans executed a planned withdrawal from Krinkelt –Rocherath to the Elsenborn Ridge itself, the German high command pulled out the SS panzer divisions. Denied the vital road network in the northern portion of the "bulge," the Germans now had to depend on other roads in the center of their penetration, around Bastogne. This was where they sent their armor. But paratroopers of the 101st Airborne Division already had arrived at Bastogne. They would see to it that Hitler got no more at Bastogne than he had at Elsenborn.

The elements of the 2d Division remaining in Krinkelt, Rocherath and Wirtzfeld withdrew during the night according to division plan. The 38th Infantry occupied the front-line positions overlooking Wirtzfeld. The 2d Battalion of the 23d held a secondary defensive line along a ridge which included the town of Berg, between Elsenborn and Wirtzfeld. We would occupy secondary positions on the left.

The next morning I joined the provisional company, made up of men who had thus far rejoined the battalion, four hundred yards to the northwest of Elsenborn where they were digging in a secondary line. I was overjoyed to find thirty-five of my men, including Lieutenant Brock, Lieutenant Goffigon and Sparky. We traded information back and forth on survivors of the action of the first day of the German offensive. Almost all of the men had heard rumors that I had been either killed or captured.

Enemy artillery shelled us all day, but there were no casualties. A ragged column of GIs rapidly descended a high ridge to our left front around noon. We thought they were running from a German attack, and it was difficult to keep our men from moving to the rear. Everyone was nervous. A call to battalion verified that the retreating troops were from a unit that had just been relieved by another. It was only then that the nervous men were content to continue preparing the secondary positions. I had not trembled so violently at the sound of enemy artillery since leaving the pillbox positions in my first action, and now we all shuddered even at the sound of our own artillery pieces belching out their answering rounds.

At three o'clock we received orders to move across country to Nidrum, a small town lying between Elsenborn and Bütgenbach. The secondary defense orders had been changed. The 1st Battalion would occupy the positions we had been preparing, and we would occupy a secondary line overlooking the dam and lake between Berg and Bütgenbach. The 1st Division was on our right, the 99th on our left (holding only a regimental front, as was the battered 2d), and the 9th Infantry Division was on their left. There would be no breakthrough now to Elsenborn.

Regiment had assembled another contingent from our battalion at Nidrum. With their number I found I had a company of approximately one hundred men.

We dug in for the night on a barren ridge between Nidrum and Berg, overlooking the dam and lake. The night was cold, but a thaw had melted the snow. Here and there a patch of white clung to a shallow draw or the bottom of an abandoned slit trench. Alerts from battalion came during the night to watch out for enemy tanks. Several were reported to have broken through at Bütgenbach, although the accompanying infantry had been stopped. Enemy shells showered our position all night, sending whining fragments close over the shallow slit trench where Savage and I huddled in a futile attempt at sleep.

We improved our foxholes on the bare hill the next morning, making roofs from fence posts and covering them with straw. A heavy snow carpeted the hills during the night.

I was called to battalion headquarters in Nidrum the next morning, Thursday, December 22, to reconnoiter for a new defensive position along the northeast edge of the town. It was not until late in the afternoon that the move was approved, however, but I was delighted. The defense was designed to combat a breakthrough should it come through the 1st Division sector, and now we would occupy an area with numerous houses.

Sparky moved the company into the new positions at dusk. The platoons hurriedly went into position and began to dig in for the night. Each platoon had at least one house in which the men were rotated for sleeping, and all men could wash and shave. My CP was set up in a house near battalion headquarters. Foxholes were soon equipped with makeshift stoves, and we settled down for what we hoped would be a long period of rest.

I began to evaluate our losses in the fierce opening day fight in the Krinkelter Wald. Initially, approximately eighty men were listed as missing, but each day brought a new list of names from rear hospitals of men who had been wounded and evacuated or were victims of trench foot. The list of missing in action finally narrowed down to twenty-four men, including Lieutenant Wilson, First Sergeant Albin, Technical Sergeant Smith, Carlson (the medic), Lampton (the weapons-platoon runner), Sergeant Dieterich, and three of my cooks, Technician Fourth Grade John L. Ballew, a Texan; Technician Fifth Grade Noble R. Peters, of San Antonio, Texas; and Technician Fifth Grade Clark W. Shealy, of Winsboro, S. C. Many of my key men were hospitalized, including First Sergeant Neubert Blackburn, Staff Sergeant Neafach (the supply sergeant), Technical Sergeant Garcia and Technical Sergeant Winegardner (the platoon sergeant and guide of the 3d Platoon), and Staff Sergeant Elliott (the mess sergeant).

The losses necessitated replacement of men in the key

positions immediately. Technician Fifth Grade Richard Black, of Easton, Pa., became supply sergeant, and Private First Class Purdue took over Black's duties of armorer-artificer. Lieutenant Middlebrook became 3d Platoon leader, and Private First Class Naranjo, the battalion runner who had once served as a company clerk, became acting first sergeant. I depended upon replacements for my mess personnel, since our food was cooked for some time by E Company's kitchen. Eventually, we received replacements for our kitchen equipment, and Staff Sergeant Threadgill returned from the hospital to rebuild our mess staff as mess sergeant. Other replacements continued to join us, including two former members of the company, Technical Sergeant Carl Whelchel, of Gaffney, S. C., and Technical Sergeant Benney Stephen, of Wilkes-Barre, Pa.

Our battalion was awarded the Distinguished Unit Citation for its defense in the Krinkelter Wald, and a number of men in the company were awarded Bronze and Silver Stars for gallantry, including Silver Stars for Lieutenant Goffigon and me. Others were posthumous awards. Private First Class Cowan, the light machine-gunner who had performed his duty so faithfully and fearlessly at the firebreak, was killed in action the next day, but he received the Distinguished Service Cross that was later changed to the Medal of Honor, and Private First Class Lopez, the M Company machine-gunner attached to K Company, also received the nation's highest soldier honor, the Medal of Honor.

We had turkey on Christmas and New Year's Day. The division post office held up all packages that were not delivered during the breakthrough and delivered them on Christmas morning. Two feet of snow covered the ground, but we were situated comfortably. Many attended special Christmas and New Year religious services held in the town creamery and thanked God for the blessings of which we were fully conscious.

Showers were later set up in the creamery and clean clothes were available.

Enemy artillery continued to blast the center of the town, but few rounds fell on my company position. Enemy planes were active until after New Year's Day, but their attention was directed toward the dam to our left front or the camp at Elsenborn in our rear. We saw several planes brought down by our pilots and the anti-aircraft gunners of the attached 462d Antiaircraft Battalion. Buzz bombs sputtered overhead at intervals throughout the day and night.

On January 2 I went with the other company commanders and the battalion staff to reconnoiter the area held by the 2d Battalion, but the anticipated move was not made. Two days later I went on reconnaissance to Bütgenbach and beyond the town to the positions held by a battalion of the 26th Infantry, 1st Division, but the move was cancelled even after we had moved up part of our equipment. We were overjoyed that we were not to move, but we could sense that some type of action was brewing for us. The *Stars and Stripes* told of offensive action all along the front to seal off the German penetrations in "the Bulge," and we knew that we could not escape for long.

Sparky was transferred to K Company, and First Lieutenant Ewell L. Smith, Jr., of Dallas, Texas, was transferred from K Company to be my executive officer. Captain Cowan, the former B Company commander, became battalion operations officer when Captain Montgomery was transferred to the 1st Battalion as executive officer.

The days and nights became long and boring, but one look at the snow-drenched countryside and the bitter days of cold and snow were enough to convince us that we were fortunate to be here. The enemy shelling became less and less frequent. On January 11 another group of replacements arrived to bring the company once more to full strength.

On January 14 the other two battalions of the regiment moved to the vicinity of Weismes, Belgium, as the vanguard of the 23d Infantry Combat Team. Colonel Tuttle went to Weismes on reconnaissance and returned at dusk. I received a telephone call to have the company prepare for movement at dawn the next morning, and I felt a sinking feeling in the pit of my stomach. Again we were preparing for an attack. I was to report to battalion immediately for orders. Our period of rest was over.

Colonel Tuttle outlined the plans. The 30th Division and the 1st Division, minus the 26th Infantry, had already jumped off the initial phase of an offensive aimed at re-

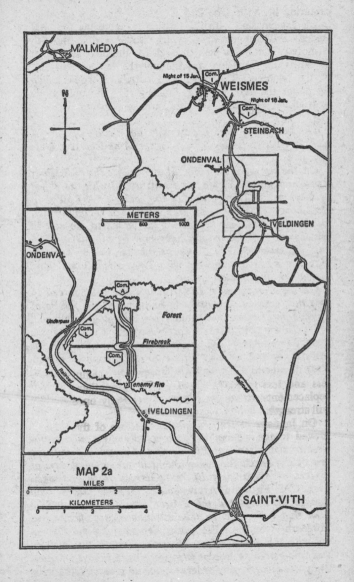

MALMÉDY

Night of 15 Jan. Com.

WEISMES

Night of 18 Jan.
Com.

STEINBACH

ONDENVAL

IVELDINGEN

N

METERS
500 1000

ONDENVAL

Com.
A

Forest

Underpass

Com.

Firebreak

Com.

Railroad

enemy fire

IVELDINGEN

Railroad

MAP 2a

MILES
0 1 2 3

KILOMETERS
0 1 2 3 4

SAINT-VITH

capturing St. Vith. The 23d Combat Team was attached to the 1st Division with the mission of capturing the vital Ondenval–Iveldingen Pass, which would enable the 7th Armored Division to pass through for the final assault on St. Vith. Our battalion was initially the reserve battalion of the regiment. The other two battalions would begin the attack the next morning, January 15. We would move by trucks at dawn to an assembly area in Weismes.

The passage of time has brought the picture of this attack into better focus, both from the American and German sides.

On the northern shoulder of the bulge, the U.S. First Army had started to attack on January 3d with the object of meeting the Third Army in the center of the bulge at Houffalize. Ten days later the First Army commander, General Hodges, had broadened the attack to the east to include the V Corps, commanded now by Maj. Gen. Clarence R. Huebner. The V Corps mission was to take St. Vith and eventually link up with Third Army units along the base of the German bulge.

On the German side, Hitler at last had been forced to face the facts. On January 8th, he admitted the failure of his counteroffensive and authorized grudging withdrawal of the Fifth and Sixth Panzer Armies. Eventually the Sixth Panzer Army was to withdraw through St. Vith for transfer to the Eastern Front to help counter a new Russian offensive. Though the German field commanders, including Field Marshal von Rundstedt, wanted to pull back all the way to the Rhine, Hitler insisted on a stubborn delaying action for every inch of the bulge and another stand at the Siegfried Line.

In the Ondenval–Iveldingen area, only a few miles southwest of the Elsenborn Ridge where Company I and the rest of the 2d Division had fought in the opening days of the counteroffensive, a different German force had taken over. The Fifteenth Army, under General Gustav von Zangen, had replaced the Panzer divisions of Sepp Dietrich that had failed to take Elsenborn. Specifically, the Fifteenth Army's LXVII Corps defended around Ondenval with the 3d Parachute Division. Though this division was understrength, the paratroopers were skilled veterans. They were under strict orders to give no ground. Otherwise, yond Ondenval. The 2d Battalion was to attack on the right to take the town. A highway from Ondenval crossed the wooded ridge to the next town of Iveldingen, providing the pass that was the regiment's ultimate objective.

Resistance had been stiff thus far in the towns, Lieutenant Prinds told me. His company had almost forty per cent casualties, but many of them were from frozen feet.

Word came soon that the 2d Battalion had taken Ondenval without a fight. The enemy had pulled out during the night, leaving only a few snipers to delay the advance. We could hope that perhaps the pass would be taken before we were committed.

Actually, the enemy's 3d Parachute Division *had fallen back to the Ondenval–Iveldingen pass itself because the U.S. 30th Division, on my regiment's right flank, had begun to threaten the rear of the paratroopers. But the Germans were determined to hold the pass. The* LXVII *Corps commander, General Otto Hitzfeld, was rushing* *ops of the 246th Infantry Division into the line to help* *inst the 30th Division. And the next day, January* *th, the* LXVII *Corps would come under the Sixth Pan-* *Army. Then General Dietrich himself would be re-* *ible for holding the pass long enough for the panzer* *ions to escape to the east via St. Vith.*

spent the day setting up our temporary defenses in ittle farm town. The weapons platoon found two mortars which the Germans had been using, evi- captured in the breakthrough. A dead GI lay be- stack of antitank mines a few yards from my CP. r man told me he was from Antitank Company and ed while clearing the mines.

just got a letter from home last night," the soldier is wife wrote that she'd just had his first kid. He ven get to answer the letter."

ant Middlebrook sent a runner to my CP that . A civilian woman in one of the houses his pla- pied was going to have a baby. He thought it was soon. He thought I should call a medical officer. talion medical officers were busy when I called,

the Americans might break through the pass to St. Vith, cut off the Sixth Panzer Army, *and prevent withdrawal of the panzer divisions from the Ardennes.*

The weather was piercingly cold when morning came, but there was no additional snow. We covered approximately ten miles by truck, although I could tell from my map that the town was no more than four miles by direct route from our starting point. We could hear the dull pounding of heavy artillery pieces as our trucks stopped on a tree-lined road near the town of Weismes. It was two miles into town, but we must walk from here. The road was under observation.

We trudged slowly along the snow-covered, icy highway, expecting at any moment to hear the dreaded sound of incoming shells. Colonel Tuttle met us at the edge of town, and Sergeant Wolfgang, again our billeting guide, joined us to lead us to the assembly area. There was no shelling, but the freshly-sprayed dirt around the shell holes beside the road kept me in a constant state of alert. Our route took us through the center of the town, past tanks and tank destroyers painted white and ill-shaven infantrymen wearing dirty white robes as camouflage, and beyond the village square to a large L-shaped three-story building. Branches fallen from the massive trees littered the streets; yellow spots showed high on the tree trunks where shells had torn the branches away. Sergeant Wolfgang led us into a door of the building and up a dark stairway into a large room. Shelves, stacked with civilian hats, lined the walls. We were in a former hat factory. Five minutes later three-fourths of the men had equipped themselves with fantastic civilian straws and felts.

I was called immediately to battalion to go on reconnaissance.

Captain Cowan oriented me on a large map of the area. Four hundred yards to the southwest of Weismes the 2d Battalion had succeeded in capturing Road Junction 109, two farmhouses at a junction of trails that had held out stubbornly since it was by-passed two days before by elements of the 30th Division. The battalion was now engaged in taking the portion of the town of Steinbach which lay to the right of the railroad track to the southeast, while Company C was fighting to capture the part of the town on the left of the railroad. My mission was to reconnoiter defensive positions in the vicinity of RJ 109, which the reserve company of the 2d Battalion was now vacating, with the idea that I might occupy the positions for the night.

Salberg accompanied me on the reconnaissance, and we returned to the hat factory around four o'clock. Again there was a message for me to report to battalion headquarters. Captain Eisler, the L Company commander, waited for me there. We were to go immediately to RJ 109 and reconnoiter the route to the town of Ondenval to the southeast with the possibility that we would attack at two o'clock in the morning to capture the town.

Captain Eisler and I assembled our platoon leaders and moved to the road junction, careful to follow the tracks of a tank destroyer as we neared the houses since the area had not been cleared of mines.

Dusk was approaching and a heavy fog settled down suddenly, making it impossible to see over two hundred yards in the direction of Ondenval. Our maps told us that we were over three-fourths of a mile from the town, and the route was evidently a mass of uncharted mines and enemy defenses leading down into a draw and up again toward the town. Eisler and I exchanged disapproving glances. A night attack under the circumstances would be virtual suicide. A night attack necessitated long hours of preparations and detailed reconnaissance, but there was little we could do except express our fears to Colonel Tuttle and hope for the best.

Hot food was brought to the company from Nidrum by jeep and trailer. We laid plans after supper for the two o'clock attack. I Company would guide on the right of the snow-hidden trail from the road junction to Ondenval. L Company would be on the left. I assigned platoon dispositions and issued additional ammunition and waited for the seemingly inevitable order which would send us out on the mission.

Captain Cowan telephoned at ten o'clock, and my CP group waited expectantly as I took the phone. C and G Companies had finally taken Steinbach, he said, which, for some tactical reason that I did not question, did not necessitate the taking of Ondenval that night. I should have the company turn in for the night, prepared to eat

Bazooka

a five o'clock breakfast in the morning, and th relieve Company C in the defense of Stein o'clock.

My face beamed with a jubilant smile group yelped with joy.

It was cold and dark when we lined of twos outside and moved down the fasting on hot cakes by candlelight. The made sucking noises as we walked.

After leaving Weismes we passed an occasional gutted house on the r arrived shortly after dawn at a small ing near a railroad underpass. The and a gaping bazooka hole at the showed daylight all the way thro Company's CP.

Lieutenant Marvin H. Prinds er, showed me the disposition men took over. A and B Com yond the town without resista to join them to continue wooded ridge far to the fr

so we waited anxiously through the afternoon, expecting at any minute for the baby to come. The only man we had who knew anything at all about such an event was one of the aid men who had read a medical book once on the process.

The Battalion Surgeon, Captain Edward T. Matsuoka, of Honolulu, arrived before the baby, despite our fears. I sent him immediately to the house where the civilian woman waited. We joked back and forth among ourselves about I Company becoming a father.

Captain Matsuoka returned in a few minutes, however. Her time was not near, he said. She was evidently feigning such illness in order to get transportation into Weismes, but she could walk perfectly well.

I Company would not have a baby. We found it difficult to hide our disappointment.

The area around my CP became a veritable parking lot for all vehicles that had business beyond the underpass. I expected the enemy to shell the area all afternoon, since his observation was evidently perfect. He held the high ridge beyond Ondenval, marked here and there by towering wooded peaks, a terrain feature which commanded all the surrounding area. A shelling did come just before dark, but there was no damage.

It was dark when I received a telephone call to report to battalion. A jeep was dispatched to pick up Captain Eisler and me and took us back into Weismes to battalion headquarters. The other company commanders were there when we arrived, and Colonel Tuttle began the order. We knew even before he began that the 3d Battalion would attack!

The 1st Battalion, attacking on the left of the Steinbach–Ondenval–Iveldingen highway, had suffered heavy casualties, but had advanced to take a narrow neck of woods fifty yards from the main forest. Their major opposition had come from their left flank where the main forest extended for several hundred yards in the direction of the attackers. Lieutenant Prinds, the C Company commander, had been killed. The 2d Battalion, attacking on the right of the highway, had advanced to the bottom of a draw near a point where the highway wound again beneath the railroad track. They were held up by intense small-arms fire and heavy shelling from the wooded ridge to their front.

Our battalion was alerted to attack at any time after seven o'clock the next morning, passing through the 1st Battalion to take the wooded pass and continuing on to Iveldingen. If the final attack order was received, we would attack in a column of companies, I Company following Company L. L Company would swing right after entering the woods, and I Company would be committed then on their left flank. The time of our attack depended upon the rapidity of the advance of a battalion from the 30th Division on our right.

Once again I had received an attack order, and the realization of my inexperience made me afraid. The old phrase, "This is it," ran through my mind again and again. The last such order I had received had been negated by the German breakthrough near Krinkelt. There seemed little possibility of anything happening this time to keep Company I from attacking.

We returned to our companies, and I gave the information to the platoon leaders. We set the time for breakfast at six o'clock, and I curled up on the cement floor of our basement CP and went to sleep.

14

ATTACK!

One of the men awoke me at six o'clock. I blinked my eyes several times and tried to realize where I was. The realization came and with it a feeling of revulsion that the war still went on, and today we would attack. I wanted to turn my face back toward the wall and sleep on and on.

We had hot cakes and syrup again for breakfast, but transporting the food from Nidrum in an open trailer had made them more cold than hot. We ate standing in the cold outside the CP, and I watched bearded, dirty men eat the cold flapjacks with cold syrup, one ear half-cocked for the sound of an incoming shell. I wondered if the time would ever come again when men could sit down to a hot meal in pleasant surroundings and not wonder if it would be their last.

I waited expectantly by the telephone after breakfast. The call which would tell me that the attack plans laid the previous night would go into effect might come at any time. Colonel Tuttle drove up in a jeep at eleven o'clock, however, and wanted me to go with him on reconnaissance to Ondenval. We drove through the underpass and into the town. He directed the driver to pull up before a building on the right of the road where a sign said "Inspire Red." It was the 1st Battalion's forward CP.

Lieutenant Colonel John M. Hightower, of Las Cruces, N. Mex., the battalion commander, had been preparing to go up to A Company's positions when we arrived. He said that it was impossible to get a good view of the surrounding terrain from the town since the skies were overcast and visibility was poor. He didn't think A Company knew where the hell they were anyway, and he wanted to see for himself. I might come along since I would be attacking through the positions later in the day.

We walked along the left edge of the highway the remaining distance through the town, the colonel's long, swinging steps making it difficult for me to keep up despite my own long legs. He was a giant, towering six and one-half feet tall and weighing two hundred and twenty pounds. Even if he had worn no insignia of rank one could easily have guessed that he was a ranking officer. His confident swagger and infallible manner were constant sources of amazement to the men of his battalion.

The highway curved gradually to the right as it neared the last houses in the town. It continued downgrade to the enemy-held underpass, a hundred yards past the bottom of the draw to our front. At the underpass it entered the dense fir forest and began the climb to the crest of the ridge where, according to our maps, it turned abruptly to the left and ran parallel to the far edge of the forest for three hundred yards before curving again to the south for its entrance into Iveldingen.

We turned off where the road first curved to the right, following a trail to the left to the top of a small knoll, and then turned sharply to the left to cross the railroad track. Beyond the railroad the trail was lost in the snowy wastes of an open field leading to the enemy-held woods.

We followed a path beaten by soldier feet in the snow across the field. I looked apprehensively at the woods which now lay to our right. A gunner located in the edge of those woods could easily spray the entire open space with fire. The huddled body of a dead GI, partially covered with powdered snow blown there by the wind, lay beside a fence half-way across the field. I wondered if some enemy gunner in the woods had killed him, but the tall battalion commander did not seem to give it a thought.

We reached a knoll covered with bare scrub bushes. A portion of the knoll had been cut away sometime in the past to provide earth for other construction. Two mortar squads from Company A now occupied the dug-out area. The colonel spoke briefly with them and continued past the knoll toward a small promotory of tall fir trees which jutted out from the main body of the woods on the left to form a narrow neck of woods fifty yards from the main part of the woods to the south.

One of the mortarmen cautioned us about going across to the neck of woods. "They've been shooting across there all day from the left."

Colonel Hightower seemed to ignore the remark and continued. I followed him somewhat apprehensively.

The narrow neck of woods, twenty-five yards across, was filled with a profusion of foxholes in varied stages of excavation. The men were digging as we approached, half to improve the positions and half to keep warm. The colonel talked with them, asking how they were feeling and if they had a good breakfast. They told him "Yessir," they had hot cakes, and would he please be a little more careful walking around? There had been snipers firing in the area all morning.

The colonel moved on toward the left, looking occasionally toward the enemy woods fifty yards away. We reached the left flank foxholes where the promontory joined the main woods. We had covered an area which could ordinarily be adequately covered by little more than one rifle platoon, but that was all that remained of A Company.

The men on the left flank were insistent that the colonel keep down. Sniper fire had been particularly intense here. There had been a machine gun firing at them from the dense brush thirty-five yards to the left front last night. The colonel dropped calmly to a kneeling position.

We retraced our steps, and an aid man overtook us at the edge of the woods. He was supporting another soldier with blood streaming from his forehead. There *were* snipers in the area.

Colonel Tuttle gave me the final orders for the attack at Colonel Hightower's CP in Ondenval. L Company would pass through A Company's positions at four o'clock, preceded by a ten minute artillery barrage. I would follow L Company as soon as they entered the main woods, swinging to their left. Our objective was a firebreak running east-west which bisected the woods at the halfway point. Here we would dig in for the night and continue the assault in the morning.

Our battalion had top priority on all artillery support.

The capture of the Ondenval–Iveldingen Pass was the top Corps objective, and the Corps commander wanted it pushed with all possible vigor.

It was two o'clock when I returned to my company CP and assembled the platoon leaders for the order. No time remained for them to make a reconnaissance, so I tried to describe the route they would take after passing Ondenval. The line of departure would be the line now held by A Company. The 1st Platoon would attack on the left, the 2d Platoon on the right, the 3d Platoon in support and protecting the left flank. Lieutenant Goffigon's left flank would guide on a north-south firebreak which, according to the map, they would encounter after entering the main woods. One section of heavy machine guns from Company M would be attached initially to each assault platoon, and our own light guns would go with the 3d Platoon. There would be little use for the 60mm mortars in the woods, so they would remain with my rear CP group, advancing by bounds upon my call.

Packs would be assembled and left with a guard from the CP group at the CP. Gas masks would be carried in keeping with a recent division order, but blankets would be left at the CP to be brought up after the position was secured for the night. Each man would take three meals of K-rations. Intra-company communication would be by 536 radio. Salberg, Savage, and Private First Class Charles, carrying the battalion radio, would accompany me in the forward CP group.

I was too busy with the various details of the movement to think much about fear. I tried to recall the various phases of an attack that I had learned in training, but I was fully conscious of my lack of experience. I was thankful that there were things to do to keep me busy, and I wondered what the men, who had only to get their personal equipment ready, were thinking. I completely forgot that I had not eaten even so much as a K-ration for lunch.

The company lined up at three o'clock in columns on either side of the road. I moved along the column, talking here and there with the men, calling a name when I was sure of it. There were so many men in the company now whom I did not know by name. We had received over a hundred replacements after the breakthrough. It was difficult to tell by their faces who were the replacements and who were the veterans. There was the same weary anxiety on the faces of all of them, but perhaps the smiles did come quicker from the veterans.

We had to wait for L Company to pass as we neared the underpass. Even as we waited a heavy fog began to envelop the snow-carpeted hills and the slush-covered roads. Darkness would come early tonight. Visibility was so poor that I knew our column was safe from enemy observers in the towering peaks to the south. When K Company attached itself to our rear, the double column stretched from Weismes to Ondenval.

I reported to Colonel Tuttle that I was ready. He checked my plan of attack and told me that a platoon of tanks and a platoon of tank destroyers were available on call, but he knew no method of employing them until the next day when we would have passed through the woods.

I waited outside the CP for the head of my company as L Company filed down the highway and cut left on the trail leading to the railroad track. I looked at my watch. It was fifteen minutes until four o'clock. The artillery barrage would begin in five minutes. L Company was moving into position now. The time was drawing near. *Oh, God, be with us in this attack!* Almost ten minutes until four now. I recognized Savage and Salberg in the column. I joined them and we moved toward the edge of town.

The big guns from the rear suddenly opened up, and I heard the shells whistle over and crash into the woods around the underpass and on the town beyond the woods. L Company's rear elements came to a halt. Their lead platoons must be on line with A Company's positions, I thought. We moved to the cover of the houses along the right of the highway. The big guns boomed steadily.

Four o'clock. The artillery shifted from the underpass but continued to shell the road junction beyond the woods. I heard Captain Eisler on the battalion radio:

"Hello, Charlie Three; hello, Charlie Three; my lead platoon has entered the woods. No resistance. Over."

For one brief, exultant moment I thought that perhaps the enemy had withdrawn from the woods. But no, that was too much to hope for. In the all-important but little section of war in which we were for the moment engaged, that would be like asking for the war to end.

I moved with Long to the point where the trail to the left joined the highway. I pointed toward the thin line of woods held by A Company and showed him his route. Men from L Company's support platoon lay half-crouched in the ditches beside the trail. A single rifle bullet sang over our heads and cracked as it passed as if someone had fired a small-caliber revolver close by my ear. We ducked quickly to the other side of the highway. No, the enemy had not withdrawn from the woods.

"Hello, Charlie Three; hello, Charlie Three." It was Captain Eisler again. "Lead platoon is entering opposition, but advancing slowly with marching fire. Am committing 2d Platoon."

L Company's support platoon still had not moved. I surmised that Captain Eisler was holding the platoon in the rear to move forward upon call. I signalled for the company to follow and moved across the highway and up the trail. A robot bomb buzzed across the top of the wooded ridge before us and flew at a dangerously low altitude across the town. It crashed into the hill to the rear of Steinbach with an explosion that seemed to rock the ground on which we stood and reverberated back and forth against the surrounding hills.

The boom of enemy guns in the distance gave us warning, and we plunged into the ditches beside the trail. The barrage which followed centered on the knoll where the trail turned to cross the railroad track. We lay there a few minutes after it was over. I sighed with relief when I saw that every man rose to continue.

When we reached the railroad track, the 1st and 2d Platoons jockeyed into position in the open field. They moved quickly into an approach march formation.[1] Small explosions that sent the snow cascading in all directions around little black puffs of powder and noise appeared unpatterned over the field. The men fell face downward in the snow and rose again when the barrage lifted. The Germans were firing light mortars.

---

[1] An open formation from which deployment for the attack after meeting opposition is relatively simple.

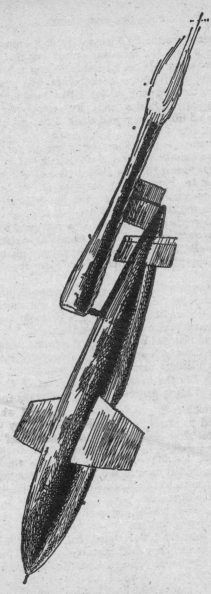

V-1 Buzz Bomb

One man from the 2d Platoon lay in a crumpled heap and did not rise. His face was buried impassively in the snow. I looked at him as I passed. He was a new man, a replacement received the week before. He was the first man from the company whom I had seen killed, and a mixed feeling of horror and pity swept over me, but there was no time to stop and think. I did not even know the man's name.

How strange is war. Some of us can go for days, and weeks, and months in war and never be killed or wounded, but another man is killed in his first taste of war.

Three more light mortar barrages fell at intervals as the platoons circled to come upon the A Company positions from the rear. I saw no one hit. I found cover during the barrages in the dug-out area occupied by A Company's mortarmen and ran the remaining distance to the narrow neck of woods where the lead platoons were reorganizing prior to crossing the open space into the forest.

I saw Captain Eisler. He said his platoons had already reached the east-west firebreak, wiping out four machine-gun outposts on the way, but one platoon continued to meet sharp resistance around the underpass.

The lead platoons began to cross into the main woods. I looked at my watch and saw that it was five o'clock. The time was speeding past. Already it was getting dark. The dense fog and the overhanging branches of the thick fir trees would bring darkness even more quickly in the forest.

I followed the assault platoons across the open space. They had found no opposition. Everywhere there were foxholes, but they were half-covered with snow and unmanned. I saw the north-south firebreak which I knew should be the left flank of the 1st Platoon, but the last men in the platoons were going across it. Someone had gotten mixed up in directions.

"Hello, Mac Six," Long radioed. "We've reached the objective. No opposition."

For a moment I was elated, but then I realized what had happened. They had mistaken a second north-south firebreak for the objective. I signalled for Savage, Salberg and Charles to follow, and I ran and stumbled through the snow until I reached the head of the column.

Battalion was questioning over the radio, wanting to know why we hadn't reached the objective. Since there seemed to be no opposition in the woods, I directed the platoons forward in column along the second firebreak. That would be quicker. We could move over to the right after reaching the objective. I started off with the head of the column.

"Goddamit, Captain," Savage said, "you've got to stay farther back. At least get some scouts out front."

His admonition reminded me that it was foolish for me to lead the column. The foolish days of "leading" one's troops into battle were past, even though correspondents persisted in telling of daring generals who preceded their troops, firing from the hip or brandishing a bayonet. I had had no feeling of bravado, but it seemed obvious that the woods were undefended. I dropped back to the rear of the 1st Platoon.

The lead platoon advanced three hundred yards and reported that they had reached the objective. I moved again to the head of the column and saw that the two firebreaks formed an intersection. I directed the scouts to follow the clearing to the right until they should reach the north-south firebreak which should have been our left flank. We would dig in there for the night.

The column started forward and then stopped abruptly. A slow, moaning voice came from the patch of small firs growing beyond the narrow ribbon of white that was the firebreak.

"Help! Help!" the voice cried, each word slow and deliberate. "Save me. Save me."

Every man stopped as if each had dropped an instantaneous anchor, and rifles dropped to the ready position as if by instinct. Darkness was almost completely upon us, and the men peered in vain toward the patch of firs to determine the source of the voice.

"Help me," the voice continued, the words heavily accented and spoken so mournfully that I could have sworn I felt the hair bristle on the back of my neck. "I am wounded. Help me."

"Come on out with your hands up," someone yelled.

"I cannot come," the voice said slowly, as if it were torture to utter each word. "I am blind. I cannot see you."

"Come out or we'll shoot."

"I cannot come. Please come and get me. Do not shoot. I am blind. I cannot see."

The same thought must have entered all our minds. This was a German trick to lure us into the open fire-break. I ran forward to the head of the column, apprehensive lest someone should decide to go out into the open toward the voice.

"Come out with your hands up or I'll shoot your nuts off, you Nazi sonofabitch!" a soldier yelled.

He fired a single shot into the underbrush.

The fir branches stirred. A dark figure emerged slowly from the brush, and I could see that it was a German soldier with his hands raised high above his head. He wore no cap or helmet, but a dirty, blood-stained bandage stretched across his forehead. Choosing each step carefully, he advanced across the firebreak.

"Do not shoot. Do not shoot."

Two of my men grabbed him roughly and searched him for weapons.

"I have no gun," the German said in carefully chosen English. "My comrades have left me when I am wounded."

"Bring him along," I said, designating two men to walk with him. "We'll send him back when we get where we're going."

I noticed for the first time the bodies of two Germans near the point where we had stopped. One still breathed. An aid man examined him briefly.

"Nothing we can do," he said. "He's dying fast."

I wondered how they were killed.

We continued along the edge of the trees until we crossed the north-south firebreak. I halted the column and sent a patrol from the 1st Platoon to continue to the west until they contacted the left flank of L Company. I reported our location to battalion and assigned defensive sectors to the three rifle platoons. Our main defense would face to the south, but the 3d Platoon would defend our flank along the north-south firebreak, facing east. Numerous abandoned slit trenches filled the area, and the men began improving them for the night.

I turned my attention to the prisoner, directing the two men who were with him to take him to the A Company positions. I had lost contact with the rear CP group by radio and wanted them to contact Lieutenant Smith, who should be at the A Company positions now. The men were afraid they could not find the positions. Our circuitous route through the woods had confused them, but they said they would try.

"Would you be kind to give me cigarette?" the prisoner asked.

"Why you Nazi sonofabitch," one of the guards answered, kicking the prisoner in the rear, "of all the goddamned nerve. If it wasn't for you and all your —— kind, all of us could be smoking now."

The patrol from the 1st Platoon returned. L Company's left flank was fifty yards beyond the right flank of the 1st Platoon. They were digging in for the night.

K Company reported by radio that they contacted the left flank of my 3d Platoon and were setting up their defense along the north-south firebreak. The night was quiet except for the scrape of shovels upon frozen ground and the distant pounding of artillery.

The two men who had taken the prisoner to the rear returned. They had made a quick trip.

"Did you get him back OK?" I asked.

"Yessir," they answered and turned quickly toward their platoons.

"Wait a minute," I said. "Did you find A Company? What did Lieutenant Smith say?"

The men hesitated. One spoke out suddenly.

"To tell you the truth, Cap'n, we didn't get to A Company. The sonofabitch tried to make a run for it. Know what I mean?"

"Oh, I see," I said slowly, nodding my head. "I see."

Captain Cowan called over the radio at nine o'clock.

"The orders are changed," he said. I should continue through the woods until we reached the highway and dig in there for the night, reporting to battalion upon arrival so they could send a tank-dozer to clear the highway of mines. The highway would be our supply route.

I cursed beneath my breath. We had reached our objective, but now we must continue. The men had practically finished digging in for the night. It was six hundred yards through the dense woods to the highway, six hundred yards of dark fir forest and deep snow where the enemy might lie in perfect ambush. Something inside me revolted against continuing forward, and I begged battalion to reconsider until daylight.

"There's nothing we can do," Captain Cowan answered. "Regiment's orders. L Company is already on the highway."

I knew from the report of my patrol that although L Company's right flank might be on the portion of the highway that ran through the woods, they were as far from the highway where it ran beyond the woods as was my company. I told Captain Cowan.

There was a moment of silence.

"Our information is that L Company is on the highway," Captain Cowan continued. "The Colonel says to get going."

There was no alternative now. Battalion thought I was bluffing.

I jumped into a partially-completed foxhole and turned on a flashlight to look at my map. Two men threw their overcoats over me to shield the light. According to my map, the north-south firebreak on our left should continue to the south, reaching the highway six hundred yards from our present location. But, in reality, there was a dense growth of small firs where the firebreak should have been. There was only one other route. We would move east and follow the second north-south firebreak down to the edge of the woods and the highway.

We moved out again in a column of platoons, the 2d Platoon leading so that I might shift them easily to the far side of the firebreak when we reached it. Lieutenant Brock was not certain he knew the route. I said I would lead the column. Savage objected, but I moved off behind two scouts who stepped out ten yards ahead of me. Perhaps there was nothing in the woods. Everything was quiet enough. I might as well lead the column so we could get there quickly and get set up for the night.

We reached the north-south firebreak and the 2d Platoon crossed and took up a close approach-march formation on the other side, facing south. The 1st Platoon moved into position on the right. I joined Long at the head of the 1st Platoon, and we moved cautiously through the woods, the whiteness of the snow making it possible for us to half-see where we were walking. Two scouts preceded us by five yards. The night was quiet, so that the crunching noises we made when we walked seemed amplified by the stillness.

We had gone slightly over two hundred yards to the south when the scouts stopped dead in their tracks and signalled quiet. I was about to ask what was causing the delay when I heard a German's voice.

"Halt!" the German cried and spouted a stream of guttural German. He could not have been over twenty-five yards away.

We dropped quickly to the ground. The German cried "Halt!" again and repeated the flood of German. I crawled up next to Long.

I said, "Sounds like we've hit an outpost or something. Deploy your two lead squads to the right and close in. I'm moving back with the radio to the head of the 3d Platoon."

Savage's warnings against leading the column now seemed exceedingly wise. If the Germans opened fire, I would be pinned to the ground, helpless to contact the other elements of the company except by radio.

Long began to deploy his forward squads to attack. I signalled for the three headquarters men to follow and turned to move toward the rear.

A burp gun stuttered. A flood of fiery tracer bullets blazed among the trees.

We fell face downward into the snow. The bullets traced a fiery path two feet above the ground. My men did not return the fire, and I was glad. The confusion would be terrific, if they opened up, I thought. The night was quiet again.

I rose and motioned for Savage, Salberg and Charles to follow. We had taken only a few steps when the burp gun opened up again.

"I'm hit, Captain!" I heard Charles scream, and he dropped to the snow. "I'm hit!"

I was conscious of a sudden pain in the calf of my right leg, as if someone had hit me with a giant club swung by powerful arms. I realized that I, too, was hit, and a sudden flood of fear engulfed me. We were two hundred yards forward of any friendly troops and eight hundred yards inside the woods. A momentary vision of a night spent bleeding in the freezing forest swept through my mind. A warm liquid flowed over my leg and into my boot. That would be blood, I thought.

"I'm hit, too, Charles," I said.

15
PURPLE HEART

My leg felt numb, and I dropped to the ground. The firing ceased. Charles said he was hit through the right hip and could not walk. Savage took the battalion radio, and I designated two men to carry Charles. We would have to get back to the 3d Platoon now.

I believed I could walk. I stood and put my weight on the wounded leg. A nauseating pain swept over me, and I thought I was going to faint, but I tried keeping the leg stiff and found that I could walk.

The men around us lay flat upon the snow in little bunches, as if they gained some solace through sharing their fears with each other. My brain was whirling. Should we continue the attack? How badly was I hurt? Had we hit a German patrol, or an outpost, or had we stumbled upon a main line of defense?[1]

I hastily decided to continue to the rear out of the line of fire and direct the attack upon the German position from a less restricted spot. We moved toward the rear, two men supporting Charles with his arms about their shoulders.

A sudden burst of small-arms fire came from our right rear, and the woods echoed to the crack of machine-guns and rifles. The fire was coming from the direction of the defensive position at the junction of the firebreaks which we had left. Bullets whined low over our heads

---

[1]Some years after the war, I revisited this area. As I retraced Company I's route through the woods, I was astonished to learn how close we had come to our objective on that confused night in January 1945. We had been less than 50 yards from the edge of the woods and not more than a hundred yards from our objective, the highway on the other side of the woods.

and buried themselves in the trees and the snow around us.

My first thought was that K Company had contacted our rear elements and, thinking they were Germans, had opened fire. We heard battalion talking on the radio, asking K Company what time they wanted to pick up their bedding rolls for the night.

"We've got no use for bedding rolls," K Company answered. It was Lieutenant Flaim. "We're in a fire fight."

Savage turned the butterfly switch on the radio and broke into the conversation with a distressed voice.

"Lieutenant Flaim," he cried. "Lieutenant Flaim, this is I Company. You're firing at us. This is Item Company. This is Item Company."

"Goddamnit, I said we're in a fire fight. We can't use any bedding rolls now."

"Lieutenant Flaim," Savage continued, "this is Savage. You're firing at I Company. Make your men quit firing. You're firing at I Company. You're shooting hell out of Item Company."

The radio was silent for a moment.

"The hell we are! If we're firing at I Company, then why'n hell don't you quit firing back?"

I was frightened with the realization of what he had said. We were receiving fire from K Company, but they were not firing at us. The enemy had slipped in behind us!

For some unexplainable reason my men had not opened fire in either of the directions from which the bullets came. I silently thanked God that they had not started shooting. The confusion would have been trebled, and I could visualize GIs firing at one another in the darkness.

The men were milling about in an aimless fashion, some moving to the rear, others shifting to avoid the group that had collected along the firebreak. I wondered if I could ever bring order out of the confusion. It seemed an impossibility with fire coming at us from front and rear in the darkness. I made a sudden decision.

"Call Long and Brock on the radio," I told Salberg. "Tell them we're withdrawing to the positions we just left. We'll reorganize and try it again from there."

Salberg contacted Long, and the men began to move toward the rear, stumbling and falling over one another in

the darkness so that I wondered if they would stampede
like cattle.

Salberg said, "Brock's radio must be out."

He tried again and again, but he could not contact him.
I stumbled to the edge of the firebreak and called across
to where the 2d Platoon should have been. There was no
answer. I tried again. No answer.

I decided that they must have already moved to the
rear; if not, they would surely hear us and follow. I
joined the milling mass of men, stumbling forward until I
reached the 3d Platoon. We crossed the east-west firebreak, and I directed Middlebrook to turn to the left and
follow our former route to the west to the positions beyond the next firebreak.

Two men moved out as scouts. I followed closely behind them, my leg beginning to pain fiercely. I stumbled
headfirst into an abandoned foxhole, and my face was
buried in the snow. A blinding light suddenly lit the forest for a moment, and I heard the explosion of a concussion hand grenade not five yards from the hole in which
I had fallen. Then came the guttural burst of a burp gun,
and the bullets whined over my head. The men behind
me dropped into the snow. A soldier yelled, "I'm hit!" All
was quiet.

I waited a moment and then tried to climb from the
foxhole. I could not make it without the use of my right
leg. I asked someone to help me, and a soldier extended
his hand. I looked toward the direction of the firing. The
two men who had preceded me as scouts had caught the
full burst of the grenade. Both men were dead.

*Good God! Are there Germans everywhere in these
woods? Everywhere we turn there are Germans, and I
am running. Always I am running from dirty, stinking,
killing Germans. Will I never stop running from Germans?*

I called for the column to follow again and changed
our course back along the edge of the north-south firebreak. We would move to the rear to avoid this enemy,
and then we would turn west again and head for the other
firebreak over the same route the platoons had erroneous-
ly taken in the opening phases of the attack.

We moved quickly through the woods. The wound in
my leg grew increasingly painful, and I found it difficult to

keep up with the pace the other men were setting. I fell again and again into abandoned foxholes and found it impossible to climb out without assistance. Two men were carrying Charles, and another was helping a man who had been hit in the foot when the last firing occurred.

The clearing that was the second north-south firebreak loomed ahead of us. That would be where K Company was digging in initially, and I wondered if they were still there and if they would fire at us. I told Savage to contact them on the radio and tell them we were coming across. They said, "Roger." We hurried across the firebreak, but K Company was not there. They had evidently moved to our former position at the junction of the firebreaks.

It became almost impossible for me to walk. Each step brought a wrenching pain through my entire leg, and beads of perspiration broke out of my forehead. My mouth was dry, and I reached down and ate a handful of snow. I longed desperately for a cigarette.

I decided to move the company to the A Company positions to reorganize. I was still missing the 2d Platoon, but I trusted blindly that they had seen us withdrawing and would follow.

I called across the fifty-yard open space to announce to A Company that we were I Company men withdrawing. An unseen voice, evidently satisfied that we were friendly troops, told us to come across.

The open space had been a cultivated field before the snows came, and the ground rose again and again into minute ridges. I tripped over what I thought must surely be each ridge and fell sprawling again and again into the snow. Technical Sergeant Wiley Post, of Jacksonville, Texas, the 3d Platoon sergeant, saw my plight and told me to put one arm around his shoulders. He helped me into the narrow neck of woods where the platoon leader from Company A waited for us.

I called battalion on the radio and explained the situation, asking for litter bearers for the two wounded men who could not walk. There was no denying my own case now. I could not return with the company after we reorganized.

Lieutenant Smith was not with A Company. The platoon leader said he had moved forward earlier with the

Weasel

mortars and the rear CP group to our former position at the junction of the firebreaks. I placed Lieutenant Goffigon in command of the company until he should be able to contact Lieutenant Smith. I told them to dig in with A Company until they received further orders from battalion. Sergeant Post would take me to the aid station.

It was a slow, painful walk back to Ondenval. We met the "weasel,"[2] flying a Red Cross flag, going forward for the two men who could not walk. They offered to pick me up on their way back, but I said I thought I could make it.

We had passed the battalion CP when I decided that I could not make it any farther. My leg had grown stiff, and the pain was almost unbearable. Sergeant Post ran ahead to the forward aid station and returned with two aid men and a litter. They carried me into the aid station. The light inside blinded me and the heat from the stove engulfed me, and I thought I was going to lose consciousness.

They seated me in a chair and someone gave me a drink of water that felt wonderful going down my parched throat. Technical Sergeant Martin J. Gwin, of Bellevue,

[2] A jeep-sized vehicle equipped with tractor-type treads.

Texas, removed my soaked combat boot and cut the trousers from my leg at the knee.

I looked down at my leg. The bullet had made a bloody three-inch gash on the right side of the calf of my leg. The imprint of the bullet was pressing the skin out on the opposite side of the leg, but the skin there was not broken.

"You're lucky, Cap'n," Gwin said. "It didn't hit an artery, or you'd have lost more blood, and I think it missed the bone, too, or else you couldn't have walked back."

They moved me to a stretcher at the rear of the room, and Gwin gave me a dose of sulfa tablets.

"I'll wait and let them give you morphine in Weismes, unless it's paining you too much," he said. "Here's something that'll hold you 'till then."

He gave me half a glass of rum. I swallowed it and felt warm inside.

The door opened and eight men entered, carrying another soldier on a stretcher. I recognized Captain Roy G. McCracken, of Pueblo, Colo., the Antitank Company commander. He had been hit slightly by a steel fragment just above one knee.

"Where'n hell was I Company?" he asked me. "Regiment told us you reached the highway an hour ago, and we started up in a tank-dozer to clear the road."

"I can't see why'n hell they told you that," I said. "We never did reach the highway."

"We passed L Company," he continued, "and didn't see anybody for a helluva ways, and then we saw some men by the road and thought surely they were from I Company. We pulled up to talk to them and they opened up with a bazooka. It grazed the tank and caused some light casualties, and we hauled ass."

I wondered who had told them we had reached the highway.

Two men lifted my stretcher from the floor and carried me out the rear of the house, placing the stretcher on a rack over the engine of an aid jeep. They placed the litter casualty from Antitank Company beside me, and the driver started the engine. We moved out down the highway toward Steinbach and Weismes.

I looked up into the dull grey sky, and the cold wind crept beneath the closely-pinned blankets and chilled me.

I shuddered and thought of the company. Where were they now? Did Brock's platoon get out? Had I done right in withdrawing, or should we have stayed and fought it out? It seemed that I was always running. Perhaps it was all my fault.

There had been a brief moment of exultation in the aid station when someone had reminded me that now I could get a nice rest in the hospital, but now a nausea of fear for the welfare of the company enveloped me. I felt, somehow, like a deserter.

Strong hands removed our litters from the jeep at the rear battalion aid station in Weismes. The heat inside felt good after the ride in the cold air. I had spent the early hours of many long nights in bull sessions at the aid station, and I knew most of the men well. Lieutenant Roftis, the Medical Administrative officer, gave me a hypodermic of morphine, and then proffered a half-glass drink of highly-prized bourbon. Private First Class Wendell Cumberland, of Lubec, Maine, copied the information from the casualty tag which hung on my jacket.

The bourbon and morphine had begun to take effect when they lifted my stretcher into the rear of an ambulance with three other casualties. I was a bit drunk. The man beside me was again the stretcher case from Anti-tank Company. A heater made the ambulance warm. We talked of the fight in the woods, trading experiences in the manner of all GIs just removed from battle, until my eyes closed involuntarily, and the gentle swaying of the ambulance rocked me to sleep.

Cold air entered the ambulance, and I realized that we were at the regimental medical collecting company and a soldier wearing a red cross on his arm was checking our diagnosis tags and closing the doors again. If we had not been progressing well, an emergency operation could have been performed here.

Our next stop was the division clearing station, a miniature hospital set up under tents. A heavy rain had begun to fall, and the corpsmen placed blankets over our heads before removing us from the ambulance. They placed my stretcher on a table inside the tent and a medical officer checked my wound and rebandaged it.

I suddenly realized that I was famished. I had eaten only a K-ration for breakfast, and it was now two o'clock the following morning. A corpsman brought me a large broiled pork chop between two thick slices of bread. My mouth watered hungrily, and I consumed it ravenously.

An ambulance arrived from an ambulance company, and I was loaded aboard again.

Our next stop was the rear division clearing station in Verviers. A medical officer explained that this was not a normal stop on the evacuation route, but the holding of less serious cases here for treatment had become 2d Division's policy to expedite their return to duty without the lengthy process of passing through replacement depots.

I was carried to an operating table in a room of the building that was being used as the clearing station. A medical officer injected a local anesthetic and removed the bullet from my leg. Strangely, the bullet had turned around inside my leg, and the butt of the bullet was forcing the skin outward on the opposite side. The medical officer wiped the blood away and gave the bullet to me as a souvenir.

I remained at the clearing station through the remainder of the night and the next day. Shortly after supper two corpsmen came for me and carried me "piggy-back" downstairs to the operating room. I was being transferred to an evacuation hospital in Verviers, which would have been my normal disposition after the forward clearing station.

As I waited for an ambulance a group of casualties arrived. A number of them were from I Company. Their injuries were not serious; two men had been hit with small shrapnel fragments which only slightly broke the skin, and others were suffering from light cases of frozen feet. Lieutenant Brock was among them.

"We had a helluva time after you left, Cap'n," Brock told me and explained at length the details of the remainder of the night and the following day.

"My platoon ran into two German patrols on our way back to A Company. No one was hurt, but we got about ten Germans. The Krauts were all over the woods the rest of the night, and they counterattacked in force at daylight with three tanks. They hit mainly on the flanks, and raked the open field near A Company with fire all morning. No one could move over it. They even fired at stretcher bearers, and the German tanks fired at the weasel when it tried to evacuate casualties. We couldn't get up any food or ammunition, but the men held somehow.

"The counterattack ended around noon, and the 1st Battalion attacked through us and took Iveldingen with almost no resistance. The woods around our positions were black with dead Germans.

"The weather was hell. It started raining last night, and turned to snow and sleet this morning. It was a regular blizzard when the 1st Battalion passed through us at noon. Some of the worst wounded froze to death before aid men could get them out."

He knew of no other men from I Company having been killed, but he knew there were a number seriously wounded.[3]

They were all laughing at the Antitank Company commander now that it was over. When we had moved out from our midway point in the woods around nine o'clock, he led his company up to the junction of the firebreaks where we had been. He saw a group of men standing there and walked up and tapped one of them on the shoulder in the darkness. "Is this I Company?" he asked. The answer had come in a flood of German: *"Was ist los? Was ist los?"* Both groups hit the ground and began firing. They had contacted a German patrol of about forty men.

The ambulance arrived, and I was moved to the 97th Evacuation Hospital, located in a large school building in Verviers. I had no sooner become settled on a canvas cot in a ward on the top floor than two corpsmen came to take me to the X-ray room. There they X-rayed my leg and found that the bullet had missed the bones entirely.

A tall, brunette nurse from North Carolina began to give me penicillin injections when I returned to the ward, waking me every four hours during the night. As soon as

---

[3]It is difficult to establish precisely, even now, long after the war, what German force counterattacked with tank support. It seems probable that the infantrymen belonged to the same *3d Parachute Division* responsible for defending the pass. But because the corps directing the paratroopers had come under the *Sixth Panzer Army*, some armor had, more than likely, become available. In any event, after my regiment's 1st Battalion had passed through and captured Iveldingen, the 7th Armored Division began to roll. The armor took St. Vith on January 23d, the day after Hitler finally ordered the *Sixth Panzer Army* to leave the Ardennes for the Eastern Front.

it was dark the next night, I was loaded again into an ambulance and moved to the 46th Field Hospital in the same town. I was going to the 46th to await a hospital train for the rear, a corpsman told me.

I spent an almost identical night and day in the 46th Field. If I had been wounded more seriously, I might have received another operation or have been equipped with a plaster cast. At least half the patients in the two hospitals were severe cases of trench foot, or frozen feet, their feet purple and swollen almost twice their normal size. There was evidently little difference in the diagnosis, but for frozen feet you qualified for a Purple Heart. The most severe cases of either might become gangrenous, possibly resulting in amputation.

We were loaded on a hospital train the next night. A pleasant but business-like nurse in GI coveralls came around to continue the penicillin injections and told us that we were on our way to Paris. We should arrive in twenty-four hours.

The nurse, sometimes in company with a medical officer, came through the car every four hours to administer the penicillin. The patients laughed good-naturedly as the medical personnel hardly gave them time to awaken before they stuck them with the big needle.

"I got these shots once before," a soldier laughed, "but it wasn't on account of frozen feet."

The nurse stopped to help the patient on the lower stretcher across the aisle from me with his cigarette. He thanked her but refused assistance.

I began to talk with him. He was a lanky farm boy from Kentucky and had been assigned to Company G of my regiment only the week before. The Ondenval offensive was his first action. He had been hit almost directly by an 88mm shell while digging in in the draw to the south of Ondenval. It got him in the right shoulder, practically severing his arm, but the doctors had told him it would be all right in time. It was enclosed in a large cast which encased his body.

"It was four hours before they got me out," he drawled. "I almost froze, but that wasn't so bad. Another 88 came in and did this."

He shifted the cigarette to his mouth and lifted the

blanket with his free left hand. His right leg had been severed above the knee.

French civilians assisted the ambulance drivers to unload the train at the Paris station. Ambulances were designated for various hospitals in the Paris area. Two ladies in Red Cross uniforms passed out coffee and doughnuts. We were famished; they had fed us only dry pressed-meat sandwiches on the train.

My ambulance bounced along the Paris streets. I looked anxiously through the small windows in the rear in an effort to catch a fleeting glimpse of some historical landmark which would assure me I was at last in the fabulous city, but I could see only the dimmed lights of other passing trucks and ambulances. Like the majority of GIs, we had by-passed Paris on our trip to the Siegfried Line. This might be my only chance to see the city.

The convoy of ambulances pulled up in a schoolhouse courtyard bathed in floodlights. A squad of medical corpsmen joked among themselves as they lifted the stretchers and placed them in a large glass-enclosed entrance. A medical officer checked the diagnosis tags and marked a ward number on them. Another crew began to transport the stretchers which the officer had examined up a flight of stone steps to the wards indicated.

I was deposited on the third floor in a small room with two beds. The clean white sheets and the bouncy wonderfulness of the bed were almost too good to be true. I ran my grimy hands over the white sheets caressingly. It was the first bed with sheets I had seen in five and one-half months.

A small, pretty brunette nurse came in and made me comfortable for the night, as if just being in the luxurious hospital bed were not enough. She was Second Lieutenant Marie Pierce, of LaFollette, Tenn. The other patient in the room was Lieutenant Donald McDonald, of Minneapolis, Minn., and we talked until Lieutenant Pierce returned and told us to turn out the lights.

The next morning Lieutenant McDonald and I were both moved to an officers' ward on the fourth floor, shared by about twenty officers. New arrivals came almost every day, but others were shipped out to other hospitals.

Ours was the 194th General Hospital on the Boulevard Murat near the Pte. de St. Cloud.

We were classified each day by Major Yash Venar, of Cleveland, Ohio, the ward surgeon, according to the progress which our wounds had made. Patients in Class I were to go back to duty, Class II to a convalescent hospital on the Continent, Class III to a general hospital in England, and Class IV, cases which would require a minimum of six months treatment, to the Zone of the Interior, the fanciest name I had heard for the United States.

On the first day my wound was examined in the operating room, followed several days later by suturing. The sutures were removed ten days later, preceded by a continuation of the penicillin injections. I was able to walk after one week, though with a decided limp at first, and soon obtained afternoon passes into Paris.

Private First Class Charles, my radioman who was wounded with me in the woods the night of January 17, was admitted to the hospital, and I visited him every day until he was shipped out by plane for further treatment in England. The wound in his right hip had caused a temporary partial paralysis of his leg.

I followed the *Stars and Stripes* avidly for news of my division but there was little to tell me that the outfit was pursuing a vigorous offensive that retook Wirtzfeld, Krinkelt, Rocherath and Wahlerscheid, eventually carrying them to the vital Roer River dams and subsequently to the Rhine River.

Orders came on February 10 transferring me and the three lieutenants in my ward to a convalescent hospital located in a former Luftwaffe headquarters building in Étampes, thirty miles south of Paris. We made numerous trips back into the city *via* free rides to American soldiers on the French railway, until on February 26 we were transferred to the 3d Replacement Depot in Étampes. A few days later I was placed in command of a group of two hundred hospital returnees and loaded on French "40 & 8s" for a ride that took me once again to Verviers, Belgium. We ran into snow soon after crossing the Belgian border, but the replacement depot in Verviers was located in heated buildings, and the men slept on canvas cots, a far cry from the earlier days in Normandy when the depots were set up in the Normandy fields and the food was atrocious.

Our return to the front continued by truck convoy on March 7, a long, cold ride which took us through the battered city of Aachen and south through the shambles of the Siegfried Line border towns to Kalterherberg, Germany, a muddy farming town with unpaved streets located a few miles south of Monschau and ten miles north of Elsenborn. Radio reports of the rolling First Army advance cheered us, and we received the news three days later, as we loaded on trucks for another forward movement, that elements of the First Army were across the Rhine.

We rode through the ruins of towns wrecked by the First Army steamroller smashing toward the Rhine and halted again in Rheinbach. We were close enough to the front again to hear the boom of the big guns at night and to see the orange flashes on the horizon, and the old feeling of fear in the pit of my stomach gradually returned. The weather was improving now, and the snow was gone. I hoped that I had seen my last European snow.

Trucks from the division called for us on Monday, March 12, for the final move on the return to duty. Our route took us past stores of abandoned German ammunition and equipment, overturned vehicles and half-completed roadblocks attesting to the rapidity of the First Army advance. We arrived in Sinzig on the Rhine River, two miles southwest of the famed Remagen bridgehead where the 9th Armored Division had forged the first Rhine crossing. I reported immediately to regimental headquarters.

I learned at regiment that Captain Oscar L. Goodson, of Eagle Pass, Texas, had taken over the command of Company I. The news was disheartening. I wanted so badly to return to the company, but with another captain already in command, it seemed unlikely.

The adjutant gave me the news a few minutes later. I would not return to the company. I was to command Company G.

BOOK TWO

COMPANY G

16

MEET COMPANY G

I spent the night at regimental headquarters and went by jeep the next morning to visit Company I. I found them in a large country villa on a high hill five miles to the northwest, and it was like a reunion with old friends to be with them again.

Almost all the men whom I remembered were there. There had been few serious casualties since the night I was wounded, and none had been men whom I had known intimately. I was more than pleased to see Sergeant Savage and the men from the headquarters group again and to find that Lieutenant Antey, who had been 3d Platoon leader in the pillbox positions, had been reassigned to the company.

I reported to 2d Battalion headquarters in Sinzig in the afternoon to Lieutenant Colonel William A. Smith, of Laramie, Wyo., the battalion commander. He had been a major when I left the regiment in January. He was a tall, slightly heavy young man who wore glasses. He welcomed me to the battalion and called for the G Company executive officer, First Lieutenant Laurice L. Loberg, of Fargo, N. D., to show me to the company.

The company was billeted in houses a few blocks from the battalion CP. The days that followed were warm, spring days filled with sunshine, and I considered myself fortunate to be with my new company for several days before going into combat. I had little of the uncomfortable feeling of not being accepted because of inexperience now, but I did want to learn to know the men as much as possible before going into action.

Sinzig (which the men called "Zig-zig on the Rhine") was within enemy artillery range, but the Germans were directing all their efforts against the Remagen bridge site nearby, and except for enemy planes which we could see raiding the Remagen area each day, there was no enemy action. The men would scream and curse at our invisible antiaircraft gunners, turning away disgustedly when they failed to down the enemy planes. We did not see even one plane shot down over the area, but each morning's news broadcasts told of numbers of German craft having been downed over the bridge the preceding day. We wondered how they did it. Perhaps they used mirrors.

I began to like my new assignment with Company G, but I could not avoid yearning to return to Company I. The men had liked their former company commander, Captain John M. Stephens, of Tyler, Texas, and I knew it would be difficult to replace him. He was a dare-devil type of leader and had received the Distinguished Service Cross for action at Ondenval. He had been wounded by mortar fragments in the leg on the drive to the Rhine.

I noticed one distinct difference immediately between G and I Companies and looked upon it at first with disfavor. Where Company I had insisted upon few formalities toward officers, G Company maintained an officer's mess, a table with china and silverware set up wherever the kitchen was located and presided over by Private First Class John Citrone, of Boston, the company commander's runner. Citrone left a few days after my arrival on a pass to Paris, but his duties were taken over temporarily by Private First Class Hester F. Townsend, of Woodbine, Ga., a nineteen-year-old drawling Southerner who talked with the help of his hands. I thought of changing the mess arrangement, but the other officers were accustomed to it, and it was definitely nicer than sweating out a chow line. And in later days the "mess" became little more than a plate prepared for me before the main part of the company came to the meals—Townsend had an amazing faculty for losing the silverware and dishes.

First Sergeant Clarence C. Quinn, of San Antonio, Texas, was on pass to London at the time of my arrival, and his duties were assumed by Staff Sergeant John R. Henderson, of Bedford, Pa., the hefty, good-natured twenty-year-old supply sergeant whom everyone knew as "J. R."

We scanned the *Stars and Stripes* and listened to the radio each day for news about the Remagen bridgehead, because we knew that it was only a matter of time before our division would be committed. The order did come on March 22. Our objective was to push south to enable the Third Army to cross the Rhine without a fight at Coblenz. The 38th Infantry had already been committed.

We moved four miles to the south by truck to Oberbreisig and spent the night, moving by foot the next afternoon to a point on the Rhine south of Niederbreisig. It was a four-mile hike to the river. We carried blanket rolls and overshoes, due to battalion order, but few men believed in the necessity of carrying overshoes in the balmy spring weather, and the discarded overshoes traced a path like the bread crumbs of Hansel and Gretel from our origin to the water's edge. A battalion salvage crew retrieved them later.

We crossed the Rhine in groups of forty on LCVPs manned by Army engineers. Men joked and imitated the sounds of artillery shells whistling overhead. All of us were fully conscious of our good fortune in crossing to an already established bridgehead.

Our road march continued on the opposite bank parallel to the broad, swiftly-flowing river. Tall mountains rose on our left, and I wondered in awe if the enemy were defending the high hills. If so, we were in for quite a fight.

We passed through two towns taken two days before by the 9th Armored Division, past gaping holes in stone buildings, littered German equipment, and signs screaming *"Achtung! Minen!"* encircled by strips of white cloth.

We reached our destination at dusk—an open field on the eastern edge of the industrial town of Wollendorf. Several houses were in the vicinity, but when I tried to persuade battalion to allow us to billet the men in houses, I was informed that the town had been assigned to the 9th Armored. We could not use the houses, even though they were empty, but they finally consented to locating the company CP and the kitchen in houses. The men pitched pup tents in the open field, the sweat from the six-mile walk drying and chilling them in the dampness of early evening.

Church services were held in the field the next morning, but when I left the CP to attend, a call came for me to report to battalion with my maps and to have the company alerted to move as soon as the services were over.

At battalion we got in jeeps and rode to the southeast, arriving after a six-mile drive over curving roads to a group of small stone houses, resembling an American housing project, on a hill beyond the town of Nieder-bieber-Segendorf. Three rows of trim cottages ran east-west across the hill and one row of smaller wooden houses stood fifty yards to the south. Captain Henry L. Calder, of Dallas, Texas, the battalion adjutant, assigned certain houses for each company, and with my interpreter, Private First Class Walter G. Harms, we began to clear the houses of civilians, telling them to move to the row of wooden houses across the way for the night. Most of the civilians seemed apathetic toward moving, as if they had been doing this all their lives, but others grumbled and insisted on taking most of their household goods with them. One woman was ill and had a three-month-old baby, so we allowed her to remain in one room of her house.

Harms remained to direct the company to the billets upon their arrival, and I went with Colonel Smith and the other company commanders to reconnoiter the terrain to the front. Colonel Smith outlined the plans briefly before we departed. Three divisions would launch a coordinated attack. We would be on our division's right flank, with the 1st Battalion attacking through woods on our left and the 9th Armored on our right. Our initial objective was the town of Heimbach in the valley to our front, followed in succession by the towns of Weiss and Bendorf-Sayn (on the Sayn River). We would cross the line of departure at 4:45 in the morning.

Our reconnaissance took us across two hundred yards of open field to a group of five buildings and a brickyard beside an east-west highway at the crest of the hill. The bodies of three dead Germans in the trail beside one house seemed to perturb no one enough to move them, and our jeep dodged to the right of the trail to avoid them. To the left were the burned-out hulks of four American light tanks. A soldier nearby said that a German SP gun in Gladbach, the town to our left front, had knocked out the tanks that morning.

The 38th Infantry had taken Gladbach after a stiff fight. We drove into the town, avoiding spots in the road marked "Mines" and *"Achtung! Minen!"* From the attic window of a tall building we could see artillery pounding our next day's objective with high-explosive and white-phosphorous shells. Three houses were burning. Between us and Heimbach lay another east-west road, and we could see OD-clad GIs digging in along the road for the night. The highway cut abruptly to the south across an open field to Heimbach,[1] where a leafless orchard offered some concealment on the right of the road. We thought we could see white flags fluttering from the buildings in the town.

We returned to the billet area and found that the companies had arrived. I called for my platoon leaders: First Lieutenant Thomas D. Bagby, of Glen Allen, Va., 1st Platoon; Staff Sergeant Thomas W. Patton, of Tulsa, Okla., acting 2d Platoon leader in the absence of the officer who was on pass to Paris; Technical Sergeant James Barnes, of Saluda, S. C., 3d Platoon; and Second Lieutenant Earl Speed, of Dallas, Texas, Weapons Platoon. Technician Fifth Grade Raymond Hess, of Pittsburgh, Pa., my transportation corporal, drove us by jeep to the brickyard beside the east-west highway.

We dismounted beside a house on the far side of the road. An ambling trail ran along the right of a high brick wall and connected to the front with another trail which led to the point where I had seen GIs digging in earlier. We might well have driven our jeep down the forward-sloping trail. The GIs to our front were making no effort at concealment. Jeeps ran here and there in the open valley, the high enemy-held hills to the south looking down upon them menacingly but ineffectively. We walked around without regard to concealment and sat with our maps unfolded beneath a barren fruit tree on the forward slope of the hill and pointed and conversed about our objective.

This was a strange war, I thought. We were acting as if we were on maneuvers. Wandering about in the open on reconnaissance would have made the founding fathers of the hectic Normandy and Siegfried days snicker in de-

---

[1] A veteran of World War I, who read the first edition of this book, informed me that this open field at Heimbach had served as a parade ground for a U.S. unit occupying Heimbach in 1919.

risive amusement. And the weather was comfortably warm, and we would sleep this night in houses. This was a far cry from the gruelling days in the Siegfried Line.

Had I been able to look across the line at the German situation, I would have understood why the war in this sector had taken such a turn. During the early fighting in the Remagen bridgehead, the Germans had concentrated their only really effective forces against the north flank of the bridgehead, for they expected the U.S. First Army to attack northward directly against the vital Ruhr industrial area. This was a major error which would have the effect of shortening the war considerably. The First Army commander, General Hodges, intended instead to strike in the center and on the south flank. He would then swing northeast as part of a pincers movement made with the Ninth Army north of the Ruhr. The aim was to encircle the vast industrial area. Only the day before the start of the attack of which my company was a part, the German army group commander, Field Marshal Walter Model, shifted his last panzer division from the southern flank of the bridgehead to the northern flank. The result: virtually nothing left to oppose our thrust.

We returned to the billet area at dusk, accompanied by a jeep-load of Rhine wine which Corporal Hess had found in a cellar while we were on reconnaissance. The company kitchen, run by Staff Sergeant Johnny E. Hairston, of Temple, Texas, had already moved to our new location and was feeding supper. We ate inside one of the blacked-out houses by flickering candlelight.

Private First Class Edgar Philpot, of Bark Camp, Ky., one of the headquarters radio operators whom we called "Junior," had discovered that a German "civilian" living in the house which our CP occupied was a *Wehrmacht* soldier in disguise.

"He said he got discharged from the Army three days ago," Junior said. "Sonofabitch had a knife on him *that* long"—and he indicated with his hands—"so I ran him in."

I had no sooner finished eating than battalion called for me to receive the final attack order.

The order was brief. Company G would attack on the

left of the highway leading into Heimbach, with Company F on the right. A platoon of medium tanks would attack with each company. Immediately after capturing the initial objective, we would proceed to the town of Weiss, which showed on our maps as a portion of Heimbach. Then we would go on to Bendorf-Sayn, the village on the Sayn River which lay at the far end of the broad valley to our front, and be prepared to continue the attack upon order. The line of departure would be the road where we had seen the GIs digging in.

"The *Bürgermeister* of Heimbach came into the 38th Infantry lines at dusk carrying a white flag," Colonel Smith said. "He begged them not to shell the town any more. He said the German soldiers had already left."

We laughed hollowly. It made things look easy—*if* you could believe the *Bürgermeister*.

We would attack the next morning at 4:45.

Someone awakened me at three-thirty the next morning. It was cold in the room, and I shivered as I climbed from my sleeping bag. My mind was dulled with sleep, and I wanted to climb back into the warm sleeping bag and sleep on and on. I wanted to scream to hell with the war and go back to sleep. The sudden jolt of awakening was like emerging from a wonderful, peaceful world into a world of forbidding reality. There would be men hurt today, perhaps killed—men from my own company. It could be me. That seemed remote and impossible, but it did not remove my fear for the others.

There were many responsibilities. Had I given the platoon leaders all the information they would need? How was my attack plan? Was there some important detail I had forgotten? Would Heimbach be defended? Would our attack be discovered as we crossed the flat, open field toward the town? Oh, God, if we could but rush from the house into the attack without thinking again. It was the waiting and the thinking and the wondering that got you.

The men were sleepy-eyed and yawning as they ate breakfast in the dark. Somewhere a moon was shining, but a foggy, overcast atmosphere completely hid it from view.

We assembled at four o'clock. There was a clattering and rustling of equipment and low curses as men sought to find their places with their squads. F Company was forming across the street. They moved out, and we followed. We would go forward in column until we reached the 38th Infantry's lines.

The men kept close together as we moved across the open field toward the highway beside the brickyard. I heard the tanks catch up with the tail of the company. Their motors churned and fretted, and their tracks voiced the clattering indignation we all felt at early morning war.

We crossed the highway and moved along a faint trail down the forward slope of the hill into the valley. I was leading the company with the men who would comprise my forward CP group in the attack. A platoon of Negro soldiers from F Company were immediately ahead of us. They swung along as steadily and quietly as the rest of us. We were wondering how they would react to their first combat. They had been selected from volunteers in rear-area organizations, some taking reductions in grades that had been as high as first sergeant, to serve as fifth platoons in one company of each regiment of several infantry divisions.

The Negroes ahead of me moved off the trail to the plowed earth on either side. I saw a string of white tape across the center of the trail, and I knew that the sign indicated mines. I passed the word to the men behind me, and each man stepped off the trail as the word reached him.

The men ahead of us stopped. I moved to the side and passed the rear platoons of F Company and found the company commander, Captain John M. Calhoun, of Athens, Tenn., at the head of the column. He had reached the line held by the 38th Infantry and was waiting for his tanks to pull around the column to join him. His lead platoons began to deploy into the approach-march formation.

I hurried again to the rear to lead my company around F Company to get into position. I could hear the motors of the big Shermans churning derisively as the lead tanks turned off the trail to join F Company's forward elements. A deafening explosion broke the monotony of the tank motors. A streak of flame and a billowing mass of smoke sprang from beneath the left track of the lead tank. For a moment I thought an artillery barrage was beginning to fall, and I started instinctively to fall to the ground. Then I realized what had happened. The lead tank had hit a mine.

A crowd of men milled around the tank as I reached it. Two men were climbing from the turret.

"Anybody hurt?" I asked.

"Nobody hurt," one of the tankmen said. "Shook us up. That knocks the tank out 'till we can get it repaired. Sonofabitches oughta mark their goddamned mines."

I found the head of G Company and signalled them forward. We passed the disabled tank, and I told the tank platoon leader to swing around the disabled tank to join us in the attack formation. He said he would have to take it slowly. There might be more mines.

We reached a shallow ditch at the road junction where the highway from Gladbach turned abruptly to the left to lead into Heimbach. The assault platoons began to move into position—Lieutenant Bagby's 1st Platoon on the right, Staff Sergeant Patton's 2d Platoon on the left, Sergeant Barnes' 3d Platoon echeloned to the left rear to move forward by bounds and protect the left flank. My weapons platoon and an attached platoon of heavy machine guns from Company H followed in the rear. I took my place in the rear center of the assault platoons.

I looked at my watch. It was twenty minutes until five o'clock—five minutes until jump-off time. Faint streaks of dawn were appearing across the horizon. I wondered if the tanks were coming.

I told Private First Class Joseph Abad, of Hackensack, N. J., my SCR-300 operator, to contact the tank platoon leader.

"The Colonel's talking to F Company now," he said.

The Colonel signed off, and I heard him give our call sign.

"Are you all set, Mac?" he asked.

"All set except for the 'cans,'" I said. (I wondered why we always called tanks "cans" over the radio. A German monitor would know as well as what we were speaking of.)

"Well, get back there and get them up," he said. "Regiment's already champing at the bit. Red is all set to go on your left." He meant the 1st Battalion.

Abad contacted the tank platoon leader. He was trying

to find a route around another mine field. They would get up as quickly as they could.

It seemed that Colonel Smith called every minute after that. Were we all set now? Had the tanks gotten there?

My watch said five o'clock, and I cursed. Already we were fifteen minutes late, and each minute was bringing more light to the grey streaks on the horizon. Men were no longer shadowy outlines but dimly discernible figures in the darkness. A burst of small-arms fire far to our right front told me that the 9th Armored had already jumped off and had met opposition. We were stalled at the starting point.

The radio sputtered and I heard Colonel Smith call for both assault companies. "You'll have to go without the cans," he said. "I told regiment you jumped off fifteen minutes ago. Get going."

A mounting angry fear swept over me. Suppose our attack were discovered as we crossed the flat, open field toward the town? The field was perfectly designed for raking small-arms fire. Without tank support we would never get into the first buildings. And if there were Germans in the town, they were certainly alerted now. An enemy doesn't ignore the churning of tanks and the explosion of an antitank mine to his front in the early morning hours.

But there was no alternative. Abad radioed the tanks, and I told them our orders. They said they would overtake us before we reached the town. Junior told the platoons over the 536 radio to move out. The dark outlines of men moved forward through the rapidly dissipating darkness.

The men moved quickly, goaded by the realization that each passing moment spelled added daylight to the enemy's advantage. The spread approach-march formation placed men as far as I could see in every direction in the dim light.

One thought kept drumming at my brain. *Let them reach the buildings! Let them reach the buildings!* I knew that if we could gain a foothold in the town without fighting, we would have a much easier battle. *Let them reach the buildings! Let them reach the buildings!*

I heard the noisy clatter of tanks behind us, and I breathed an inward sigh of relief. The steel monsters churned past us and took their places in the assault formation—three forward and two back—like waddling ducks going to water.

The bulky shapes of the first house rising from the flat field grew nearer. The platoon radio sputtered, and Lieutenant Bagby spoke:

"Hello, G six; hello, G six; we've entered the first houses. No trouble. Happy Easter! Over."

"Good going," I mumbled. It sounded trite, but I could think of nothing better to say. The news was what I had been anxiously waiting to hear. "Move on through as quickly as possible, if there's no trouble. The 3d Platoon'll mop up. Over."

"Roger. Out."

I could see the men moving around the houses, and I double-timed forward with my CP group. A tank loitered beside a house, and the commander called for doughboys to precede it down the narrow main street. Civilians were being lined up with their hands high in the air. The GIs were making a thorough job of it—everyone not in OD uniform must keep his hands high above his head.

The dull grey dawn lighted the landscape. The soldiers moved quickly through the town. Here and there a building showed the marks of the night's shelling. Somewhere near the center of town two houses were enveloped in smoke from smoldering flames. The sounds of doors being broken down and single shots dispensing with locks informed the awed civilians that they had done wrong in locking their houses.

I continued down the left side of the street, keeping close to the buildings for protection should snipers open up. We reached a battered church on a small square, and I looked at my map. This was where Heimbach ended and Weiss began. The forward riflemen had almost completed taking our second objective, and there was no resistance. I thought of the *Bürgermeister*. The poor man had been telling the truth and no one believed him.

The 1st Platoon took two sleepy-eyed submissive prisoners from a basement. The 2d Platoon sent a yawning German soldier clad only in his trousers running down the debris-littered street toward our rear. Two Frenchmen in French Army uniforms chattered wildly.

"Mon Dieu! Ils sont là. Les Americains sont arrivé! Merci! Merci!"

A procession of twenty half-dressed *Wehrmacht* soldiers moved rapidly down the street toward the rear, goaded by loud shouts from their guard, Private First Class Joseph Weylandt, and GIs whom they passed. Weylandt's face was wreathed in smiles, and his arms and pockets were loaded with German pistols. We came abreast of the prisoners.

"Found 'em all in a cellar," Weylandt called to us. "I got beaucoup pistols. Want a pistol, Cap'n?"

He tossed me a shiny Mauser .32 automatic. A pistol was the ultimate to souvenir-hunting GIs.

We continued down the street. The buildings began to thin out into single houses, and I looked at my map. We were near the edge of Weiss and about a mile from Bendorf-Sayn, our third objective. A curving blue line on the map indicated the Sayn River. That thin blue line would be the enemy's defense, I thought.

Some inner sense told me that this carefree offensive could not last much longer, but the laughing shouts of the happy GIs around me would not let me be afraid. I joined in their laughter, and men shouted, "This is a helluva war!"

We reached the last house in the town, and the lead platoons held up to reorganize. An orchard with slightly rising ground stretched before us on the left of the road. Beyond that rise would be the next town and perhaps the enemy defense. The platoons reorganized, and the big tanks crawled noisily into position. Someone in F Company fired a BAR at three fleeing Germans in an open field on the right of the road. I signalled forward, and the scouts moved out, their rifles held in readiness for whatever might happen.

Don't scouts have fun? There's nothing between them and the whole German nation but the muzzles of their rifles. They get first choice of the liquor and the loot and the fraternizin'. Everybody wants to be a lead scout. Like hell they do, brother! Like hell!

A brazen sun was shining now, but a low mist clung tenaciously around the blue hills to our front. The men moved quickly through the orchard. The scouts crossed the rise to the front. I expected at any moment to hear the dreaded sound of enemy fire, but the silence was broken only by the roaring motors of the tanks.

BAR

The last men in the forward platoons crossed the crest of the small hill. They should be almost inside the first houses of Bendorf now, I thought. I halted the CP group in a sunken trail running across the crest of the hill and told Junior to ask for reports from the assault platoons.

Suddenly, a tank fired from somewhere to our front, and a big shell whirred low over our heads. A machine gun chattered. A round of tank fire ripped the limb from a tree above our heads. A burp gun said "Brrrrrrrrp! Brrrrrrrrp!"

There was no question now. We had hit their defenses, and the Germans, too, had tanks.

17

"IT HAS BEEN HARD FOR US"

We dropped to the cover of the sunken trail. The men behind us took cover in an abandoned quarry. The shells from the enemy tanks whirred close overhead, and small-arms fire chattered loudly. I wondered if the assault platoons had been caught on the open face of the hill, or if they had succeeded in gaining the comparative safety of the houses. I took the platoon radio from Junior and called for Lieutenant Bagby.

"I've got men in the first two houses," he said, "but we can't get any farther. Their tanks are on a wooded hill to the left of town, and they're blasting hell out of the houses."

The artillery observer set up his radio, but the orchard obscured our view. I asked Bagby if he could adjust from where he was, and he said he would try.

I was trembling slightly from excitement, but I was not deathly afraid as I had once been in the pillbox positions. The opinion often expressed among GIs that after any man was wounded once he was never any good in combat again did not hold true in my case. I was more calm than ever before, but I was also more cautious.

Three of our tanks were on the forward slope, and I wondered why the Germans did not knock them out. I attributed it to the screening effect of the trees in the orchard. One of the two rear tanks pulled up beside us. There was a deafening explosion, a burst of flame, and dirt and smoke blew back into our eyes. I thought for a second that the tanks were hit, but then I realized that the gunner inside had fired the big 75.

I heard Captain Calhoun tell battalion that he was

caught in the open field on the edge of the town. He was drawing SP fire from the same direction as we were, but it was small-arms fire that had him pinned to the ground. I reported our situation.

Lieutenant Bagby could not see the first three rounds of artillery. The observer called for a smoke round, but he still could not see it. I tried to call Sergeant Patton on the platoon radio, but he interrupted.

"Send somebody to the left flank," he cried, distressed. "There's a whole bunch of Krauts coming in on our left!"

I called back to Sergeant Barnes in the quarry, and his men moved quickly to the left and entered the first of two houses that stood beside the sunken trail to the left before the ground rose to the wooded hill. I could see them moving beyond the house into a garden before they were lost from sight.

I motioned for the CP group to follow me, and we ran to the left, bending low lest our head and shoulders show above the banks of the sunken trail. I had to get where I could see what was going on.

We entered an open gate in a brick wall around the first house. Two men investigated the house but said they could see nothing from inside. I went into a small barn in the rear and climbed to a second-floor room that was filled with potatoes. Windows in the rear and on the right side afforded a clear view of the area to our front and right flank. The artillery observer began to adjust fire on the hill to our left front from which the tanks were firing.

Lieutenant Bagby reported that he had succeeded in getting all his men inside houses, but when they attempted to move across the open space between houses, they were smothered with small-arms fire. Patton had some men still on the edge of town in the orchard. Two men were wounded. He thought he could advance, however, if he could get the tanks to go with him.

I tried to reach the tanks over the radio, but to no avail. Through the right window I saw a man rise from a shallow dip in the ground and run toward one of the tanks. I saw that it was Patton. He held a hurried conversation with a tanker inside the turret, then ran back to the scant protection of the dip in the ground, a burst of enemy small-arms fire following his path.

"The goddamned tankers say they can't come forward," Patton panted over the stuttering platoon radio. "I can move in, if the tanks will come with me."

I tried again to call the tank platoon leader on the battalion radio, but there was no answer, and Colonel Smith interrupted for a report on the situation. He said he was sending E Company around my left flank through the woods to hit the hill from which the tanks were firing. I told him I thought my 2d Platoon would make it in a few minutes, if I could get the tanks forward. He said E Company had already started forward, and he wanted them to continue.

Sergeant Barnes reported over the 536 radio that his men were in the garden to the left of the barn where I was located. They had gotten there just in time to stop a flanking movement against Patton's men by about twenty-five Germans. They had pushed on to a two-story villa beyond the garden, but a German tank had chased them out with direct fire. Several men had suffered scratches and bruises from falling plaster and glass, but no one was seriously hurt.

I tried a third time to get the tank platoon leader on the radio, but there was no answer.

One of the headquarters men said, "I'll go tell him."

I looked around. It was Private First Class Sidney Fein, of Brooklyn, N. Y., a small Jewish boy who wore glasses and squinted when he talked. It was my first experience with the fact that Fein was afraid of nothing.

He ran quickly across the intervening open space to the first tank, and I could see him rapping on the side of the tank to gain the attention of the crew.

He left the tank and ran back toward us. The big tanks raced their motors and started forward. I wondered what magic Fein had used.

He climbed the ladder to the barn loft, the pockets of his green fatigue trousers bulging with various items which he seemed to have a mania for collecting.

"What did you tell him?" I asked.

"I told them you said they'd better get moving or you'd be down there and shoot hell out of them with a bazooka right smack in their tails," he said.

I laughed.

The fire from the infantry weapons suddenly increased.

The forward platoons were beginning to roll. I heard F Company report to battalion that they had entered the town. E Company was meeting stiff resistance on the hill to our left but was advancing slowly.

Lieutenant Bagby said his men were going forward. Sergeant Patton's radio operator called for two litter squads, but the platoon was pushing forward. They had ten prisoners. I could see men from Sergeant Barnes' platoon in the garden on my left rounding up about twenty Germans.

The artillery observer removed the long aerial from his radio, and I started forward with my CP group across the orchard. We passed the two wounded men from the 2d Platoon. Both were hit in the leg and were waiting patiently for litter bearers. Two walking wounded from the 2d Platoon passed us going toward the rear. We entered a street that ran at an angle toward the highway which entered the town on our right. A house and barn burned in a furious blaze of smoke and flame on the left side of the street. Two Germans lay side by side in the middle of the street. One looked at us curiously as we passed. The other was dead.

A horse broke out of the burning barn on the left, and we watched dumbfounded as a grey-haired old woman emerged from the flaming house. She caught the horse and led him blindfolded back into the barn, locking the gate behind him. The animal squealed in terror. Just as calmly, she turned and re-entered the flaming house and locked the door behind her.

"Maybe she's dying for dear old Adolf," someone said.

We stopped in a house on the corner where the street joined the main highway. Two sides of the house were gone with shell blasts from a Sherman tank. The rooms were a ruin of broken furniture and dust from crushed and fallen plaster. We paused while I called for a report from the platoon leaders. The men from my forward CP group began to search the debris in the building for valuables.

"We're approaching the bridge across the river now," Patton's radio operator reported. "We can see the bridge from where we are——"

A deafening explosion rocked the shattered building and its two remaining walls trembled.

"They just blew the bridge to hell'n back," the radio operator said.

I reported to battalion that my men were at the bridge, and I heard F Company follow with a like message. We moved again in the wake of the assault platoons, their path marked on either side of the street with gaping holes in the buildings where the big tanks had blasted the opposition.

When I reached the bridge, the men from both assault platoons were gathered in a milling group, some sitting calmly on the sides of the remaining portion of the bridge smoking cigarettes, others laughing and joking with each other as they sauntered casually about the area. I listened half-expectantly for enemy fire from beyond the fast-flowing stream to disperse the group, but no fire came.

Private First Class Weylandt appeared on the other side of the bridge waving a bottle of champagne. His pants legs were soaked to the knees, evidence that he waded the shallow river to reach the other side.

"Look what I got!" he yelled to the others. "There's a Kraut civilian over here who said he'd sworn he'd give a bottle of champagne to the first American to cross the river. Who wants to join my bridgehead?"

I talked with the four platoon leaders and took stock of our casualties. The 1st Platoon had two men wounded slightly, and three men from the 3d would qualify for Purple Hearts without evacuation. The butt of Sergeant Patton's rifle had been shot away as he carried it on his shoulder, but he was uninjured. Four of his men were wounded, however, and a fifth, one of his assistant squad leaders, had been shot in the head by an enemy rifleman as he rounded the corner of a building. He had died immediately.

Battalion wanted to know if we could get tanks across the river, but one look at the blown bridge was enough to know that it was impossible at this point. Captain Calhoun said there were no bridges to our right, and E Company had not reached the river yet.

A concrete conduit rising a few inches above the level of the water stretched across the stream to the left of the shattered bridge. It would provide a dry crossing for the foot troops, but the tanks must wait until the engineers could bridge the stream. The steep banks on either side made it impossible for them to ford the obstacle.

Colonel Smith arrived, and we studied our maps. The main portion of the town lay ahead of us beyond the stream. I should move Company G across a second stream which joined the river one hundred yards to our left front, directing my three rifle platoons up three separate streets which led to the outskirts of the town. There we should establish a defensive position, being prepared to move upon order to the crest of a wooded hill rising high against the sky beyond the village.

We lined up in single file and crossed the conduit. I directed my 1st and 2d Platoons to deploy once again in an approach-march formation after crossing, and they moved out across a wooded marshy area leading to the second stream. The scouts advanced cautiously but rapidly, but there was no sign of the enemy.

The bridge across the second stream had been partially demolished, making it impossible for the tanks to cross there even if they bridged the river, so I radioed the information to battalion.

A towering castle with ancient stone walls stood guard over the junction of the two streams, its high towers ending picturesquely in the stone sides of a cliff behind it. Four men checked it for enemy stragglers. Lieutenant Bagby's 1st Platoon moved up a side street to the right to take up their defensive position. The 2d Platoon continued up the narrow main street, lined on either side by closely-grouped shops and dwellings. I saw by my map that the street broadened out as it climbed the high hill to the rear of the town, eventually becoming a highway which led across and beyond the hills to the rear.

I sent Sergeant Barnes' platoon along a dirt road which curved to the left of the castle and would bring him abreast of the wooded hill which E Company would occupy on the opposite side of the river.

I followed the 2d Platoon up the main street. Curious civilians lined either side of the street, some standing brazenly along the old walls of the buildings, others peering cautiously from behind closed windows. The street curved to the right as it climbed the hill, and I lost sight of Patton and his men.

A moment later the sound of rifle and machine-gun fire echoed down the twisting street. Patton had evidently run into trouble.

The buildings on either side of us disrupted the weak platoon radios, and I could not contact Sergeant Patton. We moved forward quickly, calling over the radio as we went, until we established contact. They had run into German machine guns in the last scattered houses of the town and were having a stiff fight. I said I would send our light machine guns to help and called for them from the weapons platoon. They hurried up the street toward the sound of the firing.

Battalion radioed a change of orders. The 1st Battalion had gone cross-country and captured Stromberg, a small town astride the high ridge to the southeast of Bendorf-Sayn. They were to continue the attack to the southeast and would need both platoons of tanks which we had been using. The tanks had found an undamaged bridge opposite E Company and were waiting for us there. I was to take my whole company along the route which my 3d Platoon was now traversing and move with the tanks to Stromberg. And quickly. The 1st Battalion was ready now to continue their attack.

I tried to call the platoons, but I could contact only the 1st and 2d, and Sergeant Patton said he did not know if he could disengage himself from the fire fight.

I told him to get out as quickly as he could. "Then move back to the castle and follow us around to the left. You'll be the support platoon. If you can't get away soon, we'll start on up the hill without you. Just leave the Krauts. F Company will take care of them."

"We've got three prisoners in the basement of a house," Patton said, "and we have to cross a hundred yards of open field to get back out. We'll never make it with the prisoners."

"Roger," I answered. "Do what you can."

We moved back to the castle and followed the circuitous route around the left. We overtook the 3d Platoon as they halted at an abandoned factory near the bridge where the tanks were crossing the river.

I looked up at the high hill which we must climb. Horseshoe curves in the ascending road gave it a mountain-like appearance. The side of the hill was almost vertical. It would be a fatiguing climb, even if we met no opposition, and determined enemy opposition might hold us up for days.

The easiest way to climb the hill would be to ride, I observed, congratulating myself upon the intelligence of it, and we would stand almost as much chance against possible opposition if we rode as if we walked. I was beginning to ache from the day's walking, and I could tell by the expressions on the faces of the men that they were exhausted. We had walked over five miles as the crow flies already, and we certainly had not been riding crows. Also, it was four o'clock in the afternoon, and it would not be long until night.

I radioed my decision to battalion. We would ride the tanks up the hill and into Stromberg.

The plan was agreeable with the two tank platoon leaders, but Captain Dan J. Manning, Jr., of Northampton, Mass., the E Company commander, cautioned me that the last of the German tanks had retreated up the hill not more than fifteen minutes before. The information half-frightened me, but I did not tell the tank platoon leaders lest they object to carrying the doughboys up the hill.

The tankers had received a replacement for the lead tank that had hit the mine before daylight, and we now had ten tanks. My 2d Platoon had not yet joined us, so I radioed battalion to direct them to follow us on foot to Stromberg. We loaded on the tanks and the tankers signalled that they were ready. Their treads churned up clouds of dust on the dirt road, and we began the ascent.

Lieutenant Bagby rode on the first tank with one squad from the 1st Platoon. I rode with the CP group on the fourth tank. The men laughed and joked, recalling thrilling experiences astride the big monsters on the dash to the Rhine River. They were evidently unconcerned with the thought that the huge hill to our front might prove to be a formidable enemy defense.

I longed to share their jovial attitude, but I could not put the thought of the recent departure of the enemy tanks from my mind. They might wait in ambush at any one of the sharp horseshoe bends on the wooded hill and literally blow us off the side of the hill.

The big Shermans churned the dust with their treads, and their heavy motors echoed back and forth through the deep ravines in the surrounding hills. I hid my face in my hands. We could scarcely breathe for the dust. The road ran to the left for two hundred yards before making its first abrupt turn to the right. I could see around the first curve and look down from my perch atop the fourth tank at the other tanks behind us loaded with tired but alert GIs.

The lead tank stopped at the first bend in the road to the left, and Lieutenant Bagby and his forward squad dismounted. They rounded the curve cautiously on foot until a soldier in rear signalled "all clear." The tank lunged forward and picked up its cargo. The long column started to move again up the precipitous side of the hill. The little town of Bendorf-Sayn lay far below us beside the winding silvery ribbon that was the river.

The lead tank halted again when the road horseshoed again to the right, and the riders dismounted. They found holes in the road and probed for mines, but the suspected mines failed to materialize.

We halted two more times before reaching a straight stretch of road which continued to the crest of the hill. In the distance I could see the far edge of the woods. Alert eyes on every tank scanned the dense woods on either side of us for signs of the enemy.

Lieutenant Bagby's tank halted again at the edge of the woods.

"There's a farmhouse and some buildings ahead," he said over the platoon radio. "I'm going forward with one squad to investigate."

We waited impatiently on the tanks. Someone dug out a chocolate bar from a K-ration and offered me a bite. "Vooley-voo choc-o-lot?" For the first time I realized I was ravenously hungry. We had not eaten since the early morning breakfast.

My fear of an enemy defense on the high hill was gone now, for even if the enemy occupied the buildings ahead, we had safely ascended the hill. A flight now would be comparatively easy.

The advance squad signalled forward, and the lead tank moved off. The farmhouse was on the edge of Stromberg. The squad had recognized the OD uniforms of other GIs.

We turned the tanks over to the 1st Battalion. Our own battalion staff arrived closely behind us, and Captain Herbert C. Byrd, of Albuquerque, N. Mex., the battalion operations officer, designated areas of the town for each company to defend for the night.

Sergeant Patton's platoon arrived, tired and dusty from the tiring uphill walk from Bendorf-Sayn. The prisoners were not with them.

Company G today committed a war crime. They are going to win the war, however, so I don't suppose it really matters.

I went with the platoon leaders on a hurried reconnaissance of our designated sector, and we set up a hasty defense for the night, chasing the civilians to their cellars and finding room in houses for every man.

"There's an old man and his old lady in our CP who say they won't go to the cellar," Harms told me. "They say the Americans are here now and there won't be any more boom-boom."

"Tell them either they get to the cellar or we turn 'em over to the MPs," I said.

That did the trick. They evidently thought military police were the American equivalent of the Gestapo. I wondered what I would have done had they refused again to go to the cellar.

The kitchen arrived with a hot supper. I ate quickly to allow time for a visit with the rifle platoons before dark, and moved from house to house, talking briefly with the men. They were tired but jubilant over the success of the day's attack. Everywhere there were little individual stories of today's war.

I found myself becoming closely cemented to this new company. There always would be a spot in my heart for Company I, but there would be a place now for Company G as well. The successful attack on Bendorf-Sayn had raised my spirits and given me a confidence in my personal ability in an attack which I had not had before, and an integral part of that new confidence was this group of dusty, weary, smiling men. I still could find no glory in war, but there was much less evil in a successful attack than in a perpetual defense or a retreat. It made you feel elated, some way.

I stopped longer at the house where the men from the squad of the sergeant who had been killed were preparing for the night. I had not known the sergeant personally, but to these men he was an important character in the little war that revolved around themselves. There was an undertone of sadness as they talked, but there was no bitterness. The sergeant had died like any one of them might die at any time. There was a war on, you know.

An SP gun shelled the town during the night, but except for one shell that clipped off the corner of one of the buildings occupied by the 1st Platoon, they landed in the rear portion of the town. We had a hot breakfast early the next morning, and I was called to battalion for a reconnaissance. We would take over the defense of Nauort, the town to the southeast which the 1st Battalion had taken the afternoon before. The 1st Battalion would continue the attack to the next town, and then the regiment would await further orders.

With Harms to serve as interpreter, I joined the reconnaissance party. We moved by jeep to Nauort along a road that ran astride the high ridge on which Stromberg was saddled. To our right we could see the high blue hills stretching on into Germany, and I thought that if the enemy had any artillery left, he would surely shell this road.

Nauort was another sprawling farm village, but we succeeded in finding one house without a manure pile in the front door and which battalion did not claim as their command post. The company arrived on foot from Stromberg with the news that they had been shelled twice on the open stretch between the towns, but there had been no casualties. I directed the platoon leaders to defensive positions around the northeast edge of the town, and they began to obtain billets in the outer fringe of houses. Our kitchen arrived and set up in the town *Gasthaus* next door to my CP.

I visited the battalion CP after supper. Colonel Smith had received the news that two armored divisions had broken out of the Remagen bridgehead that morning in what might prove to be the final drive across Germany. Resistance had been negligible, but the two spearheads had become confused after reaching a point several miles beyond the *Autobahn* and had run directly into each other. They would bivouac there for the night but would continue the drive the next morning. Our regiment would follow the 9th Armored for any mopping-up operations which might develop. The mission of establishing a bridge-head for the Third Army at Coblenz was no more—the Third was already across the Rhine.

It had become clear that the First Army could have broken out of their bridgehead at almost any time, but they had been waiting for at least one of the other armies to cross.[1]

I brought the news back to my CP and we telephoned the information to the platoons. We all were firmly convinced that the war was in its final stages and could not possibly last much longer than one or two weeks.

We loaded on two-and-one-half-ton trucks the next morning with Dernbach, a small town to the southeast two miles beyond the *Autobahn*, as our objective. The drive was slow over unimproved roads to avoid confusion with the rear elements of the armored divisions, but we arrived shortly after noon. Our column halted beside a big building which was evidently a Catholic school or hospital on the edge of town.

Two middle-aged, pleasant-faced nuns walked toward one of the trucks which carried men from my company. A group of men were unashamedly relieving themselves beside the road.

The nuns spoke in obviously rehearsed English.

"We are so happy you have come," one of them said, choosing her words carefully. "We have waited so long for the Americans. It has been hard for us."

"Not you but us, lady," a surly GI answered. "Go back to your Nazis."

The two nuns looked blankly at each other and jabbered excitedly in German.

---

[1] The First Army, in reality, had been held up by the Supreme Allied Commander. General Eisenhower had kept the army ready to assist, if necessary, the British assault crossing of the Rhine north of the Ruhr. After the successful crossing of the British 21st Army Group on March 24th, General Eisenhower removed the restriction. Thereupon, the First Army commander, General Hodges, turned loose the two armored divisions, one operating under the III Corps, the other under the V Corps, of which my division was a part.

18

REAR-ECHELON BASTARDS

Our convoy rolled on into the center of the town, and we were surprised to find that we were the first American troops to enter Dernbach. The armored spearheads had stayed on the *Autobahn*, by-passing the town. The civilians gathered curiously around our trucks and talked rapidly and in low tones to one another.

I designated platoon sectors. A truck from battalion rode up and down the main street, collecting prisoners as the men unearthed them in their search for billets. My 2d Platoon sent word that a German soldier was in bed in one of their houses, claiming he was too sick to be moved.

I went to investigate and found the soldier in an upstairs bedroom surrounded by members of his family. He claimed that he was at home on a sick leave from the Army. I jerked back the covers of his bed. His shirt had been replaced by a nightgown, but he lay in bed wearing the trousers of a German soldier. The women sobbed violently as we hustled him outside to a waiting jeep.

Battalion transmitted an order from regiment that no soldier would be billeted in houses with civilians. The regimental CO was making a strict interpretation of the Supreme Headquarters directive on non-fraternization. I transmitted the order to the platoons, and the streets were soon filled with disconsolate civilians moving light household goods to the homes of their neighbors.

Three middle-aged women who occupied the house which we chose for the company CP began to sob violently when Harms told them they must move. They took my hand and pleaded earnestly to allow them to live in one room of the house. I tried to act tough, but my youthful face must have betrayed my efforts, and I felt peculiar inside. I could not avoid thinking how I would feel if invading soldiers were chasing my own family into the streets . . . but, then, these people had asked for it.

"Tell them to get the hell out," I told Harms, and I turned and left the house. There was one advantage in not being able to speak the language. I could leave the dirty work to my interpreter.

The 1st Platoon CP group were the proud inhabitants of a two-story villa with a crude bathtub and shower in the attic. Battalion was occupying the more modern sector of the town, as we had come to expect, and the other houses which we occupied did not possess even indoor toilet facilities. Bagby invited me over to take a bath that evening. As I waited my turn in a line of grimy men from the platoon, we consumed a bottle of rich red wine which persistent GI searchers had looted from its carefully chosen hiding place in a niche in the cellar wall.

Regiment directed a training schedule the next morning, and I assembled the company for close-order drill on a sloping green hill on the edge of town. The varied uniforms, with marked contrasts of laundry and pressing, emphasized the mockery which we felt for this type of work when we had the opportunity to rest. *Tomorrow we may be fighting the Germans again. Today we are doing close order drill. Damnit!*

We moved unexpectedly the next day by trucks, only to wait long, chilly hours under overcast skies by the road as rear elements of the armored division ahead of us tied up the roads. Oftentimes we were within sight of the wide ribbon of concrete that was the *Autobahn*, with sparse traffic on it. The *Autobahn* was in the Third Army sector and by command of General Patton its use was restricted to gasoline vehicles of the Third Army. Even that was not enough to convince us that it was necessary to hustle and bustle to cross an IP[1] at a given time, only to spend long hours waiting by the roadside later. *Hurry up and wait!*

GIs joked to drivers of passing single vehicles, "Is your trip really necessary?"

---

[1] Initial Point.

The side highway which we followed changed into a dirt road, dusty from hundreds of heavy vehicles, and the *Autobahn* disappeared in the rolling hills to the southeast. The column progressed in leaps and bounds, sometimes no more than a few hundred yards at a time. The soldiers invariably dismounted, building small fires by the roadside and heating K-rations over the flame. Darkness came, and with it the chill of evening, and the bonfires of troops ahead of us marked the route which we were to follow.

As night fell we could see the orange flashes of artillery on the horizon, and the sounds of their firing told us that the war was not far away. I made out the outlines of fighter planes on an air strip through the inky blackness. A small town with burning buildings told us that here the advance elements had met resistance earlier in the day. Fires burned in the next town, but we turned to the north on the edge of the village and the fires died away to our rear. The column slowed to a virtual halt and maneuvered to keep from being crowded into the ditch by a column of American tanks with dim cat's-eyes glowing in the darkness. We picked up speed again. Three miles farther we pulled off the road into a grain field and dismounted. It was eleven o'clock. This was our destination for the night.

Our guide, Sergeant Donald Jenkins, a former schoolteacher from Seven-Mile Run, Pa., met us at the road as we moved from the field. He was our battalion billeting guide and had arrived only a few minutes before the main convoy. The town was Altenkirchen, a backwoods farming town which Sergeant Jenkins described as a "cow town." It was only thirty-six miles from Dernbach, yet we had travelled all day. The town behind us where we had met the tanks had been the scene of bitter fighting by a by-passed German garrison.

We moved down the dark street to the area designated for our billets. Sergeant Jenkins waved his arm at the general area, and I hastily divided it into platoon sectors. The sleepy men began to hammer loudly on closed doors with harsh commands to "open up, you German sonso'-bitches." Sleepy civilians appeared at the doors, only to join their excited comrades a few minutes later in moving about the dark streets to find neighbors' homes which had not been invaded. Harms gave the occupants of our prospective combined CP and kitchen ten minutes to *gehen heraus*. The terrified civilians made it in five.

The rough order system seemed to be what we needed. Not only had the houses been evacuated rapidly without argument, but a partially full bottle and another untouched bottle of choice cognac had been left on the table beside the bed which Sergeant Henderson designated for me. Now we were evidently using a language these civilian Krauts could understand.

The kitchen had supper ready by midnight. We would leave the next morning at seven o'clock, and the company must be fed again before leaving. The kitchen force prepared for a sleepless night. I checked to see if all platoons were billeted properly and went to bed at two o'clock.

We had fried eggs for breakfast, the first in months.

The order for movement was changed three times during the morning, each time seemingly at the last possible moment, and it was noon before our column finally moved off down the road. After three miles we reached a river with a partially-blown bridge and a town on the opposite banks which bore the marks of heavy shelling. The enemy had evidently attempted a stand on the river line, but the armored dreadnaught had rolled on.

The second day of travel was a repetition of the first, except that the ride seemed colder and the halts seemed even more frequent. A column from the 80th Division of the Third Army somehow became entangled in our column, and it was hours later before the situation was set right. Here and there we passed a town which bore signs that the enemy had attempted a fight, but for the most part the towns were unscathed. An occasional enemy vehicle with littered papers and equipment sprawled around it lay upturned beside the road. Callow German youths looted vainly through the rubbish. Occasionally we saw a dead *Wehrmacht* soldier, his skin turned a sickly green in death. Empty K-ration cartons and C-ration tins littered the shoulders of the roads, and the German children searched vainly for chewing-gum and cigarettes through rubbish which had been searched countless times before them by others like them. In the scattered intervals when the convoy moved we passed an occasional group of Frenchmen, or Poles, or Russians, or Belgians, who would wave their arms violently and shout hoarsely, their fingers upraised in the V-sign for Victory.

"You Rooskie?" the GIs would shout from the speeding trucks, and the liberated slave laborers would shout happily in return, "Polski," "Français," "Belgique," or "Yah, Yah, Rooskie!"

MPs at intersections or GIs standing beside the road came to accept the cries as well. The soldiers on the trucks would shout to a harried MP, "Rooskie?"

The MP would answer, "Yah, Rooskie," or "Me Deutsch."

German civilians watched apathetically from windows and balconies or hurried about their business. This American Army had been rolling by for hours now. The dust and the roar of motors had become routine. If you displayed a white flag on your house, that was all that was necessary.

Buxom *fräuleins* became accustomed to passing shouts of "you *schlafen* with me?" and some kept their eyes to the ground and hurried on, and others looked up and laughed.

Rumored reports on the rapid advance of the armored spearheads filtered to us at every halt. We were ten miles behind the front when we started out, but we were forty or fifty miles behind now. Hell! we might never catch up. Passing men from rear echelon units lining up for evening supper with mess kits and in neat regulation uniforms brought jeers and derisive laughter from the infantrymen.

"Hell, corps headquarters was in that town. Jeez, we're rear-echelon bastards now."

Again the *Autobahn* with its speeding traffic appeared on our right. How we longed to move out on the big four-lane highway and join the rapid flow of unimpeded traffic. But our convoy halted within sight of the highway, and we watched the vehicles speed by.

Darkness seemed the signal for which the slow-moving column was waiting. The trucks sped and careened dangerously over the small curving highway, each driver trying desperately to keep the dim taillights of the preceding vehicle in view, his own visibility reduced to almost nothing by the black-out driving. If we were to do most of our traveling at night anyway, I wondered why they didn't allow us to wait until night to begin. At least we could sleep in the daytime.

But the column was held up again in the middle of a dense fir forest. I learned that a truck was stuck up ahead where exploded mines had destroyed the road. We shivered for two hours in the damp, chill darkness. When we finally moved off again, we progressed only a few hundred yards. A soldier with a flashlight stood by the road directing the trucks to turn off into a cleared space in the woods. It was midnight. The Colonel had decided to bivouac for the night in the woods. The men cursed. *With all the goddamned towns around——*

A group of fifteen Germans was waiting by the road to be taken prisoner when we had finished breakfast and moved out again the next morning.

We by-passed rear elements of the armored division, and some unknown priority allowed us to move on the *Autobahn*. It was a thrill to speed down the wide ribbon of concrete after the slow riding over the side roads. The *Autobahn* was lined with displaced persons and former slave laborers making their way toward our rear. The men on the trucks tossed cigarettes and chewing-gum from K-rations to them. They scrambled madly for the prizes, and then the winners raised their hands toward us in an enthusiastic V-sign for Victory.

We turned off the *Autobahn* to the northeast after twenty miles and followed a dusty country road through thick woods that had evidently been a large German ammunition dump. Ammunition of all sizes and calibers was stacked in small piles throughout the forest.

We neared our destination and passed through a "cow town" occupied by Company I. The men waved cheerfully at me as we rolled on through the town. We crossed a hill with a white flag fluttering in the breeze and came upon the dilapidated little farming town of Dennenrod beyond the hill.

The billeting detail met us in the center of the town.

"What a deal this was," Sergeant Jenkins said. "We rode through town in our jeeps, and then we saw two German soldiers in a house on the far side of town. When we came back through, there were Germans everywhere waiting to give up. We were the first Americans here . . . nine men. We took one hundred and nine prisoners."

We hoped that we would not stop here for the night. It was the poorest town we had encountered, and it was only midday. We set up the company in the old houses, however, and the kitchen put the final touches on the noon meal. The orders came after lunch. We would move on.

We moved comparatively rapidly, even though we did not see the *Autobahn* again, arriving at our destination at four o'clock. It was another small farming town, Slidern, but more modern than Dennenrod. My company CP was set up in a small brick bungalow near battalion headquarters, and we attached the electric lights of the house to the captured German generator which battalion carried.

Colonel Smith warned me that we were on the left flank of the First Army's left spearhead which had joined with the Ninth Army to trap thousands of Germans in the Ruhr pocket. There were rumors of a German attempt at breaking out of the pocket, and we would be directly in the path of such an attempt. I should plan my defenses accordingly.

The rumors had some basis in fact. Field Marshal Walter Model, faced with the imminent encirclement of his entire Army Group B of some 400,000 men in the Ruhr industrial area, ordered on March 27th that the Fifteenth Army assemble several armored divisions for a thrust into the north flank of the U.S. First Army's fast-moving columns. Unfortunately for Model, he had lost touch with the situation. One corps of General Zangen's Fifteenth Army had been crushed, another was in serious condition, and a third was entirely out of communication with the army headquarters. Not long after receiving Model's order, Zangen and his staff were forced to flee their command post and hide in a nearby woods while American armor raced by. Not until night came was Zangen able to escape. He did so by sandwiching his vehicles into gaps in the American column. A major counterattack, as Model wanted, was by this time out of the question. Shortly before all resistance ceased in the Ruhr, Model committed suicide.

The 1st Platoon drew the choice billets again. One of the houses had a modern bathroom, and I accepted Lieutenant Bagby's invitation to a bath. That made my second bath in less than a week, and I was beginning to tire of the frequency.

The next day was April 1 and Easter Sunday. Chaplain Anderson, the regular 2d Battalion Protestant chaplain who had also conducted services for the 3d Battalion when I was with them, held the Protestant services in a large hay barn next to the battalion CP. Men of Catholic faith were provided transportation to the town which regiment occupied.

We moved the next afternoon at one o'clock eighteen miles to Mengeringhausen, a large town that would provide ample billets for all of us. G Company was assigned a sector on the northern edge of town.

Captain Byrd, the operations officer, called me the next morning to send out a combat patrol of approximately one platoon, supplemented by a machine-gun section, to comb the woods to the north for enemy stragglers trying to escape from the Ruhr pocket. He sent an overlay by runner of the route the patrol should take.

I decided to go with the patrol and called the 3d Platoon to assemble at the company CP. The two jeeps arrived, and we mounted the two light machine guns on the antiaircraft mounts. The men from the platoon crowded into the two trucks.

I rode in the lead jeep with Private First Class Roy Shepherd, SCR-300 operator who would keep us in touch with battalion in case we ran into too much trouble, and the gunners for the machine gun. Our driver was Private First Class Clem E. Todd, from Georgia. The two trucks followed and the other jeep acted as a get-away vehicle in the rear under Staff Sergeant Savino Soniga, of Gonzales, Texas, the machine-gun section sergeant, and Staff Sergeant John Day, the 3d Platoon guide.

We moved slowly along the road for two miles until we came to a crossroads. A lone stone house stood at the intersection, the dense fir forest stretching behind it. Two Frenchmen ran from the direction of the house, waving wildly for us to stop.

"SS! SS!" they shouted. "SS!"

I halted the column and dismounted to talk with them. They were forced laborers working for the farmer who lived at the crossroads. They said there were several German soldiers who lived in the woods during the day and

came to the farmhouse for food at night. Three of them had been at the house and had run as we approached. Their insistence that the Germans were SS troops worried me.

Sergeant Barnes motioned for his platoon to dismount, and the men took up and extended formation on either side of the road. They moved off toward the woods, and I followed closely behind in the lead jeep, the machine gunners alert for trouble.

The lead scouts found the three Germans a few yards inside the woods, waiting submissively to be captured. Instead of SS they were three elderly men from a *Wehrmacht* labor battalion.

Lieutenant John W. Whitman, of Renovo, Pa., the 2d Platoon leader, who had been on pass to Paris, had rejoined the company when I returned from the patrol. He took over the command of his platoon, and I shifted Sergeant Patton to take over the 3d Platoon. Sergeant Barnes outranked him, but Patton had been recommended for a commission that should be through at any time. The two

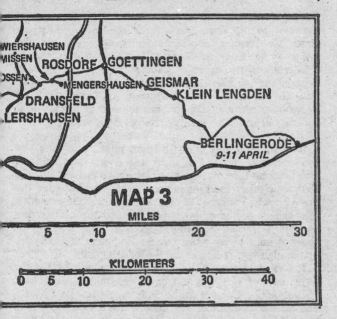

WIERSHAUSEN
MISSEN
ROSDORF GOETTINGEN
OSSEN MENGERSHAUSEN GEISMAR
DRANSFELD KLEIN LENGDEN
LERSHAUSEN

BERLINGERODE
9-11 APRIL

MAP 3

MILES

5 10 20 30

KILOMETERS

0 5 10 20 30 40

noncoms were close friends, and neither objected to taking orders from the other, and Sergeant Barnes had consistently refused a commission. Staff Sergeant Walter A. Cantwell became Lieutenant Whitman's platoon sergeant.

Lieutenant Bagby called the CP to tell me that his platoon CP had come equipped with a bathtub again, but, sorry, no water.

I was called to battalion after supper for a company commander's meeting. The battalion was alerted for movement the next day. It looked like trouble. The armor had met stiffened resistance on the approaches to the Weser River, and the 23d Infantry would attack. We would move the next morning at 8:30.

With encirclement of the Ruhr complete, reduction of the pocket became the responsibility of other units. The Ninth Army and two corps of the First Army, including our own V Corps, headed east across Central Germany toward the Elbe River. We could not realize it at the

*time, but the entrapment of hundreds of thousands of
Germans in the Ruhr pocket was the end of German
hopes for forming another defensive line east of the
Rhine. In the Ruhr the Germans lost all of Model's Army
Group B and two corps of another army group. In prisoners alone the Germans numbered 317,000 men, more
than the Russians took at Stalingrad. As infantrymen, we
would have many another anxious moment in the war, but
never again would we face a cohesive enemy front.*

It was 11:30 before our column pulled out. The sky
was overcast, and the weather was dreary and cold. A
lone German fighter plane flew high above the column, but
alert antiaircraft machine gunners held their fire when the
plane kept its distance. We reached a small village hidden
in a valley. A line of high hills guarded the horizon beyond it. I learned that this town had been the limit of
advance until today when our 3d Battalion had attacked
up the highway leading across the towering hills.

It was night when the 3d Battalion finally captured the
large town of Hofgeismar from a determined garrison of
SS defenders. Colonel Smith ordered me to go forward
and take over a sector for defense from Company I. A
rain and the cloudy skies had brought an early darkness,
and we could see only a few feet ahead of us. Our
column moved across the hill and down a tree-lined highway toward the town, past fallen branches and an occasional gutted house standing gaunt and ghostly against the
dark horizon. Fires were burning in Hofgeismar.

We pulled the trucks up beside a series of large stone
buildings that looked like army barracks. I dismounted
and began to look for someone from I Company whose
position we were to take over, but the darkness was inky
black and I could see no one. A tracer bullet from a sniper's rifle whistled over our heads, tracing a burning red
pattern through the blackness.

I called the platoon leaders into a building, and we
looked at the map by flashlight. We were in the right location. I designated defensive areas, and the platoons
moved out.

Lieutenant Loberg, my executive officer, located a
clean portion of the barracks to serve as our CP, and the
men settled down on hard German Army bunks for the night.

Lieutenant Bagby called over the 536 radio.

"I haven't got a bathtub this time, Cap'n," he said, "but we've got a mighty attractive *fräulein* and a cellar full of champagne and cognac. Want to come over?"

When morning came, the sun was not shining but the rain had stopped. I received a call during breakfast to report to battalion as soon as I had finished. I found the Colonel in an upstairs room from which we had a clear view of the rolling hills to the east. The other company commanders arrived, and we spread our maps for the order.

F Company would attack at nine o'clock to take the next town to the east, Karlstadt. The 1st Battalion would then advance to Karlstadt, passing through F Company to attack along a road to the southeast. E Company would also pass through F Company, moving to the northeast to take the town of Hombressen. G Company would follow in reserve closely behind E Company.

I returned to the company and gave the order to the platoon leaders and returned to battalion to await the outcome of F Company's attack, overjoyed that we had drawn the reserve company position for today's action.

Fox Company found no resistance in Karlstadt. From the vantage point in the battalion CP we could see the head of the column which was the 1st Battalion moving out from Hofgeismar toward the town of Karlstadt.

Someone pointed to three dark spots on the forward slope of the hill beyond the distant highway.

"There're tanks up there!" he shouted. "Take a look with the glasses."

A puff of smoke came from the nearer object on the hill. Dirt cascaded beside one of the trucks in the column. There could be no question now. The dark spots on the hillside were German tanks!

"They're Mark IVs," someone with field glasses said.

The other two enemy tanks began to fire, and the shells ripped up the dirt around the vehicles in the column. At any momont one of the tanks or tank destroyers or one of the trucks loaded with soldiers might be blown to pieces. The tanks and TDs stopped and turned the muzzles of their guns toward the menace from their flank, opening fire. The trucks sped around them and raced toward the cover of the buildings in Karlstadt.

Mark IV

Shells burst to the right and left and forward and rear of the speeding trucks, but I saw no hits. The inaccuracy of the enemy fire was hardly believable.

An explosion from close outside the building shook the house. Three tank destroyers had pulled up beside the house and were blasting away at the enemy a mile away on the hillside.

The tanks and TDs on the road seemed to realize that they had help. They turned again toward Karlstadt and raced toward the town. The Germans followed their paths with shells, but the tanks and TDs went unscathed.

The shells from the TDs firing from below the window where we watched churned the earth around the Mark IVs, now maneuvering on the hillside like bugs on the surface of a pond. A sudden burst of orange flame sprang from the nearer tank, and flame and smoke billowed up. One of the TDs had scored a direct hit from over a mile away. The two remaining Mark IVs beat a hasty retreat into the obscurity of the woods beyond the field.

The show was over We left our reserved seats in the window of the house. We would become the actors now. It was our turn to run the gantlet to Karlstadt.

19

ACROSS THE WESER

I followed close behind the last truck in E Company's column in a company jeep driven by Private First Class Joe Rowe, of Oklahoma, watching the left flank apprehensively for the return of the German tanks. As we neared Karlstadt, the vehicles ahead of us pulled to a halt. The lead trucks had evidently stopped in the town to unload their GI cargoes, not realizing that they had left my company exposed on the open road to the mercy of the enemy tanks, should they choose to return. I told Rowe to pull around the last E Company vehicle and move on into town.

A wrecked jeep stood beside the first house on the sloping hill that led down into the main part of the little farm village. One GI sat erect in the back seat. A companion hung limply over the steering wheel. The marksmanship of the enemy tanks had not been as poor as I had thought. The jeep had absorbed a direct hit. The occupants were dead.

I heard tank fire behind me, and I realized that the Mark IVs were firing again, this time at the rear trucks that were carrying my men. Rowe drove as fast as possible on the narrow road with the line of E Company trucks on the right, and my column reached the safety of the town unscathed.

I found the head of the column and contacted Colonel Smith. E Company would continue the attack immediately down the main highway to Hombressen. The highway ran on the floor of a narrow valley walled on either side by sharply rising wooded hills. F Company would place men on either side of the valley to prevent an ambush, and I would follow E Company toward the ob-

81mm Mortar

jective. At the junction of streets in the center of Hombressen, E Company would go to the right, clearing the southern half of the town. G Company would take the left fork, clearing the northern half. Our role as reserve company had been short-lived.

A section of 81mm mortars under First Lieutenant Jim Raney, of Pasadena, Texas, was set up beside the highway on the edge of Karlstadt. An artillery observer called for fires on the objective, and the 81mm mortars added their crunching explosions to the roar that echoed up and down the narrow valley.

We moved down the highway with single columns on either side. A man from E Company met us bringing two Germans in black SS uniforms with their hands resting on their heads. Neither of the Germans could have been over sixteen years old.

The town proved to be infested with snipers, but there were no other defenses. It was a long, tedious process clearing the snipers from the houses and barns, and the minutes wore on into hours.

It was two o'clock in the afternoon when the last sniper was cleared from the sector. I called the platoon leaders and assigned their locations for the defense until we should receive further orders. I hoped that we could spend the night in the town.

On the hill to our right front we could see the lead tanks of E Company's column move out of Hombressen toward a gently rising wooded slope to the east. The lead tank was half-way up the slope when an explosion came from the woods and a shell ripped up the dirt to the right of the tank. The soldiers riding on the tank jumped to the ground, but the tank kept moving. Another explosion came from the woods, and the tank burst into a sudden, hideous orange-colored mass of flame. *Isn't it funny how you feel sorry for a wounded tank as if it had a human's sense of pain?*

The other tanks turned back toward the town. I did not know what was happening, but meeting the fire from the woods had evidently caused a change in plans. E Company did not press the attack up the hill.

The afternoon settled down to a drowsy quiet. Civilians straggled back into the town from the woods beyond where they had gone to take refuge from the shelling. The information that the Americans had arrived and there would be no more "boom-boom" must have spread quickly.

Technical Sergeant Samuel D. Dillard, of Woodruff, S. C., the platoon guide of the 3d Platoon, came over to my temporary CP to invite me to a feast of eggs. I accepted with pleasure.

The platoon had found a basketful of eggs. Their preparation would have won no blue ribbon for sanitation, but they tasted good. I must have eaten five, and the men from the platoon were gorging themselves. They seemed happier over finding the eggs than they would have been had they found a cellar full of cognac.

Private First Class Leon W. Fulton, one of my radio operators who had only recently returned from his second trip to the hospital from wounds received in action, came over to the platoon to tell me that battalion was calling. It was Major Vern L. Joseph, the former exec with the 3d Battalion who was now with the 2d. He was with the battalion rear CP and was relaying a message from Colonel Smith.

"This is Joseph, Mac," he said. "There's been a change in plans. You're to hold where you are until relieved by the 38th Infantry. Load on their trucks and move back to Karlstadt. I'll have a guide meet you there."

My questions for further information were denied. He did not want to give any more information over the radio.

Officers from the 38th Infantry arrived shortly on reconnaissance, and the troops were not far behind. I talked with the officers.

"I understand your outfit is crossing the Weser tonight," one of them said.

I was shocked. Then that was our mission, establishing a bridgehead across the Weser River. If there was any main line of German defenses between the Rhine and the Elbe River, it would be the Weser. Visions of flaming tracer bullets from a dug-in enemy across a river as we assaulted in a night attack flashed before my mind. We had had it easy for a while now. Tonight we would get the works.

The big trucks rolled swiftly over the narrow highway, but the race against darkness was lost. It was dusk when we arrived at the town of Veckerhagen on the west bank of the Weser. My battalion radio was able to pick up the forward CP again.

"Have you eaten yet?" Colonel Smith asked over the radio.

"Not yet, but I understand our kitchen is set up here ready to feed us now."

"Eat as quickly as possible," the Colonel continued, "then load up with all the ammunition each man can carry and at least two days supply of K-rations. Is that clear?"

"Yessir. Roger."

"There're guides at your kitchen to show you where to find the boats. Come on across."

Come on across? Just like that. I swallowed.

"What's that, sir?" I asked incredulously.

"Across the river," the Colonel said again. "A guide'll meet you on this side. E and F are over here already."

The news was startling, but I was relieved. I wanted to jump and shout with joy. So there would be no night assult against the river line. We would move across without opposition to a bridgehead already held by friendly forces. It was almost too good to believe.

The men formed quickly for supper, but complete darkness had fallen before we finished the meal. The night was damp and misty and dark.

Major Joseph had explained the crossing of the river to me. The 1st Battalion had gone through the woods to Veckerhagen with little resistance, and when there seemed to be no opposition on the other side, they radioed the information to regiment. E Company was having trouble beyond Hombressen, so they pulled E and F Companies out and shoved them across in assault boats. The Germans hadn't fired a shot. One man was killed and another lost a leg when our own artillery fire fell short after they reached the town of Hameln on the opposite bank. It was the first First Army crossing of the Weser.

Our guides led us down a muddy back street to the river. It lay stretched before us, a wide misty expanse of swiftly flowing water. We could not see the opposite bank in the darkness. As we reached the river we heard a short burst of small-arms fire far in the distance.

The guides had missed the point where the boats were supposed to be, but a search up and down the slippery bank revealed their location two hundred yards to the north. A group of small landing craft was drawn up on a section of gently sloping shore line. We could hear the muffled sound of oars from other boats making the trip across the misty water to the other shore. Men spoke in muffled undertones.

My men loaded on boats, and we moved across. The engineer crewmen guided us easily, allowing the small craft to drift with the swift current until it approached the opposite shore. Other boats were disgorging their cargoes upon the muddy river bank. Waiting hands reached out for a line tossed from our boat and pulled us up on the sloping bank. We jumped quickly ashore.

A guide from battalion headquarters was waiting for

us beside a house near the water's edge. We waited for the other men of the company to arrive, and the guide led us up a narrow street into the town and pointed out our billets on either side of the street.

The guide said, "The Colonel wants to see you right away. I'll show you to the CP."

I found the other company commanders already assembled at the battalion CP when I arrived. We exchanged greetings around.

"Spread your map here on the table," Colonel Smith said. "Here's the situation. . . ." and he pointed to the map.

The map showed that beyond the town of Hameln the ground sloped gently upward until it reached a point approximately one mile from the river. There the contour lines on the map formed almost a solid black smudge, indicating that the ground rose abruptly into cliff-like hills. The highway leading east from Hameln made two hairpin curves after it reached the densely wooded hills. A patrol from F Company had already gone as far as a farmhouse at the first curve but had been fired upon. That must have been the small-arms fire we heard at the river.

It was obvious that anyone holding the commanding hills to the east could easily pinpoint any object that moved in the valley on either side of the river. The Germans evidently did not yet know that we had crossed the river, but the patrol skirmish at the farmhouse made it clear that they would know by morning and would set up defenses on the high ground, unless——

I looked at my watch. It was almost midnight. I suddenly realized that I was dog-tired from the nervous tension of the day although the fighting had not been stiff. Christ! how I wished we could wait until morning.

"Fox Company will lead out," the Colonel said. "You'll follow with George Company, and I'm holding Easy here in reserve." *Goddamn E Company, they always get the breaks.* "Fox Company will dig in on the high ground beyond the first curve. You will either break off from the tail of the column and go cross-country to the second curve, which is almost abreast of the first one, or pass through Fox to the second curve."

"If there're any Krauts there—which I doubt," he continued, "they won't be expecting you. They blew the bridge across the river here and evidently figured it'd be some time before we could get boats up to get across. A car full of German officers came barrelling into town right after we got here, and F Company's Negro platoon was holding the road into town. I think every one of them got a shot in. Those Krauts didn't know what hit them."

The men from F Company were waiting for us when I reached the east edge of town with my company. The column moved out, men walking without conversation on either side of the road, their heavy boots and rattling equipment belying their efforts at secrecy. Captain Calhoun had found a civilian automobile in Hameln, and since there would be no transportation until the engineers could bridge the river, he had brought it along to transport his heavier weapons. It seemed to make enough noise for a column of tanks, and I was glad when it ran out of gas half-way up the hill and had to be abandoned.

I was not afraid. At least, I had no overwhelming fear to make my body tremble as I remembered it from the pillbox positions, but instead a deep, underlying dread of the unknown which posed question after question in my mind. What was ahead of us? What the battalion staff officers did not seem to realize was that it was rough even when you hit no opposition. Your nerves were keyed to such a pitch until it was a relief sometimes to run into trouble.

We reached the point where I thought we should turn off the road to go cross-country to the second curve in the high hills above us, so I dropped back to the rear of the lead platoon, remembering my folly in the woods at Ondenval. The men jumped the ditch on the left of the road and stumbled across a gently-rising plowed field until we reached a line of underbrush and trees which marked the abrupt ascent of the hillside.

The men plowed noisily through the dense underbrush. I cautioned those around me to be quiet, but there was no stopping the muffled curses as branches slapped men in the face or sharp thorns tore at exposed hands and faces. The side of the hill was almost perpendicular, and I found myself pulling up by the bases of small trees.

The climb was slow and fatiguing. Sweat popped out on my body beneath my field jacket, and I wanted to take it off, but there was no time. The blanket roll slung over my shoulder became heavier and heavier.

The single file of men ahead of me stopped, and a call was passed down the line for me to come forward,. I by-passed the men and they dropped quickly to the ground, grateful for the opportunity for a brief rest.

Lieutenant Whitman was at the head of the column. He had halted on a small trail which seemed to wind around the hillside. He thought it was time we had reached the highway and wanted to check with me to see if my map showed this trail leading to our objective.

Two men held a raincoat over me, and I spread out my map and scanned it hurriedly by the light of a dim flash-light. The map showed no trail.

The hill continued high above us. The underbrush looked to be more dense than that through which we had already passed. The trail to the right ran downhill in the direction of the highway we had left originally.

"This isn't it, Whit," I said. "Looks like we should have reached the highway by now unless we turned off the road too soon. I believe we must be too far to the north."

Whitman agreed.

It seemed that our best bet was to take the trail to the right and follow F Company, passing through them when they stopped at the first curve in the highway.

The lead men picked themselves up slowly, fatigue in every movement of their bodies. I knew they were cursing me for leading them up the hill only to descend and have to climb it again. Nothing ever seemed to go right in the infantry.

We caught up with the rear elements of F Company just as they reached the farmhouse. There had been no fight. The Germans who had fired on their patrol earlier in the evening must have withdrawn. F Company's rifle platoons were going into position around the first hairpin curve. I talked with Captain Calhoun to decide on a point for my right flank to tie in with his left. I knew from my memory of the map that my three rifle platoons would be stretched to the limit to cover the wide area between his left flank and the second curve.

The platoons scrambled up the hill beyond the highway to find their positions for the night. The 2d Platoon would defend the second curve. I was wondering how much far-ther it was to the curve when it came suddenly into view. It didn't have the appearance I had expected from the map, but I couldn't be mistaken. The map showed only the two hairpin curves.

I could see by the luminous dial on my watch that it was four o'clock when the platoons finally were all placed for the night. I shivered in the chill night air and moved with my CP group a few yards down the slope from the highway. There was no sound of shovels digging into the earth. We would probably be here only the few hours until daylight, and the men were evidently too tired to dig in for that length of time.

One by one the members of the CP group fell asleep, until I was left alone with Private First Class Warren Bock, the nineteen-year-old weapons-platoon runner from Pittsburgh, Pa. I wanted to sleep, too, but fear of the unknown and my responsibility kept me awake. Bock and I walked up and down the road to keep ourselves warm.

The minutes ticked slowly by. I wondered what would happen if a large German force should move down the highway toward us to take up defenses on the hill. They did not know we were here, but my men could hardly be classed as a serious obstacle to anyone's advance. They were dead tired, and most of them would be fast asleep. And there were no dug-in defenses.

In the distance from the east I hard the sound of heavy motors. *Tanks! Enemy tanks!* The thought went through me like an electric shock. We were not at the top of the hill by any means, and enemy tanks could sit at the crest and shoot us off like sitting ducks. And where were our tanks? They would be sitting on the other side of the wide Weser, unable to cross until the engineers should finish a bridge, probably not until late in the afternoon. Oh, God! what if the sound of the motors did indicate tanks! *Please, dear God, don't let them be tanks!*

The sound of the motors died away. I yearned for a cigarette. Bock woke Junior to take his place on guard. I awoke Citrone, my runner, and we walked toward the farmhouse two hundred yards down the hill.

The house was battered from artillery shells that had plastered the area after the F Company patrol was fired upon. Six different men challenged us as we made our way to the house.

When we were inside, I hastily lit a cigarette and looked at my map.

Colt Automatic M 1911 A1

One glance at the map was enough to tell me that my company was in the wrong location. The curve which was now our left flank showed on the map as a short twist in the highway. We were only halfway between the two hairpin curves.

I hurriedly smoked a second cigarette, and Citrone and I headed back for the company. Faint streaks of dawn were beginning to give a dull, grey tinge to the surroundings. Since it was so near daylight, I decided not to shift the platoons to the north until we could see where we were going.

The minutes until dawn seemed like hours. The night was still and quiet. I heard the beat of feet approaching on the highway from the left, followed by the muffled voices of several people. The guard heard it too, and we dropped to the ground. The footsteps came nearer. I held my .45 pistol ready. Perhaps the 2d Platoon guards had fallen asleep, and a German patrol had slipped through on the highway. We could see an assortment of figures approaching us.

The figures came abreast of us on the highway, and I dropped my pistol. There were three women, two men and several children, jabbering excitedly in a language I did not recognize. I decided they were Russians. They passed from sight around the curve in the highway.

Dawn was approaching faster now. I awoke the CP group, and they took their unopened blanket rolls to continue the move. Citrone went with me to the 2d Patoon at the twist in the road, and we found men sleeping in the ditches. I asked Sergeant George Sabol, of Chicago, where I could find Lieutenant Whitman, and he led me to him. I told Whitman we had made a mistake and should continue to the next bend in the highway and take up defensive positions until further orders.

I moved back down the highway and contacted Sergeant Patton and gave him the same information. He prepared his men to move.

We followed a small trail which led to the 1st Platoon on the right. Lieutenant Bagby was already awakening his men. I gave him the information and turned to go back toward the highway when I noticed two figures in a clearing a hundred yards up the steep hill to the front of the platoon position. They seemed to be picking berries from a bush.

"Have you got any men up that far?" I asked.

"I don't think so," Bagby answered, looking in the direction to which I pointed. "Why those are Krauts!"

Staff Sergeant Hartwell York, of South Portland, Me., one of the 1st Platoon squad leaders, leveled his rifle at the two Germans and called out: *"Kommen sie her! Kommen sie her!"*

The Germans looked toward us. They seemed not to have noticed us until Sergeant York called to them. I thought I could see them shrug their shoulders, and they turned slowly and walked into the woods.

Two of the men started to shoot.

"Don't shoot yet," Lieutenant Bagby said. "You might start something. Two of them can't do us much harm."

Citrone and I moved back toward the highway. As we came abreast of the 3d Platoon, Private First Class Umberto R. Rodriguez, of Tampa, Fla., stepped out on the trail driving before him a German soldier with his hands high above his head.

"This bastard just wandered calmly down the hill," Rodriguez said. "He says he's out on patrol with two of his buddies."

I looked up the hill. The two Germans whom I had seen in the clearing in front of the 1st Platoon were sauntering casually down the hill. They saw us and stopped.

Rodriguez motioned to them to come on down the hill. The two Germans held a hasty consultation between themselves and casually turned and walked slowly back up the hill. I could have sworn I saw them shrug their shoulders indifferently.

"Good Lord," I said. "These guys are absolutely nuts."

"You take this one for me, Cap'n, and I'll go get the other two," Rodriguez said. He motioned to two men and they started up the hill.

Citrone motioned the green-clad soldier to move down the trail. He started forward in slow shuffle. Citrone kicked him solidly in the rear, and the soldier turned slowly and looked at us blankly. Just as slowly, he turned again and with the same slow shuffle moved down the trail. I looked at Citrone, and he shrugged his shoulders.

Citrone said, "Maybe he don't know there's a war on."

We found the CP group waiting for us beside the highway. Harms questioned the prisoner. He said he and two of his fellow soldiers had been sent out on patrol to find the American positions. They were members of a labor battalion which had been moved up the night before to halt the Americans at the Weser River. They had found the Americans already across, however, and now their outfit was digging in around a town beyond the woods to our front. He didn't know whether his outfit had any tanks.

I called battalion, and Captain Byrd said to assemble all prisoners at the farmhouse which was serving as F Company's CP.

Rodriguez came down the trail to the highway with the other two Germans.

"These guys must be balmy," Rodriguez said. "They act like fugitives from a nut factory."

A flurry of small-arms fire sounded around the curve on the left flank. I listened intently. The 2d Platoon had run into trouble. I tried to get Lieutenant Whitman on the radio, but the batteries were getting weak and the distance was too great. We walked in the direction of the firing, Citrone calling at intervals for the 2d Platoon over the radio.

A series of rifle shots sounded up the hill in the direction of the 1st Platoon. Citrone contacted Lieutenant Bagby.

"We're moving on up the hill and toward the curve," he

said. "We got within sight of the highway where it bends back and ran into a Kraut patrol on bicycles. They wouldn't give up, so we had to take care of them."

"How many did you get?" I asked, unaware that I sounded as if I were speaking of birds.

"There're five of them."

Citrone tried again to contact the 2d Platoon. The radio sputtered, and Sergeant Cantwell, the platoon sergeant, answered.

"What's the situation?" Citrone asked. He was so short and funny-looking and sounded so authoritative when he asked the question I laughed.

I heard another flurry of small-arms fire from the left.

"We were walking down the highway," I heard Sergeant Cantwell say over the radio, "when we ran into a bunch of Krauts hiding behind some stacks of firewood."

Another flurry of small-arms fire sounded from our left, but Sergeant Cantwell's voice did not seem in the least perturbed, rather amused.

"The bastards are yelling at us to surrender now," he said. "They say they've got us surrounded. Stupid sons-o'bitches."

The 3d Platoon broke into the conversation. It was Sergeant Patton.

"Hello, G six," he said. "This is G three. We can see Whitman and are moving in on his flank. We'll let you know how we come out."

"Roger," I said.

We continued down the road to the left around the curve which I had thought in the darkness was our objective. The road curved then gradually to the left, and we could not see the men from the 2d Platoon, although the firing sounded nearer. We came upon the spot where the platoon must have first come under fire. Their blanket rolls were scattered along the road where they had dropped them hurriedly to go into action.

I heard three more shots from the direction of the 2d Platoon. Sergeant Cantwell called over the radio.

"I think we've taken care of 'em now, Cap'n," he said. "We're moving on to the bend in the road. Killed six and got three prisoners. Too bad it had to end this way when they had us surrounded."

Sergeant Patton called for the 3d Platoon.

"Make that two more prisoners from the Fightin' Third."

"Roger."

The battalion radio sputtered, and Abad said headquarters was calling for me.

"Hello, Able three, this is Smitty. Get your men set to move out. I'll be up shortly. Our objective is the first town past the woods. You'll be on the left of the highway with Fox on the right. We jump off at eight o'clock. Any questions?"

I started to tell him we had been attacking already since six o'clock, but I decided that perhaps it would be best if he didn't know that we hadn't reached the objective last night.

"No questions," I said. "Roger. Out."

20

"THANK ADOLF!"

F Company joined us at the second hairpin curve in the highway. I formed my company in the woods on the left of the road, the 2d Platoon leading the assault with the 3d and 1st Platoons echeloned to the left rear to protect the wooded flank. Colonel Smith radioed to ask if we were ready, and I looked at Captain Calhoun and he nodded. I signalled to Lieutenant Whitman, and the lead scouts stepped bodly into the underbrush. *We will now take a short walk in the woods for the purpose of nature study. Please excuse our silly walking formation. We were raised in an army camp.*

My map showed that the first likely spot for an enemy defense was a north-south highway which met the road we were following at a crossroads in the woods almost a quarter of a mile distant. There might be enemy patrols between us and that point, but the crossroads seemed the only logical defensive position until we should emerge from the woods at a point overlooking the town of Ellershausen slightly less than a mile away. Our orders were to hold up at the far edge of the woods to await the completion of the bridge across the Weser and the subsequent arrival of tank support.

I tried, but I could not put the memory of the heavy motors that I had heard during the night from my mind. The harsh memory of riflemen against tanks in the gruelling Ardennes battle was stamped indelibly in my mind, and I could not avoid the overwhelming fear of meeting the Germans on such terms again.

The riflemen plowed slowly through the woods, hindered by the dense underbrush. I followed close to the

245

highway as it continued slighly south of east after making its last deliberate turn at our starting point.

I pushed around a thick bush. On the ground before me lay a tangle of bicycles and human bodies. The bodies were German and their faces were rapidly turning a sickly shade of green that seemed to blend with their uniforms.

"Must be the patrol the 1st Platoon hit," someone said, impassively. "Lieutenant Bagby's men sure got far enough up the hill."

One of the dead German's lips were pulled back, baring irregular teeth in a sickening snarl; the eyes of another stared blankly at me; a thin trickle of bood from the temple of another appeared to be still warm. I wondered why the Germans turned green so quickly after death, and then I remembered that someone had once said that it was due to a diet deficiency.

A report came over the radio from the 2d Platoon. They were coming out of the underbrush now, but they were still in the woods. So far, no trouble.

So far—I thought. They should be reaching the crossroads soon.

Colonel Smith and Captain Byrd came abreast of me on the highway.

"Call your men out of the woods to the highway, Mac," the Colonel said. "There's nothing here. That's pretty obvious. Move them over to the road where they can make some time and let's get going."

I looked at him dubiously. I wanted to scream and ask what in hell was all the all-fired rush about, but I turned to Citrone and told him to get the three rifle platoons on the radio.

"Hello, G two," Citrone began. "Hello,——"

A sudden burst of small-arms fire echoed through the woods ahead of us. Bullets whistled over head. I dropped instinctively to the ditch beside the road. The small-arms fire was so intense that I could not distinguish between German and American fire, but I wondered why so few bullets whistled over our heads. Whitman and his men must be laying down quite a volume of fire. There was no need to ask him if he had reached the highway. It was obvious that he had hit the German defenses there.

I had fallen behind when I stopped to talk with the

Colonel, so I motioned for the CP group to follow and we moved up the ditch toward the sound of the firing. I looked around for the battalion staff, but I could not see them.

"Hmph, nothing in the woods," I said to myself.

The road curved slightly to the left, and I could not see the crossroads, but I knew that we must be near. The ground had leveled out. We had at last reached the top of the hill.

The firing stopped almost as suddenly as it had begun. A few scattered rifle shots remained.

"Call Whitman," I said to Citrone. "Ask him what's happening."

Citrone called for "G two."

"We've come up against a bunch of Kraut dug in beyond another highway," Whitman said. "Looks like they've got quite a trench system."

"Do you think you can move forward?"

"We'll try it with marching fire," Whitman answered. "I think so. Cantwell has been hit. Not too bad, but you'd better get a litter, and we need some ammo."

I said, "Roger."

Abad was carrying the battalion radio. He contacted Captain Byrd.

"We'll get a litter squad right up," he said, "and we'll try for ammunition. No transportation but F Company's auto, but I'll send it back."

I sent two men to the Weapons Platoon to collect all M1 ammunition they could spare. It was not enough. I sent them back to get any spare ammunition from the 1st Platoon.

The barrage of small-arms fire began again. There was the same rapid crescendo as before, echoing back and forth through the woods.

The picture of what was happening in the woods a few yards from me was clearer now even though the low-hanging branches of the trees obscured the view. The Germans were being given very little opportunity to fire their weapons. The platoon was laying down such a terrific barrage of fire that they were forced to keep their heads down in their trenches. And the 2d Platoon riflemen would be jumping up and running forward one by one, hiding here behind one tree, hiding there behind another, while their comrades fired and awaited their turns to move forward.

The firing suddenly stopped again. I noticed the litter squad kneeling in the ditch behind me. Whitman sent a man to the highway to guide the litter bearers and bring the ammunition. Two of the aid men moved forward in a half-crouch and entered the woods, their red crosses against a white background on their helmets glistening as they moved.

A burst of small-arms fire came from the right of the highway. The enemy's line must extend to the right as well, and F Company had run into trouble.

Whitman's platoon started to fire again, and the woods crackled with the sound of the firing.

The aid men emerged from the woods carrying Sergeant Cantwell on a stretcher between them. I stood up to talk to him.

"I'm sorry as hell, Cap'n," the sergeant said, and I could see that he was making an effort to keep his face from showing the pain which he felt. "Just got in the way, I guess."

"Nice going, Cant," I said. "Hurry back to us."

He had a painful wound in the side, but the aid men thought there was no danger.

Two men from battalion headquarters arrived with their arms full of bandoleers of .30-caliber M1 ammunition. I sent it back to be distributed among the 1st Platoon and told the men from battalion to bring us another load. At the rate Whitman's platoon was firing, we would need several loads before we reached Ellershausen.

"Send the litter squad back," Whitman called. "I've got two more men wounded."

Fulton ran back to overtake the little squad. The two men returned with him and re-entered the woods, emerging a moment later carrying Private First Class Carby J. Simpkins, who was wounded in the upper leg. Private First Class Herbert I. Flam walked with them. He had been hit in the left shoulder. Both men had been hastily bandaged in full view of the dug-in Germans by the courageous platoon aid man.

Captain Calhoun was just across the road with his forward CP group, and we decided it would be best to coordinate our next assault in order to reach the crossroads at the same time. Thus, neither company would be endangered by enemy fire from the flank after reaching their respective portion of the enemy position. He said he would order his platoons forward when they heard Whitman's men open fire again. I radioed the information to Whitman.

The sudden fusillade of fire from the woods came once again, and I knew that Whitman's men were endeavoring to make this their last assault. F Company answered with a small-arms barrage on the other side of the road. The rapid fire was sustained, and then slowed down gradually until I could hear only scattered shots.

"We've crossed the highway," Whitman radioed. He was breathing heavily. "Patton's on my left. We're going on."

I signalled the CP group and the Weapons Platoon forward, and we moved the few remaining yards to the crossroads.

The woods beyond the north-south highway became a dense forest of big firs. German dead and equipment were scattered in and around a series of trenches which zigzagged back and forth beneath the heavy branches of the fir trees. The damp red earth piled high in front of the trenches showed that they were freshly dug. Five wounded Germans in immaculate uniforms except for blood stains here and there screamed and moaned for medics. A German officer, still wearing his officer's cap with its shiny, black visor, saw as we passed that I was an officer. He called to me for help and pointed alternately at a decoration on his blouse and a bleeding wound in one leg. The decoration must have meant something, but I did not understand, and I was revolted at his appeal to me as a member of the "officer class."

We passed on. There was no time to care for the stupid officer. The aid men in the rear would care for him in time.

Small-arms fire sounded again to the front. Whitman had run into trouble again, and the noisy chatter of small-arms fire told me he was pulling no punches.

"They're trying to hold up at a firebreak," he radioed. "Patton's platoon's up beside me now. We can handle it OK."

I wanted desperately to go farther forward to where I could see what was going on, but I knew that it would be necessary for me to be almost atop the forward riflemen before I could see anything through the dense woods, and I remembered again the folly of moving too far forward the night I was wounded. I contented myself with cautioning the CP group to be alert for snipers that the lead platoons might by-pass.

The firing stopped to the front, and I knew that the 2d Platoon was pushing forward again.

Captain Calhoun called over the battalion radio. His men had come upon a two-hundred-yard clearing on the right of the road. The woods beyond would most probably be defended, and he wanted permission to move his company through my sector. It offered concealment all the way to his objective.

I said, "Roger," and saw his men move across the highway ahead of us. I radioed Lieutenant Whitman that they were coming through our area.

I reached the firebreak where the lead platoon had met its second resistance. Two dead Germans lay as they had fallen, but there were no foxholes or trenches.

We passed through a few more yards of dense trees before we came abreast of the clearing on the right of the road. The route in our sector offered only slightly more concealment, and I could see the last of F Company's assault platoons moving up and mingling with my forward elements where the woods became dense again. The intervening space was carpeted with high grass and ferns, but the majority of the trees had been felled. Scattered rifle shots and the occasional staccato chant of a BAR came from the woods beyond the clearing on F Company's side of the highway.

We moved across the thin stretch of woods and overtook the rear elements of Sergeant Patton's platoon resting wearily beneath the trees. An occasional enemy bullet whined over their heads, but it did not seem to disturb them. Several men from the platoon were assembling a group of prisoners which grew ever larger as more Germans stumbled across the highway from the dense woods beyond the clearing. There seemed to be no pattern to any of the action. The riflemen bringing in the prisoners were from Whitman's platoon, but an occasional F Company

Panzerfaust

man brought in a group. The Germans began to form in a ragged platoon formation, their hands high above their heads while GIs frisked them for weapons and valuables.

I found Sergeant Patton and asked him what happened.

"We were coming across the open stretch there when these Krauts opened up from across the road," he said. "Whitman didn't want to wait on F Company, so he headed on in after 'em. The woods must be packed with the bastards."

Colonel Smith radioed to find out the situation. When I told him, he urged me to get moving again. I shifted Patton's 3d Platoon into the attack with the 1st guarding their left flank and told them to hold up when they reached the far edge of the woods. I would drop the 2d Platoon back into the support role as soon as they finished clearing the sector beyond the road.

A shell burst suddenly in a tree high above my head. For one agonizing moment I thought about the enemy tanks, but I heard no sound of motors and no second round. I decided that it was a round from a *Panzerfaust*.

One by one and in groups the German prisoners straggled and ran from the woods across the road. Finally, Lieutenant Whitman emerged.

"Goddamnit!" he said. "Goddamnit! Goddamnit! I had those Kraut in there talked into surrendering when F Company came in shootin'. Damned Krauts jumped back in their holes and started fighting again. Goddamnit!"

We had another quarter of a mile to go through the woods, but the 3d Platoon fired only a few shots at fleeing Germans who were trying to reach the town beyond the woods. I caught up with the 3d there when they stopped. The highway curved at the point it emerged from the woods and ran at an angle across our front as it entered Ellershausen, a cluster of stone houses and farm buildings nestled on either side of the highway in a valley surrounded on three sides by low fir-covered hills. A few frightened Germans were fleeing across the open fields toward the town, and the infantrymen sat calmly at the bases of trees and shot after them as if they might have been quail on the rise.

I realized for the first time that the sun was shining brightly. We had been in the woods since the attack began, and I had not thought once of the weather.

Battalion sent forward a platoon of heavy machine guns from H Company with instructions to place them along the forward edge of the woods with my own light guns in positions from which they could place overhead fire against Ellershausen. The gunners went into position quickly and began to fire. The woods echoed with the loud chatter of the six machine guns firing at occasional targets that presented themselves in the valley to our front. Six additional guns opened up from the woods on the south side of the town, and I knew that F Company had been ordered to the south and had been given a platoon of heavy guns as well.

Colonel Smith called for me to meet him on the highway near the point where the highway emerged from the forest. He said that replenishment on ammunition would be up shortly, and the bridge across the Weser would be completed before three o'clock. Our tanks had top priority for getting across.

Our preparatory barrage against Ellershausen would begin at 3:15 and last for fifteen minutes. At the end of that time F Company and a platoon of tanks would ad-

ned up on the rear elements of the assault pla-
My light gunners did not vary from their mission of
zing the woods to the north, but the four heavy
urned their attention to the intruder without a
nt's hesitation. I saw the tracer bullets plunging into
aystack, and the hay burst into flame. *Exit: the vil-*

cautioned the machine gunners to hold their fire until
should get past them, and I signalled my CP group for-
rd. We moved at a half-run down the slope to the draw
d the road and on toward the town. The fields on
ther side of us were littered with German dead. The
flemen had caught more quail on the rise than I had
hought.

I entered the town with my CP group. Already at least
fifty German soldiers were assembled before the second
house, their hands raised high above their heads and
dazed, startled expressions of incredulity on their faces.
Others poured from every building as eager GIs sought
them out with curses and shouts of derision. Some hurried
alone down the street toward the assemblage, terror written on their faces.

We moved on. I looked back and saw my support platoon move into the town and join in the mop-up operations.

The   e was a mass of flame. Two cows stood
    their cuds and staring without expression
   destruction. A grey-haired German farmer
   m around his aged wife and stared at the
   ars streaming down both their faces.
   ut! Alles ist kaput!" they sobbed hysteri-
d.

pressed; instead, I was suddenly angry at
ed at my own anger. What right had they
sobbing and blaming us for this terror?
they and their kind have to any emotions

f!" I shouted. "Thank Hitler!" I pointed
ouse and said. "*Der Führer!*" and laughed.
continued and guards from the reserve
to march over two hundred prisoners to
ered if the flag-waving soldier on the hill-
cceeded in surrendering.

vance under overhead machine-gun fire against the objective from the south and hit the town broadside. G Company would attack astride the highway toward the east,
also with a platoon of tanks and overhead machine-gun
fire. After clearing the town, we should be prepared to
continue the advance. Regiment had assigned another objective.

I cursed Regiment. They were always assigning "one
more objective."

I returned and gave the platoon leaders the information. The center platoon was facing a draw which the
highway entered before reaching the town and then followed into town. We decided to move out from the woods
down the draw and rendezvous with the tanks at the
point where the highway entered the draw.

The machine gunners continued their sporadic bursts
toward the town. A lone German was stranded in a shallow dip in the ground on the open hill to our left, and the
machine gunners laughingly fired short bursts slightly
above the German's head. He waved a white flag frantically after every burst of fire.

An enemy machine gunner opened up on our position
from the edge of the woods on the north side of town, but
my six machine guns gave him their attention. He fired one
more burst and was silent, but he had already revealed his
position and I assigned my two light guns the mission of
spraying the north woods as the riflemen moved in the
open toward the town.

I heard the roar of tanks on the highway to our rear,
and I knew that the time for the attack was drawing near.
I double-timed the two hundred yards to the highway and
contacted the platoon leader of the five tanks that would
be with us. He agreed to start two minutes before the preparatory barrage was scheduled to end, meeting us at
the junction of the road and the draw and continuing into
Ellershausen in time to reach the buildings just as the
artillery barrage should lift.

The preparatory barrage began as I turned from the
tanker to return to the company. Artillery shells whistled
again and again over the trees to cascade in a cloud of
dust and roaring explosion upon the hapless town beyond.
Heavy mortar shells plunked into 81mm barrels and joined
in the explosive tumult falling on the town. The sound of

the twelve machine guns and an assortment of smaller weapons reverberated over the countryside.

I ran back to the company. The 2d and 3d Platoons were in position, ready for the double-time assault toward the objective.

Three sleek P-47s emerged from the clouds, the sunlight glistening against their silver wings. Down and down they dived above the town, which looked now as if it would completely disappear in the smoke and confusion of the preparatory barrage. Their machine guns and cannon began to chatter and assert themselves above the din of the battle whose privacy they had invaded. Up and up they climbed, higher into the sky; and then as if they had suddenly spotted their prey, down, down once more, their machine guns and cannon barking derisively. Then they flew away toward the east, and we could see them dive on the next town, and one of the planes dropped a bomb.

Abad tried to say something to me, but I could not hear him above the noisy demonstration before us. I made out the word "battalion" and told him to say that we were ready.

The artillery continued to whistle and explode on the town. The mortar shells dropped unheralded upon the objective. The machine guns chattered. A freakish lull appeared in the louder noises for a second, and I heard the "plunk" of a 60mm mortar shell being dropped into a mortar tube somewhere behind me. The 4th Platoon artillery could not resist getting in on the action.

The lone German on the hillside was waving his white flag more frantically than ever.

I was ecstatic with an elation born of excitement. The men around me were laughing and patting one another on the back. This preparation was something for the book, and the unexpected appearance of the planes had added the finishing touch.

I looked at my watch. Four minutes to go before the barrage would lift. The men in the two assault platoons knew that the time was near and stood in half-crouches like animals waiting for the moment to spring. The smiles were gone from their faces, and in their places had come expressions of determination. It seemed impossible that any human being could survive the pasting which Ellershausen had taken and was taking, but the Germans al-

ways came out again when the come out.

If only they get there just as the ba

I heard the roar of the tanks tun *Any minute now.* Time stood still for an

Almost time now . . . almost time . . .

The machine guns stopped firing. The from the woods with their comrades clos The artillery and mortars fired their final the platoon of tanks race from the woods down the highway toward the draw. To the so see the lead riflemen from F Company emerge woods. Their tanks followed. They formed an a march formation on the open, downward sloping and I thought of the diagrams in the Army manuals.

My own men met the tanks at the rendezvous with split-second precision. The tankers infiltrated steel monsters into the formation and adjusted their sp to the slower pace of the foot soldier.

The light machine gunners began to fire again, the tra ers from the light guns creasing the edge of the nor forest, the tracers from the heavy guns forming an u brella of fiery steel over the heads of the advancing fantrymen. The lone German stranded on the hills waved his white flag.

The timing, the formations were perf men around me, and they looked at m The last time we had seen an attack training films back in the States. Th this way in actual battle. Somethin No, they didn't make them this w was a mirage that was ridiculo derful and so true.

The last rounds from th with a roar upon the to licked up, up into the air smoke billowed abo   the h appeared from sight   "Thank Adol lead tank followed   to the burning crossed the open spa   The mop-up mopping up.   company began

Enter: the villain.   the rear. I won stack on the hillside   side had ever su

Colonel Smith arrived by jeep and gave me brief instructions for continuing the assault. Our next objective, and the final one for the day, was to be shared again with F Company, the town of Varlossen a quarter of a mile to the east. G Company would follow the left of the road as before.

I instructed my platoon leaders to meet me at the hill on the eastern edge of town as soon as they could assemble their men, and I moved forward to have a look at the objective.

I climbed the low hill and saw that the road sloped down again into Varlossen. A lone house stood atop the hill on the left. Three tank destroyers were grouped around the house, firing at fleeing German vehicles in the valley beyond. I climbed the stairs in the house. Two light machine guns from F Company were firing from the east windows. An artillery observer was calling for fire on enemy vehicles evacuating Varlossen along a tree-lined road to the east. The noise of the TDs and the machine guns was deafening in the close room. The plaster walls of the house began to crack from the concussion of the big guns on the TDs.

The men from the platoons arrived and lined up along a wooden fence beyond the house to watch the target practice, showing utter disregard for the basic military principles of cover and concealment.

But a German tank fired in the distance and the screech of an 88mm shell whistled over our heads and exploded in the town behind us. The gallery quickly dispersed. The enemy tank fired again and again. The artillery observer said he picked him up with his glasses. He was firing from the edge of another village to the northeast, but by the time a soldier had gone downstairs to give the information to the TDs, the tank had pulled behind the cover of buildings in the town.

"No use now," the artillery observer said. "Sonofabitch will sure give us hell when he catches us on that open hill to the next town."

I was suddenly afraid of crossing the exposed forward slope of the hill leading to Varlossen. It had been an easy day as far as casualties were concerned. I wondered why regiment did not let well enough alone and forget this next objective until the next day. The Germans would pull out during the night, if we would only give them time.

I went downstairs and found that my company had assembled. F Company was forming across the road. The tanks that would support us were lined up on the road.

The Colonel called Captain Calhoun and me together for final instructions. Another round of enemy shellfire suddenly whistled overhead and crashed behind us, followed by another and another.

"They're giving them hell back there in Ellershausen," the Colonel said. "Easy Company lost a jeep and trailer in the first barrage."

The Colonel said the instructions were the same as before.

"Let me know when you're ready," he said.

I walked to the crest of the hill with Captain Byrd while the company was forming. We stood looking at the terrain before us when the next barrage came in. We could tell by the *swish* instead of whistle that it was intended for us instead of the town behind us.

The Germans had evidently found the range of the confusion of men and tanks on the hill. The shells burst all around us, and shrapnel whistled low overhead. I could hear the sound of the gun being fired in the distance, followed by the noise of the shell in flight that grew in intensity and found me holding my breath when it finally exploded on the hilltop. Fragments whined above the shallow ditch. Another burst sounded in the distance, and we knew another was on the way.

"Two bits on where she'll land, Mac," Byrd laughed falsely.

"No takers," I answered.

I winced as the shell exploded on the hilltop.

21

G COMPANY LEADING

We waited for the next shell, but it did not come. I stood up and looked around. The hill was barren, except for the TDs and tanks which had pulled back to the reverse slope. There were no casualties. I was amazed at how quickly the mass of men had found cover.

A talk with Captain Calhoun brought the decision to ask the Colonel for permission to ride the tanks into Var-lossen. The less time we were exposed on the forward slope of the hill the better, it seemed. It was obvious now that more than one enemy tank had fired. They had the range and could easily blast any slow-moving object that appeared on the other side of the hill.

"Each of you send one rifle platoon on tanks," the Colonel decided, "and both of you keep on the right of the road. The hill seems to drop off slightly on that side. Have the platoons take your extra 300 radio with them, and as soon as they're inside the town, we'll send the rest down one platoon at a time."

I designated Lieutenant Bagby's platoon for the mission since they had been in support all day. The tanks moved to the right of the road, and the men climbed aboard, careful to sit to the side and rear of the tank to give the gunners inside a clear field of fire to the front. Private First Class Shepherd from my headquarters group went with them as radio operator.

Both platoons signalled ready. The big tanks raced their motors and plunged down the hill in a race toward the town. One tank fell behind. Something was wrong with its motor. I saw it was Bagby's tank, and I knew the men riding it were cursing the misfortune that had stalled them on the open slope. I expected at any moment to hear the sound of the enemy tank, but the motor started again, and the tank raced on.

The lead tanks began to spit tracer bullets from their machine guns into the grey line of houses before them. *One hundred yards to go. Fifty yards.* The riflemen jumped from the tanks and raced on foot toward the town and disappeared from view. *They made it!* I felt like cheering.

Captain Calhoun send his 2d Platoon down the road. I assembled my CP group and the 3d Platoon and waited until the F Company men had gone two hundred yards. I signalled "Forward" and we started toward the objective on the run, a single column following the ditch on either side of the road. The pace was too fast, and I slowed to a fast walk. I listened intently for the sound of a telltale explosion in the distance that would mean the enemy tankers were opening fire. Though I planned exactly how I would drop to the scant cover of the shallow ditch, the telltale explosion did not come.

We entered the town, and I looked back and saw two more platoons following us. Still the enemy tankers did not fire.

The 1st Platoon had almost completed clearing our assigned sector of the town. There had been no fight. They had three prisoners and another who was wounded. My rear CP group arrived and took over the prisoners.

"Maybe that's all for the day," Sergeant Henderson said. "As if it weren't enough. This is some kind of record for G Company. . . . two hundred and ten prisoners and at least thirty Krauts killed."

E Company led the assault at seven o'clock the next morning riding on the two platoons of tanks astride the highway. We followed on the tank destroyers and three trucks, waiting in Varlossen while E Company took the first town and then moved on to the second. Then we leap-frogged into the first town. There had been no opposition. E Company reported all clear in Dransfeld, the second town, and we moved forward again, waiting in our vehicles at the edge of Dransfeld while the assault company moved on.

A sudden burst of machine-gun fire told me that E Company had run into trouble. I heard Lieutenant Carroll K. Heitzman, of Litchfield, Ill., the exec who was commanding the company in the absence of Captain Manning, who was on pass to London, talking to battalion over the radio.

"We're inside Warmissen," he said, "but the sonofabitches shot a machine gun from that wooded hill to the right and caught my fourth tank. Killed five men and a tank ran over another. Wounded three."

I knew that it would be a matter of minutes before we would be committed to clean out the machine gun. Being the second company to be committed was hardly better than being in the assault element initially.

I did not have to wait long for the order. Captain Byrd rode up beside me in a jeep and gave me the information. I should move my company as quickly as possible to the south and clear out the wooded hill. The men jumped quickly from their vehicles as if they had been expecting the assignment.

We moved from the cover of the buildings and saw the town of Warmissen lying in a wide, deep valley before us. High hills rose on either side. A small patch of woods lay half-way up the slope of the hill to the south, and at the crest of the hill a timberline began that extended to the southeast as far as the eye could see. I decided that the enemy gunner must have fired from the small patch of woods, the other was too far away to have caused the damage inflicted on E Company.

A platoon of machine gunners from H Company under Technical Sergeant Lamar Pate, of Mauston, Wis., set up on the edge of Dransfeld to cover our advance. We moved out in approach-march formation across a shallow draw and up the side of the hill toward the patch of woods.

The scouts came closer and closer to the woods, but nothing happened. I wondered why the Germans did not fire.

The lead scouts entered the woods, and the platoons followed close behind. I decided that the enemy gunners must have retreated to the east.

"There's no sign of any machine gun . . . no foxholes . . . no nothing," Lieutenant Bagby radioed.

We continued into Warmissen.

Colonel Smith decided to send both E and G Companies into the assault after the ambush at Warmissen. The next town lay at the bottom of the valley to the east, more a narrow chasm now than a valley. I moved G Company back through the small patch of woods which we had traversed in our search for the enemy gun and past the woods to the cleared slope of the hill. We waited there for our platoon of tanks to join us. I could see E Company jockeying into position on the high hill to the left of the highway like animated chessman.

The tanks arrived and Lieutenant Heitzman radioed that his company was ready to move out. I signalled "Forward." There seemed little danger of the enemy defending the high open area, but we might get fire from the woods line on our right. I cautioned the right platoon to be on the alert, but it was too far to our right to send a platoon to investigate.

We came abreast of the next town and halted. Sergeant Patton's platoon went down the almost perpendicular side of the valley to check the town, and I could see an E Company platoon moving down the other side of the valley to check their sector. Patton returned shortly. . . . not even any stragglers. I radioed "ready" to Lieutenant Heitzman, and we moved forward again.

The hill which my company was following ended in a pointed ridge overlooking the next town of Klein Wiershausen. E Company was assigned the mission of clearing the town alone, so I moved my company across a cross-valley and they sprawled on the hill beyond while I moved down into the town to contact battalion.

There had been no enemy troops in Wiershausen, but a group of six liberated British flyers were overcome with enthusiasm. A hay barn was burning from the supporting artillery barrage which shifted from town to town ahead of us as we advanced, and a line of elderly farmers formed a bucket brigade from the stream running through the center of the town to the burning building.

Except for the hill on the right where my company rested, and which dissipated itself in the valley a few hundred yards beyond Wiershausen, the area to our front was a wide expanse of flat valley land over five miles across. Directly to the east we could see the farming town of Rosdorf two miles away, and to the northeast the taller buildings and the towering chimneys of the city of Goet-

tingen, the 1st Battalion's objective for the day. Between
us and Rosdorf lay an *Autobahn* running parallel with the
contours of the valley.

Colonel Smith ordered E Company to continue forward
to take Rosdorf, supported if necessary, by F Company. I
was assigned the mission of taking Mengershausen, a small
farm town across the hill to the south which would otherwise be by-passed and might cause trouble for later units.
A small build-up area which my map showed to be two
farmhouses and outlying buildings lay to the east where
the hill shaded off into the valley and would be by-passed
by E Company. I should send one rifle platoon to check
the farmhouses.

I moved back up the steep hill and dispatched Sergeant
Patton's platoon to clear out the built-up area and, assisted by the platoon of tanks, join in the attack against
Mengershausen along a north-south highway connecting
the two objectives. I moved the remainder of the company across the crest of the hill and saw now that the
hill extended to the southwest more as a ridge than as a
hill. The light machine guns set up on the forward slope
overlooking our objective, which lay sprawled two hundred yards away at the base of the ridge.

I waited for word from Sergeant Patton that he had
completed his initial mission and was ready to join in the
assault on Mengershausen. The remainder of the company sprawled on the exposed slope of the hill, making no
effort at concealment, but there was no sign of life from
the town below us. The machine gunners spotted straggling Germans making their way across the wide valley,
but the range was too great to be effective, and I would
not allow them to open fire.

I heard two long bursts of rapid machine-gun fire from
far to our rear. That was strange, I thought. Someone said
maybe we were surrounded, and laughed.

We waited impatiently for the signal from Patton. A
machine gunner suddenly shouted and pointed to the crest
of the ridge to the southwest about six hundred yards
away. Six German soldiers were emerging from the woods
and crossing the open ridge.

The machine gunners had already turned their barrels
in the new direction. Their eyes watched me for a signal.

I checked the figures on the ridge with my field glasses. They were Germans all right.

"OK," I said, "let 'er go."

The machine guns opened up. The startled Germans seemed not to know whether to try to run the remaining distance to the next patch of woods or fall to the ground. The second burst decided the issue for them. They fell to the ground. The 60mm mortar crews took their cue and began to pump the little shells into the mortar tubes. The shells exploded in little puffs of black smoke and noise all around the cringing Germans.

Three of the Germans got up and made a dash for the woods. A burst of machine-gun fire cut one of them to the ground. The other two continued the race toward the woods, mortar shells dancing around them, but they did not stop. They made the safety of the woods, but the other four did not move.

We were confident they were the machine-gun crew that killed the men from E Company. They had allowed us to pass, and then had fired again at our rear elements, possibly the artillery, and then retreated. Well, they would not fire again.

I could see the men from E Company, little black dots against a field of new grain, nearing Rosdorf. I could not hear the sound of firing, but with my glasses I could see the men hit the ground. They had come under fire from Rosdorf.

It was long past time for Patton to radio us that he was ready. Perhaps his radio was weak and the intervening hill interfered. Abad walked in the direction of the built-up area, calling over the radio as he went. Finally, he got a faint answer. Yes, they were ready.

The 1st and 2d Platoons moved slowly down the sloping plowed field toward Mengershausen. They were as convinced as I that the town would be undefended. I saw the tanks and the 3d Platoon emerge from the mask of the hill on my left and move down the highway toward the objective.

I signalled the CP group and Weapons Platoon forward, and the machine gunners grumbled as they dismantled their weapons because they had not had a chance to fire again.

It did not take long to clear out the town. Ten submissive Germans were routed from a cellar. Our artillery observer radioed for his jeep, and I ate a cold K-ration while we waited.

It was three o'clock in the afternoon. Colonel Smith called with the news that the 1st Battalion had taken Goettingen without a fight, and mopping-up operations were going on in Rosdorf. I directed the 1st and 2d Platoons to load up on the tanks, and I led the column in the artillery jeep across a bridge over the *Autobahn* and into Rosdorf. We took the heavier weapons on the jeep and the 3d and 4th Platoons followed us on foot.

The 3d and 4th Platoons joined us on the eastern edge of Rosdorf, as E and F Companies completed clearing the town.

"Damn if you didn't have a close one at that bridge over the *Autobahn*," Lieutenant Speed, the Weapons Platoon commander, said.

I didn't understand what he meant and said so.

"When we came along, there was a Kraut soldier on the far side of the bridge with a *Panzerfaust*, just laughing bigger'n hell," he explained. "He had a wire attached to a five-hundred-pound bomb set to blow up the bridge when he pulled the switch."

I felt a little uncomfortable inside and said, "Why'n hell didn't he blow it?"

"I dunno," Speed answered. "Sonofabitch is crazy, I think. He thought it was funny as all hell when you all didn't see him."

We loaded up on the vehicles again, my company drawing the reserve assignment on the trucks. E Company continued to lead. The column wound into Goettingen, avoiding a highway which circled the south edge of the city, because a bridge over a small canal had been demolished.

E Company took the next town of Geismar to the southeast of Goettingen without opposition. As the rear of the column closed into town, I heard a small-caliber anti-aircraft gun from the next town firing at one of our Piper Cub artillery observation planes which circled lazily above us. The plane beat a hasty retreat.

E Company would stay in Geismar for the night with battalion headquarters. F Company would take a small town to the south and billet there for the night. G Company would take the next town in the valley to the east, Klein Lengden. I suddenly realized that was the town from which the antiaircraft gun had fired.

"There can't be anything there," Colonel Smith said, and I wondered if he really expected me to swallow that. "The 1st Battalion has already passed through the woods on the left and taken the next town around the curve beyond it. I want you to take both platoons of tanks and ride them on down and get your defense set up before dark."

I moved past a group of E Company men who were laughing about a German who had unsuspectingly driven his truck into Geismar from Klein Lengden after they had already taken the town. I continued to a slight rise beyond the town for a view of our objective while Lieutenant Loberg was moving the company up. The road curved abruptly beyond the rise. My eyes bulged at the sight of a German soldier feverishly harnessing a team of horses to a multiple-barrel 20mm antiaircraft gun not over a hundred yards from where I stood. Farther down the road toward Klein Lengden a truck was pulling another antiaircraft gun toward the town.

I ran back quickly and found a lieutenant in charge of the tank destroyers. He directed two of his TDs to move to the hill, and they began to pump away at the two targets. The German with the team of horses plunged into a shallow ditch beside the road. A direct hit on the antiaircraft gun blew it to pieces and threw the horses to the ground. Another direct hit sent the truck careening crazily into a tree beside the road.

My platoon leaders did not want to ride tanks into the town any more than I did. The memory of the tragic ambush at Warmissen was too fresh in our minds, and if the Germans had other antiaircraft guns in the town, they could cause an untold amount of casualties before we could get off the tanks and find cover. The area to our front was an expanse of flat, open field pierced by the narrow highway, and enclosed on either side with rising slopes covered with thick firs. It was a perfect setting for an ambush.

Colonel Smith agreed to change the order when he heard our disagreement. We set up my light machine guns and a platoon of heavies on the rise on the edge of

Geismar to provide supporting fire along with the TDs. I told the artillery observer to begin firing at the town and not to lift fire until we were within a hundred yards of the objective. With the 3d Platoon on the left and 1st on the right, we set out in an approach-march formation toward the town, the 2d Platoon remaining well to the rear, prepared to move upon order through the woods to the left and come in on the town from the north.

I followed the left of the highway with my CP group, and we passed the frightened German who had been harnessing his horses. Fulton relieved him of his weapon and sent him running up the hill to our rear to be taken prisoner by the machine gunners. One of the horses was dead, but the other had a gaping shrapnel wound in his side and struggled painfully to rise from the entangling harness. Junior put his .45 to the horse's temple and pulled the trigger five times, but still the terrified animal continued to struggle. Junior emptied his clip in the horse's head, and the animal twitched convulsively and died.

The lead riflemen were almost to a point where the highway curved abruptly to the left for a hundred yards before curving right again to enter the town, when I heard the deep thumping blasts of 20mm antiaircraft fire. The forward platoons dropped to the ground. We dropped to the shallow ditch beside the highway.

I saw a figure running back and forth among the tanks and prone men of the 3d Platoon. I could see the tracer bullets from a 20mm antiaircraft gun hidden behind a slight rise in the open field to the front of the platoon skim closely over his head. The man would be Sergeant Patton. He was crazy. Absolutely insane.

It was apparent that no enemy fire was coming from the town, still four hundred yards beyond the forward platoons. The only opposition was from the antiaircraft gun to Patton's front, but its flanking fire pinned the 1st Platoon to the ground as well. I wondered if there had been casualties.

I radioed Sergeant Patton for information.

"We can handle it all right, if I can get these goll-blasted tanks forward," he said. "There're two AA guns about seventy-five yards in front of us. The Krauts can't depress them enough to hit us where we are now, but we can't get any closer unless these tanks will move up and blast 'em. I'll get 'em going in a minute."

Lieutenant Bagby wanted tanks with him. I realized that the five lead tanks had shifted to the left, and the support platoon of tanks had fallen back and were well to the rear.

I tried to contact the tank platoon leader on the battalion radio, but with no success.

"I'll go get them," Fein shouted, and before I realized it, the little Jewish soldier was running across the open field toward the rear platoon of tanks. He returned a few minutes later, blithely hanging on to the side of one of the tanks and directing the commander toward the 1st Platoon.

"They didn't want to come," Fein said when he had dismounted and rejoined us, "but I told them, by jeepers, it was an order."

The tanks with the 2d Platoon began to churn about in the field, their motors racing. They lunged forward with their big cannon barking with dull, booming explosions that merged with the sound of the artillery plummeting into the town. The riflemen around them rose and rushed forward with the tanks, their rifles and BARs spitting out feeble death cries in comparison to the big cannon. The 1st Platoon took the cue and rose to move forward on the run.

My view of the happenings around the hidden antiaircraft guns was obscured by the rise in the ground and aggravated by the increasing darkness. The 2d Platoon scouts came once more into view, however, and I knew the platoon had taken care of the opposition. The other riflemen followed, and they joined the 1st Platoon in the final march toward the town.

I dreaded the moment when the riflemen would be fired upon from the town, but there was no need for worry. The 2d Platoon had broken the only resistance, and the artillery lifted and the riflemen marched unimpeded into Klein Lengden and swept through the town, sending straggling prisoners scurrying back to the western edge of the buildings to join a growing group of their docile comrades. The town was ours.

I double-timed with my CP group across the remaining distance to the objective. We found another AA gun beside a house in the center of the town, but its crew had abandoned it without a fight. We congratulated ourselves upon the capture or destruction of five multiple-barrel 20mm antiaircraft guns in the short action.

Sergeant Patton said the Germans manning the position in the field which held them up were "bastards."

"They had two AA guns," he said. "Some of them wanted to surrender, but every time a Kraut would jump out of his hole to surrender, some other Kraut s.o.b. would shoot him right in the back. Counting the ones they killed and the ones we got too, there're nineteen dead."

Patton had one man slightly wounded in the arm, but he had already walked back to Geismar to the aid station.

My Weapons Platoon and the platoon of heavy machine guns from H Company arrived from their supporting position outside Geismar.

"Sergeant Mitchell[1] was killed," one of the sergeants from the heavy machine gun platoon told me. I could not think for a moment who Sergeant Mitchell was; then I remembered that he was the pleasant, perennially cheerful tech sergeant in command of the platoon who was to receive his commission as a second lieutenant in a few days.

"An antiaircraft gun fired from the woods to the south," the sergeant continued, "and Sergeant Mitchell got hit. He was unconscious, and the aid man took him back to one of the TDs to give him first aid. The antiaircraft gun fired again and the goddamn TD backed up. Ran right over Sergeant Mitchell."

Darkness was now almost completely upon us. Lieutenant Loberg ferreted out a CP from the undamaged buildings left in the town, and I checked with the platoons on the defense for the night.

Another unsuspecting German drove a truck right into the hands of the 1st Platoon on the highway leading in from the east.

Batallion sent two trucks for the prisoners, and we crowded them all aboard with a little difficulty. There were one hundred five.

---

[1]Soldier's name in this instance is fictitious.

It was not necessary for the Germans to tell me that their outfit had received cognac rations only that morning. The bottles appeared in the hands of GIs as if by magic.

F Company led the assault on tanks the next morning, and we finally drew the reserve position. Except for our artillery whistling overhead to each succeeding town, we might have been far to the rear as far as action was concerned. F Company traveled twenty-five miles and ran into one roadblock defended by thirty Germans, but they spotted it ahead of time, and it was only a matter of minutes before they knocked it out.

My company halted for the night in Berlingerode, a large farm town. The lead elements of the column pushed on to occupy the next two towns to the north. My platoons fanned out to their assigned defensive sectors and rounded up fifteen prisoners in their search for billets.

The less fatiguing day gave the men the incentive to wash and shave that night, and they looked like a different outfit the next morning. The 9th Armored Division rolled through the town all day long, their heavy tracked vehicles churning the dust in the street outside my CP as they sped by. The men from the company amused themselves by standing by the road shouting wisecracks at the passing GIs, but they were glad to see them. The advent of the armor meant that there would be no more shooting for us for a few days, at least.

Sergeant Patton was dispatched to division headquarters to receive his commission and returned to us at dark with shiny second lieutenant bars on his shoulders. It seemed odd to say "Lieutenant Patton."

First Sergeant Quinn and two men from the rifle platoons returned to the company from their elongated passes to London. They had been bouncing back and forth in replacement depots for almost two weeks but had been unable to overtake us.

We spent another peaceful night in Berlingerode, but were alerted to move early the next morning, April. 11. The alert order was postponed, however, and it was not until late afternoon that we moved, pulling into the town of Sollstadt after dark and billeting for the night, chasing the civilians into the streets to find shelter with their neighbors.

We moved again on trucks with the coming of morning, past sleepy little German towns with every house flying a white flag of surrender, some crudely hung from windows, others on flagstaffs that had once proudly flown the swastika. We passed an occasional upturned enemy vehicle or SP gun, the dead drivers or crew lying stiff beside them. At one point bombs had almost completely destroyed the road, and the dead of a German column that had been caught by our air forces lay in grotesque positions on all sides. A lengthy halt stopped us in the center of the bombed area, and we watched impassively as two aged civilian men with a wagon lifted the stiff corpses and hauled them away.

It was dark again when we pulled into Oberhausen-Petri, a small, vile-smelling farming town three miles off the main highway. I was called to battalion the next morning at nine o'clock. The CP was in a flurry of excitement getting ready to move.

"Orders just came in," the Colonel said. "The armor has swung south, by-passing Leipzig. That's our division objective—twenty miles away. We attack along this road . . ." pointing to his map ". . . and should reach the town of Schkopau just north of Merseburg by night. We'll use the regular formation on tanks, and we must get moving by ten o'clock. G Company leading."

G Company leading! I tried to act unconcerned as the words struck me, but countless minute questions and fears flooded my brain. Riding tanks in the assault was no novelty to me, but leading the battalion in a full-scale attack on tanks was new. Where should *I* ride? How far forward, or how far back? What would happen if one of the tanks should be knocked out? I wondered how the tankers determined among themselves whose would be the precarious lead tank.

There was little time to ponder the questions. It was almost ten o'clock already. I rushed back to the company and gave the orders to the platoons. The 1st Platoon would lead. I would ride on the fourth tank with my forward CP group. The other three platoons and the rear CP group would follow in order.

Any questions? Move out.

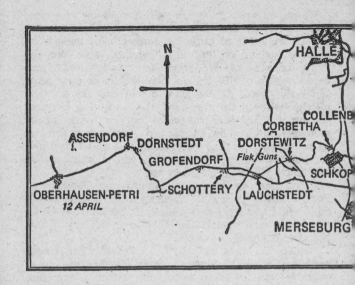

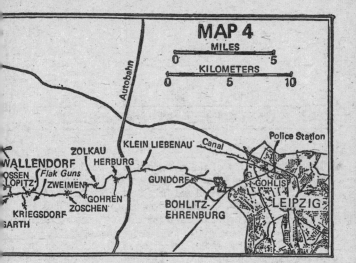

MAP 4

MILES

0   5

KILOMETERS

0   5   10

Autobahn

Canal

Police Station

ZOLKAU

KLEIN LIEBENAU

WALLENDORF

HERBURG

OSSEN

LOPITZ

Flak Guns

ZWEIMEN

GUNDORF

GOHLIS

LEIPZIG

GOHREN

KRIEGSDORF

ZOSCHEN

BOHLITZ-
EHRENBURG

GARTH

22

"SCHKOPAU BY MORNING"

The tanks in front of me were lost in a whirl of dust at a stretch of flat cultivated fields toward the first objective. Hardly before I realized we had started we had entered the twin towns of Asendorf-Dornstedt, and curious civilians were staring at us from the sides of the street. The Colonel said, "Nice going . . . keep moving as fast as you can," over the radio, and I found myself responding to the excitement and urging Lieutenant Bagby forward.

The lead tanks lurched forward, leaving us choking in their dust, and then our own tank leaped to the front, and we held on tightly lest the swerving vehicle, like some wild bronco, toss us into the dusty road. Then there were buildings on either side of us again, and we were in Grofendorf. I told Private First Class Harold Wesmiller, an eighteen-year-old soldier from Port Allegany, Pa., who had been chosen from one of the rifle platoons to be 300 radio operator, to report our position to battalion.

The tanks moved out again, their motors racing and churning their bulky bodies across another open field toward the next objective, which my map showed to be the town of Schotterey. I wondered how much longer this race could go on before we would meet opposition. The road across the open field suddenly dipped downward, and we were upon the town, finding it nestled serenely in the sunlight in a shallow valley.

An 88mm shell whirred low over our heads and exploded with a crumping noise in the field behind us. *Good morning, everybody. Welcome to another day in the Fatherland.* Our driver pulled to the right of the road abruptly and came to a sudden halt beside a high

274

stone fence. The sudden stop almost threw me from the tank, and I jumped quickly to the ground. The impact with the hard earth jarred my feet and made them burn. Another 88mm projectile whirred above us, and I heard it crash into the field. The tanks behind us increased their speed and roared toward the protection of the depression of the ground and the houses to the front.

The three lead tanks were lost from view by an abrupt bend in the street. A mass of civilians who had gathered at the edge of the town scampered like frightened flies toward their houses. A soldier guarded nine German soldiers who held their hands high in the air while submitting to a hasty search by two other GIs.

I tried to determine what had happened. The enemy gun seemed to be firing at us from beyond the village, evidently trying to catch us in the open behind the town, but he had failed. I radioed Lieutenant Bagby. He said he was on the far edge of town and had met no opposition, but he could not pick up the enemy gun.

I signalled the remainder of the company forward on foot, and the tanks followed to find better cover deeper in the town.

The GI guarding the nine prisoners said they were an enemy delaying group armed with *Panzerfausts,* but they had jumped up from their hiding place with their hands held high when the first tank approached.

"Scared s—tless," the GI said.

I pushed on through the town and joined the search for the enemy gun, but it did not fire again. Across a railroad track and three-quarters of a mile to our front we could see the next objective, the larger town of Bad Lauchstaedt. With my field glasses I could see a cluster of tanks on a hill to the north of the town, but they were facing toward the east, and they did not move. Several strange objects that looked like huge artillery pieces with their muzzles pointed toward the sky stood beyond the tanks.

"Those must be the tanks from the 9th Armored that were knocked out," Colonel Smith said when he arrived. "The armor got this far, then backed out and swerved to the south."

There seemed to be no other solution to the problem

of reaching Bad Lauchstaedt except mounting the tanks and pushing forward. The platoon of TDs set up on the edge of Schotterey to cover our advance.

The men climbed back on the tanks and held onto the sides. Their bodies and their equipment, which was strapped to the sides and backs of the tanks, almost obscured the tops of the tanks from view.

A soldier from the 3d Platoon ran up to me, a civilian beside him.

"This man is a Polish slave laborer, Cap'n," he called over the roar of the tank motors. "His uncle lives two doors from me in the States. He says he knows where some German artillery is to our front."

The tanks were racing their motors, and Colonel Smith was urging us to get moving.

"Will he go with us?" I asked.

"Yessir," the soldier answered.

"Tell him to climb on," I said and signalled for Lieutenant Bagby to move out. The soldier and the civilian climbed aboard one of the tanks to my rear.

As the column started forward a GI emerged from a house beside the street, prodding a German soldier before him. The German was carrying his trousers in his hand and trying desperately to get his captor to allow him time to put them on.

"Caught this sonofabitch trying to change to civilian clothes!" the soldier yelled and prodded the hapless German again with the butt of his rifle.

The outer buildings of Bad Lauchstaedt loomed before us, and I was elated at reaching the objective. The tanks slowed down and the men on the lead tank jumped to the ground to precede the tanks through the town.

A buxom blonde girl, her skirts billowing and revealing chubby white legs underneath, rode a bicycle down the street toward us. Lieutenant Bagby stopped her and motioned with his hands. The girl turned the bicycle around and walked back in the direction from which she had come. Bagby placed his arm about her waist, turning to wave cheerily to the rear. The soldiers on the tanks roared approval.

The tank column inched forward over the brick-paved street, slowed now by the vanguard of men on foot. I

could see the tanks on the hill to the north more clearly
—nine burned-out hulks, all facing a battery of grey-
colored antiaircraft guns that looked like stationary
models of our own "Long Toms." Their big muzzles
pointed into the sky from deep circular pits. The armor
had evidently suffered heavily at this spot, but I thanked
God that someone had taken care of the big guns before
us.

Somewhere in the distance I heard the crack-crack of
artillery fire that seemed to roll its *r*'s when it exploded.
It sounded like American time fire,[1] and I thought perhaps
the 1st Battalion somewhere on our right was shelling an
objective. A group of Frenchmen in OD uniforms standing on a street corner pointed excitedly down a side
street and cried, "SS! SS!"

The soldiers on the tanks laughed. Any German soldier to a Frenchman must be an SS. The reserve company would clean out the town later.

Colonel Smith rolled up beside my tank in his jeep.

"Nice going, Mac," he said. "You're really doing a
swell job. Just keep them moving. The faster the better."

"Don't thank me, Colonel," I said, meaning it and
disgusted that it sounded melodramatic. "Thank Lieutenant Bagby and the 1st Platoon. I'm just tagging along."

But the Colonel's encouraging words gave me a warm
feeling inside. Somewhere, if we continued, we would
come face to face with the enemy tank which had fired at
us in Schotterey, but the possibility seemed remote and
far away. I radioed Bagby to climb aboard and get moving as quickly as possible. I could see by my map that
our next town was Dorstewitz, and then we would be
within sight of the final objective for the day. And it was
not yet noon.

The column spurted forward again and the tanks
picked up speed. The road had become a paved highway
now, lined on either side by tall, evenly-spaced trees that
marked its route across a broad, open plain that was flat
except for a few gently-rising areas in the open fields.
In the distance, shrouded by a blue haze which the

---

[1] Artillery shells set to explode before contact, thereby giving deadly
air bursts. Not to be confused with the radio-controlled proximity fuse.

bright sunlight did not disperse, were the towering chimneys of factories which must be the Merseburg and Schkopau industrial districts.

We were forced to slow down at a bend in the road four hundred yards beyond Bad Lauchstaedt, turning to the left and picking up speed as we crossed a railroad track, only to lose it again as the road curved in another right angle to the right and stretched a half-mile ahead of us into Dorstewitz. The tanks ahead of us lunged forward and widened the distance between us.

I was conscious of the crack-crack of time fire somewhere behind us, ear-splitting in its intensity. I wondered how the driver inside the tank heard it above the roar of the motors, but the tank spurted forward in a sudden burst of speed that almost threw me off. Shells began to burst around us, tearing entire limbs from the trees above us. The tank picked up speed, and I found my lips moving, crying, "Faster! Faster!" A shell plowed up the loose dirt in the field beside us. Another whistled narrowly over our heads and exploded in the field beyond. Then they were crashing into the earth to the front and to the rear of us, and I was unconscious of the continuing crack of the artillery fire behind us.

An antitank gun or a tank was firing at us, I decided. I could not tell in the excitement from what direction the enemy was firing, but I thought it was from the north, and a sudden wave of selfishness made me thankful that I was riding on the opposite side of the tank. A sudden fury at my own selfish fear made me think of the other men on the tanks, and I prayed through set lips. The men around me seemed to hold on to the tank for dear life, as if tighter grips lessened their vulnerability to the enemy fire, their faces frozen in combined expressions of fear and amazement.

It had come so suddenly. We were riding along unmolested, though not without fear, and then we were suddenly running a death-gantlet of exploding shells that plowed the earth around us in every direction. I knew that one of the shells, at least, must surely hit us. *If only we could make it into Dorstewitz! If only we could make it into——*

I heard small-arms fire from the road ahead of us. I had a fleeting glimpse of a soldier lying in the middle of the highway, his arms outstretched, blood pouring from a wound in his head into a growing red puddle on the cement. Men were sprawled everywhere on the ground to the left of the road where a small trail led to the left from a culvert with raised brick sides beside the main road. I had a brief glimpse of intermingled German and American uniforms. Our tank plunged across the culvert and into the field beyond. Two other tanks were standing in the field, their machine guns spraying a shallow, bush-filled draw to the front and the houses of Dorstewitz beyond.

Our tank was clear of soldiers even before it pulled to a stop, and its machine gun began to chatter. I yelled to Wesmiller to follow me. I did not know what was happening in the confusion, but I knew that my ears were ringing from the exploding shells and the chattering machine guns, and I wanted to find cover, not only for myself but for the vital radio operator.

I ran back to the highway. The raised brick beside the culvert seemed to offer the only available cover, and I dropped behind it, motioning to Wesmiller to follow and ignoring the body of a German soldier on the other side of the low brick wall, scarcely two feet away. In a field of new green grain to the right of the road was the lead tank, smoldering helplessly. The body of an OD-clad soldier hung by the feet from the metal rail around the side of the tank.

My ears rang again from new explosions, and I could see the men in the field shouting something at me, but I could not hear them. The explosions seemed to be almost on top of me, and I thought the Germans must be getting closer than ever with the fire from the antitank gun.

I saw a soldier in the field to the left of the road with his rifle pointed directly at me, and I ducked my head behind the low brick wall. I seemed to hear three shots above the din of exploding shells and chattering machine guns, and then I heard the sputter of crackling flames beyond the brick parapet and small-arms ammunition began to crackle and explode.

I yelled again to Wesmiller to follow, and I ran ten yards to the rear where a group of men from the 1st Platoon were lying in the shallow ditch behind the other end of the culvert.

"Good God, Cap'n," one of the men said, "that German on the other side of the brick wall was tossing hand grenades at you. A guy out there in the field shot him. He must have set his ammunition belt afire."

The small-arms fire stopped except for the chatter of the machine guns on the tanks. A soldier pointed suddenly to a German lying in the ditch beside the trail near where the tanks were sitting. The German was stealthily raising his rifle.

"Look out," the GI screamed. "That bastard ain't dead!" and another GI fired round after round at the German, and he lay still.

"We'd better get away from this culvert," someone said. "They've got a damn clever trench dug out underneath. Might be some more inside."

"I'll fix that," another said. He pulled the pin from a grenade and tossed it inside, and we turned our heads for the explosion.

I saw two foxholes on the other side of the highway, and I motioned for Wesmiller to come with me. We crossed the road and jumped into the holes. They were deep enough for us to stand in without being exposed from above, but there was no loose dirt around to reveal the location. It had been cunningly carted away.

The shelling which sounded like time fire continued to explode well to our rear, and I realized that the firing was coming from the southeast instead of the north. I knew now that it was not the sound of time fire. I had heard nothing like it before. It must be from large-caliber German antiaircraft guns. *Captain, you are meeting an old friend of the Air Corps. We call him, affectionately, "flak."*

I wondered what had become of the other tanks in the column. The artillery must have commenced just as the fifth tank reached the first bend in the highway.

Lieutenant Bagby came up beside the foxhole. I asked him what happened.

"We got right here," he said, "when a Kraut rose up from behind that brick wall with a bazooka. He was too quick for us. Hit the tank right in the front. Killed the driver and two of my men. Hand grenades started popping everywhere."

The aid man was running back and forth to the men

Racketen Panzerbuchse 43

who were wounded. He went to a soldier who was lying
alone in the field of green grain near the tank. He worked
silently for a minute and then took the soldier's rifle and
stuck it muzzle first into the ground.

"That makes the driver and three of mine now," Bagby said slowly.

The machine guns on the tanks continued to spit fire
into the bush-filled draw. Suddenly, they stopped, and a
German emerged with a white flag, his comrades rising
slowly behind him and marching toward us.

"Watch those bastards! It might be a trick!"

The riflemen trained their weapons on the approaching
Germans, but there was no trick. They were eager to
surrender.

"Goddamn lousy sonso'bitches," a soldier said. "Kill a
bunch of us and then come snivelling up wantin' to sur-

render. We oughta take every one of the bastards and cut their nuts right out."

The aid man assembled the wounded in the shallow ditch on the left of the highway. There were five. None of them was seriously hurt, but three could not walk.

I motioned two men to assist me, and we moved the soldier's body from the puddle of blood in the middle of the road.

"The tanks'll be coming this way before long," I said. "This is the least we can do." I saluted the dead soldier silently.

I tried to get my rear platoons on the radio, but the range was too great. Wesmiller changed to the longer aerial, but we still could not reach the spare radio with the rear CP. Finally, battalion answered weakly, and I told Colonel Smith the situation.

"There doesn't seem to be any defense left in Dorstewitz," I said, looking up at the first buildings of the town, now only four hundred yards from us, "but I haven't enough men left to risk going in . . . hardly two squads. See if you can contact Loberg with my rear CP and have him send up my other platoons."

Loberg himself answered in a few minutes. He had had to change his batteries.

"They're giving us hell here, Cap'n," Loberg said. "This damned antiaircraft fire is worse than time fire. Killed one of the artillery observer's crew and wounded the lieutenant. Patton got it pretty bad in the arm. Seven other men wounded. I've been trying to send the other tanks up to you, but every time they move it brings in another barrage."

"Send the two rifle platoons up on foot," I said.

"They can't move either," said Loberg. "Damned Germans can see every move we make."

I thought of one other possible solution. "Try to get at least one platoon back into Bad Lauchstaedt. Have them circle way'n hell around to the left rear and join us that way. There doesn't seem to be anything to the north."

"Roger."

The afternoon wore on, but still the platoon did not appear. All was quiet except for an occasional barrage of flak against the curve where they had caught the last tanks in the column. I tried desperately to pick up the enemy positions, and I wondered what had become of the Polish civilian, but I could determine only that they were firing from the east and slightly to the south of Dorstewitz. I called for litter-bearers for the wounded men who could not walk, but the litters did not arrive. I lost contact by radio again with the rear CP group, and Fein volunteered to go back to find out the trouble. He had been hit slightly in the back of the hand by a shrapnel fragment and it needed attention.

For the first time I found out that Lieutenant Bagby had been hit by a small fragment in the left knee, and he was suffering from concussion with the possibility that one eardrum had burst. But he refused to go back until the situation should clear up.

Finally, I saw the lead scouts of the 3d Platoon appear over a gently-sloping rise to our left rear. The platoon followed, widely deployed in the open field six hundred yards away.

A machine gun stuttered. The men in the platoon hit the ground as one, with dark uniforms showing up clearly against the resplendent green of the growing grain. I followed the tracers back to their origin and saw that they were coming from an enemy machine gun that had moved into position one hundred yards to our right rear. A slight rise in the ground obscured it from our view.

My platoon radio sputtered.

"This is Barnes, Cap'n," a voice drawled slowly. "We're comin' in behind you. If that's y'all shootin' at us, for God's sake stop."

It was Sergeant Barnes taking over his old job as platoon leader now that Patton was wounded.

"It's not us shootin', but I can see you," I said. "Try to make a run for it, and we'll keep the Germans busy."

One of the 1st Platoon riflemen climbed half-way up a tree and began to fire his M1 at the enemy gun crew. The distraction stopped them from firing, and Barnes' men seized the opportunity to move forward on the run. Lieutenant Bagby told his bazooka man to fire at the enemy gun, but he had only one round, and it fell short of the target. Three other riflemen on the ground fired toward the gun, but they could not see it for the rise in the ground.

The enemy gunner turned his attention toward us, but

the rise which hid him from us prevented him from firing low enough to give us any serious trouble. The German prisoners tried to move toward the ditch for cover, but a GI kicked them and told them to "sit there and get a taste of your own medicine, you lousy bastards."

I ran over to the tank I had ridden and told the platoon leader to get set to go on into Dorstewitz with us with his three remaining tanks.

He said, "I've got orders from my company commander not to move again 'till those flak guns are knocked out."

I was angry and cursed. I went back to the radio and got battalion, but Colonel Smith would not change the tank company commander's order. We could do nothing except go on into the town without them.

Barnes arrived out of breath. I told Lieutenant Bagby to remain with five men and the wounded men to keep the enemy machine gunner occupied and told Technical Sergeant Floyd W. Campbell, his platoon sergeant, to join the 3d Platoon with the remainder of his men.

The 3d Platoon and its recruits from the 1st moved cautiously up the bushy draw and came in on Dorstewitz from the northwest. I followed closely with Wesmiller and Citrone.

I was almost overcome with relief when there was no opposition. The men scattered quickly through the town to the far edge, collecting several submissive prisoners as they went.

Sergeant Campbell called over the platoon radio.

"Good God, Cap'n," he cried. "There're twelve flak guns in the field beyond town . . . not over six hundred yards from us. They're bigger'n hell and there're beaucoup Germans running around all over the place."

The flak gunners seemed to have discovered our presence in the town simultaneously with Campbell's announcement. They turned the full force of the twelve flak guns against Dorstewitz, and the streets reverberated with the terrifying crack of the big shells exploding in mid-air to send thousands of deadly fragments whining to the ground below. Tile roofing on the houses clattered to the ground from the concussion. For the first time we realized something of what our flyers had endured, only now the weapons were even more deadly against us than against the targets for which they had been designed.

I sneaked up a narrow, curving street to the south edge of the town and entered a small house atop a low knoll. From the second-floor windows I could see the objectives before me, more than a hundred Germans milling around six huge antiaircraft guns that belched their projectiles towards us. The other six guns were hidden by a cluster of trees around a farmhouse.

I radioed the information to battalion.

"It'll take a helluva lot more than I've got to take that position," I said. "We'll have to have tanks, but you'd better wait until Lieutenant Bagby gets a mortar squad to knock out that Kraut machine gun along the road before you send 'em up."

"Hold where you are," Colonel Smith said. "I'm sending E Company on up, and we'll get the tanks there when we can."

Lieutenant Bagby radioed that our mortar section had arrived, and a few well placed mortar rounds had persuaded the German machine-gun crew to surrender. He was sending the 2d Platoon and the Weapons Platoon on into Dorstewitz, and he felt that he had best wait with the wounded men and have his ear treated at the aid station, but he would be back up for the night.

The tanks roared into the town, followed by the TDs, and Colonel Smith and Captain Byrd arrived by jeep. Litter squads finally reached the wounded men with Lieutenant Bagby and moved them to the rear. F Company arrived on foot.

The TDs moved to the edge of town and blasted away at the enemy positions, but the enemy gunners answered with such deafening barrages of the deadly air bursts that the TDs abandoned the project.

A communications officer arrived from regiment to check on wire communications with the battalion CP. A piece of flying shrapnel killed him as he stepped from his jeep into the house that was serving as the battalion CP.

The town had become a mass of broken limbs, fallen wires and broken pieces of red slate roofing. The forward walls of three houses on the far edge of town were completely blasted away by enemy fire. The big shells burst above the pond in the center of the town and sent telltale little ripples running across the water where the fragments scattered downward.

Colonel Smith sent a messenger to tell me to meet him at a house in the center of the town. I dreaded what I knew was coming, but I ducked hurriedly down the littered street. I noticed that the sun was sinking slowly behind us, and it would soon be dark.

"I just ran into your boy Junior," Colonel Smith said. "He's having a little trouble with a German major who claims he's in command of all the flak defenses around Merseburg and seems quite put out that your men took him prisoner. He kept begging Junior either to shoot him or let him shoot himself. Junior was about to let him have his way when I happened up."

"Don't feel too badly about the trouble you've run into here, Mac," he said. "The 1st Battalion has run into flak on the right, and I understand the 9th Infantry is up against the same thing on our left."

"Yessir——"

"But regiment says we've got to reach Schkopau by morning, and that means only one thing, Mac."

"What's that, sir?" I asked the question as if a heavy dread were not already inside me from the knowledge of what he was about to say.

Here it comes——

"G Company has got to take the flak guns," he said slowly. "Now."

23

SEVENTY-FIVE CENTS PER DAY

Night was almost upon us when I received the order to attack the gun positions. With the Colonel's permission I decided to wait for a complete cover of darkness to begin the assault. The artillery observer from E Company was attached to my company for the operation, since my observer had been wounded, and we moved to a house on the eastern edge of the town to await the arrival of the remainder of my company, and darkness.

From the second floor of the house I had a much clearer view of the objective. The six nearer guns were six hundred yards away, a row of low green wooden barracks lying between us and the guns. The six farther guns remained partially obscured by the tall green trees around the farmhouse. All the Germans seemed to have found cover, but the artillery observer continued to plaster the area with barrage after barrage of heavy shells.

Four hundred yards to the rear of the first battery of guns I could see a lone house atop a high knoll. One more house one hundred yards to the left front of my observation point gave some cover toward the knoll, so I decided to move my men to the house on the knoll and attack the German positions from the rear, hoping blindly that we could reach the lone house without a fight.

Darkness fell quickly. Colonel Smith radioed to find out if I was ready to move out. I started to reply when I heard a loud explosion from the direction of the flak guns and saw a sudden spurt of orange flame shoot skyward that lit up the entire area for a brief second.

I said, "Just a minute, sir. It looks from here like the Germans are blowing up the guns and taking off. I'm ready to go, but I'd like to give them a chance to leave, if possible. It's getting so dark, it'll be hell out there if they decide to fight."

"OK, Mac," the Colonel answered, seeming to have sensed some of my doubts in going up against the formidable guns. "I'm sending Easy and Fox to take Corbetha and Schkopau at four o'clock in the morning. You'll have to take the flak guns before then and be ready to follow us into Schkopau."

"Roger."

"By the way," he added, "you can tell Junior that we finally had to dispense with his German major. He tried to make a run for it."

Another loud explosion and an upward spurt of flame came from the flak guns; then another, and another. We could see figures walking on the parapets around the gun pit, silhouetted against the orange light of the fires.

I waited another thirty minutes while the artillery observer directed his barrages at the burning fires. I alerted the 2d and 3d Platoons, and they moved out in the direction of the house atop the knoll. I wondered how they would ever find it. The darkness was inky black.

I led the remaining men across the road to the small house on the route toward the knoll. We paused there to await word from the two platoons moving up the hill through the darkness. Someone lit a candle inside the house, and I went inside and checked my map. The artillery observer continued to fire single rounds at the target area, careful now to be sure that the gunners did not overshoot the target and hit the men moving up the hill.

An hour passed before Whitman called over the platoon radio. They had reached the house and taken three prisoners, but there had been no fight. Sergeant Barnes and the 3d Platoon were moving on toward the flak positions, but he was taking it slowly. The artillery observer lifted his fire.

A single rifle shot from the darkness outside the house broke the stillness. It seemed to come from the south. A guard called out "Halt!" but there was no answer. The guard fired his rifle into the air. All was quiet.

I told Lieutenant Speed and Sergeant Campbell to assemble the men around the house. We would move forward to the knoll. We stepped out into the darkness, careful to keep a close formation lest we lose one another in the black expanse on all sides of us. We could see the fires around the flak guns still burning leisurely, lower now than before, but all was quiet.

The dark outline of the house loomed ahead of us in the blackness, and I called out to let Whitman's men know we were approaching. The men from the 2d Platoon were trying to get some sleep inside while awaiting their turn to move down to the objective. A group of less somnolent men remained outside the house, violently propositioning a German girl they had found in the house with the soldiers they had taken prisoner.

I found a seat in the cellar where there was a candle. Occasional reports from Sergeant Barnes filtered over the platoon radio. They were advancing slowly and cautiously. It was blacker than all hell. So far, no opposition.

I nodded from sleepiness and looked at my watch. It was midnight. Then it was one o'clock. One-thirty. I wondered if Barnes would ever reach the flak guns, but I could not blame him for proceeding slowly. I was desperately hungry and twice again as sleepy.

Battalion called for a report. They said our kitchen truck had been waiting in Dorstewitz to give us supper since nine o'clock. I said to hold it until I notified them to send it up.

I climbed the narrow cellar stairs to the outside. I could not stay awake any longer inside the house. I stood in the cool air and listened, shaking half from fear of the unknown and half from the night chill. Sooner or later I expected to hear the sound of small-arms fire that would mean Barnes had run into trouble. How I dreaded the thought of the sound and all it embodied! It did not occur to me that it might not come.

The platoon radio sputtered, and I heard Barnes' voice come over it feebly. The batteries were almost dead.

"We're here, Cap'n. Not a sign of Kraut."

I knew he had not said that the war was over, that only one more little position on the road to Berlin was undefended, but I could hardly have been more impressed. The long hours of fearful waiting were for the moment over. It did not matter that we might meet these Germans elsewhere later, and possibly on even more precarious terms.

What mattered now was that I had one platoon inside the flak gun positions, and there was no resistance.

"Can you send two men to guide us down?" I asked.

"Yessir," Barnes said, and I could detect the fatigue in his voice, "but I can't find the barracks like you said were here, Cap'n."

"Never mind them now," I answered. "Hold where you are until I get the rest of the company down. You might run into trouble."

It was another hour before the guides found us.

"We went two hundred yards past the house," they said. "We couldn't see it in the dark."

The other platoons were waiting, and I took my place with the guides at the head of the column. We moved slowly to keep the column from becoming separated in the darkness, and when we approached the smoldering fires, we had to feel each step carefully before placing our weight on the foot. The area was densely covered with deep foxholes.

We came upon the big guns, and I could see their immensity by the smoldering light of the fires. It was no wonder that their barrages had been so terrifying and deadly. The guns were 128mm pieces, and the fuses in the shells could be set for either air or contact bursts.

We had entered, I know now, one of the most concentrated belts of antiaircraft defenses in all Europe. Fortunately for us, the troops who served the guns were men who had been considered unworthy of frontline service because of their age and physical condition. They were organized as part of the 14th Flak Division, *commanded by a Major General Gerlach, who had his headquarters in Leipzig.*

We found Sergeant Barnes' platoon waiting near one of the gun pits. Faint streaks of dawn were appearing over the horizon, and the increasing light made it easier to find the barracks. They were low, flimsily-constructed wooden buildings with bunks and straw mattresses. The men flopped down wearily on the bunks, and the air was quickly filled with snores.

I tried to contact Colonel Smith, but Major Joseph with

the rear battalion CP answered. Colonel Smith had gone forward with E and F Companies. They had now reached the Merseburg Canal beyond Schkopau with no resistance. My kitchen truck continued to wait in Dorstewitz, so I sent two men back to guide it forward.

I tried desperately not to go to sleep while we were waiting for the kitchen vehicle, but my head fell forward wearily on the table in the bunkhouse. The men awoke me when our "supper" arrived at six o'clock. Lieutenant Bagby was with the chow vehicle. It was daylight outside.

The food had been prepared for our supper the night before, and it seemed strange to be eating cold mashed potatoes and cold English peas at six o'clock in the morning, but any food was welcome. We had not eaten since seven o'clock the preceding morning. *As an officer in the United States Army seventy-five cents per day is being subtracted from your pay under the assumption that you get three squares per. Do you want I should take a letter to your Congressman?*

There were fresh radio batteries with the kitchen jeep, and I was able to contact the forward battalion CP in Schkopau.

"Everything's all set here, Mac," Colonel Smith said. "I want you to move forward as quickly as possible to take up a defense in Corbetha. Come cross-country and have one platoon clear out the houses at the crossroads between you and the town, and have the rest of your company check the big factory to the south. Leave one platoon there to hold the factory."

The company lined up in a column of twos, and we moved again past the big gun pits. To our right were the six other big guns, hardly touched by the shelling the night before. Lieutenant Whitman led the 2d Platoon toward the guns and brought back fifteen prisoners.

Loud moans from one of the gun pits beside us caught my attention, and I jumped inside to investigate. Three Germans lay inside elaborately-constructed bunker-type dugouts in the sides of the pit. They moaned so painfully that I knew I would have become nauseated had they been other than Germans. They had been wounded by the artillery barrage the night before and left by their comrades. There was nothing we could do for them. I told

Harms to tell them aid men would be up later, but I wondered how many days it would be before they would be discovered again.

We saw ten dead Germans outside the pits where they had been caught by the artillery. One German lay on the exposed hill with a blanket over his body, and I thought for a moment he was dead. When we passed, however, I noticed that he was shaking violently all over, but no one bothered to lift the blanket to see what was wrong with him.

Someone said, "Maybe he thinks he's an ostrich."

I sent the 1st Platoon to clear out the houses at the crossroads, and I followed the other two platoons to the factory, a big plant stretching the length of several city blocks to the south. A brief investigation revealed no opposition, so we moved on toward Corbetha, a quarter of a mile away.

We neared a group of low barracks buildings, and we were suddenly engulfed by a screaming horde of laughing, cheering men that I knew must be every nationality in Europe except German. They rushed from the barracks, screaming *"Americain!" "Americano!"* thrusting German cigarettes upon us. The Italians and the French embraced us, delirious with joy. We had to tear ourselves away to continue on into Corbetha.

A soberer Frenchman asked me if it was true that President Roosevelt was dead.

The idea was preposterous, and I told him as much.

"Somebody's been feedin' you a lot of German propaganda," I said.

The platoons began to clear their respective billets of civilians, and the 1st Platoon arrived, herding forty-two German soldiers before them. The captives outnumbered the captors two to one. They said they were the main portion of the troops who had manned the flak guns.

"It's a good thing they didn't start shooting," Lieutenant Bagby said. "Those two houses at the crossroads were packed."

They lined up the hapless prisoners in the middle of the street and searched them for "souvenirs." A group of slave laborers took over the search when the GIs had finished, and I thought they were going to strip the Germans' clothes from their bodies. I told the guards to march them on to battalion.

A reign of terror began for the town's civilians. The slave laborers, who had been kept in two barracks areas adjacent to the town, outnumbered the residents. Now they were free and began immediately to make the most of their freedom. Two Russians dragged a goat down the street on a leash. Chickens were "liberated" right and left.

Word spread among the civilian women that I was the *Kommandant* in the area, and they beat a steady path to our CP.

"There're Russians in my kitchen!" or "They're taking all my chickens!" or "They're killing my pigs!" they would scream in German.

I acquired a stock answer for the situation, and Harms translated for me.

"Tell them it wasn't us who brought these people here."

I directed the 1st Platoon to move to the factory as "occupation forces" until we should leave the area, and I went to the battalion CP in Schkopau.

There Captain Byrd told me that E and F Companies had been unsuccessful in reaching the canal before the Germans blew the bridges, but one platoon from F Company had gone across on a partially demolished railroad bridge. Other than occasional shelling against the bridge from flak guns, there was no opposition.

And according to the information which they had at battalion, it seemed likely that we would remain in our present locations at least overnight.

I returned to the company via the factory. Lieutenant Bagby's platoon had drawn the choice billets again. They were quartered in the mammoth administration building of the plant, which the German superintendent described as Germany's largest synthetic rubber factory. Factory workers were bringing in beds to place in the steam-heated main entrance of the building to provide bunks for every man in the platoon. A modernistic bar provided non-alcoholic beer and iced lemonade. The German superintendent was going to extremes to make the Americans comfortable—in exchange, he hoped, for protection against the suddenly-freed slave laborers.

Bagby requisitioned the plant's staff cars for his own

use—two luxurious Mercedes-Benzes and three other automobiles. He made me a gift of one of the lesser vehicles as if it might be a piece of candy.

"You got a bathroom in your CP, Cap'n?" he asked.

I wished I could have said yes, but my answer was no.

"Then maybe you'd better come over tomorrow," he said. "My manager tells me he'll have the tile showers in the basement working by morning."

The freed slave laborers held a dance at the factory that night, and a number of the men from the company attended, unofficially. I missed two men from my CP group later in the evening.

"They're 'shacking up' over at the slave camp," I was told.

I was called to battalion after lunch the next day for the attack order which we all knew must be forthcoming soon. The 1st Battalion would make a feint against the Merseburg Canal opposite Merseburg, while we, without an artillery preparation, would cross at the railroad bridge held by F Company at ten o'clock that night. The 3d Battalion would cross farther to the south. E Company would lead our attack. G Company would follow. Our final objective was the town of Wallendorf, five miles away.

Second Lieutenant John F. Reed, of Barny, Texas, was at my CP when I returned to Corbetha. He was from Cannon Company, but casualties had taken a heavy toll of forward observers from the artillery, and he had been assigned as our forward observer.

We left Corbetha at nine o'clock and walked the one mile to Schkopau. The enemy fired an intense flak barrage at the railroad bridge across the canal at 9:30, and I shuddered with the thought that our crossing might be discovered and subjected to one of the murderous barrages.

We fell in behind E Company near the battalion CP and waited for the zero hour. At five minutes until ten the column moved off again. The night was brighter than usual, but it was virtually impossible to see any distance ahead, nevertheless. To the right we could see a blaze of fire light up the sky and hear the sound of hundreds of weapons, the 1st Battalion's feint at Merseburg.

I suddenly found myself atop the railroad bridge, and I

wanted to run ahead of the slow-moving men in front of me and get off this marked target as quickly as possible. At any moment the terrifying air bursts might begin to explode above our heads.

Then I was off the bridge and walking along the marshy ground beside the elevated railroad tracks. The column picked up speed, making it difficult to keep up. The men ahead of me moved underneath a trestle and climbed a slippery bank to a dirt road. The last of my company would have crossed the canal by this time, and still there was no sound of enemy fire. I breathed more easily.

We reached Collenby, the first objective. The little "cow town" was sleeping peacefully to all appearances, and the assault elements made no effort to search the dark buildings.

We moved out again along the narrow dirt road, dark woods and bushes rising occasionally on either side. My mind began to imagine the perfect spots for ambush. We were moving too rapidly to employ flank patrols on either side of the road. The clump-clump of many heavy boots sounded on the hard roadbed, and weapons and equipment rattled noisily. Somewhere a dog barked.

But there was no sound or sign of the enemy.

We turned right on a paved highway and then off again to another dirt road leading east. The men ahead of me stopped suddenly so that I bumped my helmet against the rifle of the soldier in front of me. E Company had reached the second objective, the town of Lossen.

Now it was our turn to take the lead and capture the next two towns while E Company remained in Lossen in the defense. We by-passed E Company's rear elements, and I halted my column in the center of the little town and entered a building with my platoon leaders to check our maps.

My map showed that the next town was Lopitz, not quite a half-mile away. I directed the 1st and 2d Platoons forward, each platoon keeping one squad off the side of the road to prevent ambush. We joined the men waiting in the road outside, and the lead platoons moved off.

The lead elements halted even before the column had completed its accordion-like action of starting forward. A soldier moved to the rear with five prisoners.

"Found these on the edge of the town," the soldier said. "Lieutenant Bagby saw them standing there in the middle of the road and he walked up and asked them if they were from E Company. They didn't say one way or the other, but they turned out to be Krauts."

The column moved forward again, much slower than had E Company, and I wondered if my own wariness of all situations had infused itself into the platoons.

We found no resistance in Lopitz, and I moved inside a house to check the maps again with the platoon leaders. A grey-haired German civilian and his wife watched us warily from a corner of the room.

There was another halt on the edge of town while a squad from the 1st Platoon checked an old castle on the left of the road and brought back fifteen prisoners. The column moved forward. Somewhere in the distance another dog was aroused and barked fitfully. *Poor GI Joe. Now even the dogs have turned against you.*

The road curved back and forth, following the course of a small canal on the right.

A barrage of our own artillery whistled dangerously close overhead and crashed in the field beyond us. Lieutenant Reed quickly radioed back to stop the firing. Somebody was off his target.

The assault platoons entered Tragarth. I followed and took over a low stone house as a temporary CP, reporting to battalion that we were on our second objective. I could hear the sound of many feet on the road and knew that F Company was passing through to move on to Wallendorf.

A man from the 2d Platoon brought in two German soldiers and a civilian girl.

"Found these three in a hay barn," the soldier said and laughed. "Surprised hell outa them when I flashed a light in the barn. Had to wait for the gal to put her pants back on."

Colonel Smith followed F Company into Wallendorf and radioed back for me to follow.

"Hurry right up," he said. "Blue has hit flak guns to the south, and you'll have to get here before daylight or you'll never make it."

Grey streaks of dawn were appearing on the horizon as I led the company along the paved highway leading east to Wallendorf. It was almost light when I saw the first buildings of the town ashead of us.

I heard the sudden dreaded crack-crack of multiple flak air bursts to the south, and I could see the outlines of another town to our right by the lightning-like flashes of the exploding shells. That must be the 3d Battalion's town, and the Krauts were giving them hell.

We picked up the pace and gained the first buildings in Wallendorf before the air bursts shifted in our direction. The platoon leaders infiltrated their men to their assigned defensive sectors as the big shells burst above the buildings with resounding explosions that sent slate roofing clattering noisily to the streets.

It was six o'clock before I finally stretched across a bed in the *Gasthaus* which we chose as a CP. The shell bursts outside did not disturb me as I drifted off into sleep. The long walk and the nervous suspense of the night had made me utterly exhausted.

From somewhere in the distance I thought I heard someone calling me, but I tried to ignore it. I could not have been asleep over five minutes. Then I jumped up suddenly. Someone *was* calling me.

It was Shepherd, one of my radio operators. "They want you on the radio, Cap'n."

Captain Byrd was calling. "L Company ran into trouble trying to take the flak guns last night. That's what started all the shooting. They got right on top of the positions before they were discovered, but the Germans knocked them back with direct fire from the flak guns. They're going to try again at 7:30."

I noted that my watch said it was already 7:30.

"You're to take one platoon and move in against the flank of the position from Wallendorf to assist L Company."

"Great guns, Byrd," I said. "We'll never make it by 7:30. It's that time now. I'll wake up my men and move up as quickly as I can, but try to talk them into giving me at least fifteen minutes."

I sent Shepherd to wake up Sergeant Barnes and the 3d Platoon, and I woke Wesmiller and Lieutenant Reed, the artillery observer, to go with me. Battalion sent another radio so I would be on the same channel with the 3d Battalion. I told Shepherd to come with me to operate the extra radio, and I would send the spare company 300 with Barnes' platoon.

SCR 300

The 3d Platoon arrived at 7:45. Barnes was as dismayed as I at the sudden awakening to move into the attack. I pointed out a street on the map which led from the southern edge of town toward the objective and told him to move his platoon on to the edge of town. I took a short cut through the back yards of the houses to establish an observation post from which to direct artillery on the objective. Air bursts from the flak guns continued to explode above the town to the south, and the enemy gunners centered an occasional barrage against Wallendorf. We ran quickly from one building to another.

I reached a building that seemed to have possibilities as an OP on the southern edge of town beside a railroad track. We broke the lock on the door and went upstairs to a room on the second floor where the view to the south showed a wide expanse of slightly rising ground extending over a quarter-mile to the enemy positions. The ground was completely open except for a line of trees along the road leading from Wallendorf and a cluster of barracks-type wooden buildings beside the road four hundred yards from my OP. To cross that open space in the face of the flak fire would be virtual suicide.

To my right I could see the houses of Kriegsdorf, the town occupied by the 3d Battalion. It was even more incredible to think that anyone could attack from that town toward the flak guns. They must cross almost a mile of rising open ground without a single bush or shrub for concealment. Whoever dreamed up this attack, and with such little preparation, must have been contemplating mass murder!

Our own artillery was falling around the wooden barracks four hundred yards from me, but the enemy guns were firing from far to the rear of these barracks. I realized that the 3d Battalion in Kriegsdorf could not see the main positions and thought the barracks area was their objective.

To my left front I could see my 3d Platoon moving into a dug-out area a few yards beyond the railroad track. I could almost hear Sergeant Barnes cursing in his slow, Southern drawl at the order which expected him to cross this murderously open terrain.

I contacted 3d Battalion headquarters on the extra radio and talked with Lieutenant Colonel Montgomery, the officer who as a captain had been operations officer of the battalion when I was with them during the German breakthrough in the Ardennes.

"We're finally in position, Monty," I said, "but we'll never cross that open field the way things are now. Your artillery is hitting almost a thousand yards short."

"We've already tried once, Mac," Monty answered.

"That's what started all the shooting a minute ago. We can't get any farther than the edge of town. L Company is all shot up, and I've got I Company trying it now."

I Company! The faces of the men I had known so intimately before coming to the 2d Battalion flooded before me. So now I was working with I Company again.

"We'll try it again at 8:15," Colonel Montgomery said.

I suggested that I fire the artillery this time from my OP. "I think I can see the objective a helluva lot better from where I am."

He agreed, and Lieutenant Reed set up his artillery radio. When he had it assembled, he found that Captain William Graniss, the artillery liaison officer with our battalion, was already directing fire against the position from a building adjacent to us.

"I'm getting in on the position now," he said.

I looked toward the flak guns as a barrage of artillery whistled overhead, and the earth around the guns seemed to erupt in a series of black explosions of smoke and dust.

My watch said 8:15. I could see small black figures that must be men emerging from the cover of the outer buildings in Kriegsdorf. I radioed Barnes to get set to move out.

The air above the edge of Kriegsdorf became, suddenly, a blazing inferno of orange-colored explosions and rising black smoke. The black figures which must have been I Company disappeared. Another deafening barrage of air bursts exploded in the air above where they had been.

I radioed Barnes to hold everything where he was. The Germans had not seen them yet, but if they moved out across the open ground, they would surely receive the same terrifying reception.

24

WHITMAN SHELLS HIMSELF

I tried to get Colonel Montgomery on the radio again, but the operator said he was talking with regiment. A voice broke in with a transmission, saying, "This is Item Company," and a flood of memories passed before me. It seemed natural to hear the voice on the radio again. It was Sergeant Savage.

Colonel Montgomery called me when he had finished talking with regiment. "Regiment has been pushing us like all hell to take these flak guns this morning," he said. "I just told the Colonel I don't think it can be done from here. What do you think?"

I thought it about time that someone made that decision. "If they'll only give us time to put some accurate artillery fire on those guns," I said, recalling our experience the previous night, "we can take them without a fight. The Krauts will take off." I could not understand why we must always rush, rush, rush to take objectives at the expense of American lives. Had men, in reality, become mere numbers on a casualty report?

"I hope you're right, because that seems the only way," Colonel Montgomery said. "You try it from where you are and let me know what happens. I'll tell the old man that's what we're going to do. It won't hurt to give it a try."

Lieutenant Reed dismantled his artillery radio, and we ran to the building from which Captain Graniss was directing fire. He poured barrage after barrage full upon the German positions. With my field glasses I could see enemy soldiers running in all directions. Shells crushed the wooden barracks like matchsticks. First Lieutenant Henry S.

Compton, of Greenwood, S. C., directed 81mm mortar fire against the positions from a nearby building.

Wesmiller cried, "They're taking off, Cap'n! They're running bigger'n hell!"

I shifted my glasses to the direction in which he pointed. A horde of Germans was running to the rear and the men were disappearing across the crest of the hill behind their positions. Captain Graniss shifted his fire to catch the enemy in his flight.

I was filled with a sort of smug satisfaction over the outcome of the attack thus far. If only some of the big shots would get the ants out of their pants and take a little time to get things organized, I thought, bitterly. Perhaps they were too busy pondering the outcome of their latest recommendation for an award for gallantry sent in by some ambitious staff officer.

At any rate, there seemed to be no hurry now to take the positions. The enemy guns had ceased to fire, and a strange quiet pervaded the two towns, broken only by the overhead whistle of our own artillery, followed by its dull crushing explosions around the antiaircraft guns. Captain Graniss leisurely continued to fire at the objective.

Colonel Smith called at noon and asked what I thought of the situation.

"Do you think you can take it now with your one platoon?"

The suggestion startled me at first. I had not thought for a moment that the 3d Battalion would not now go on and consolidate the objective.

"Well, yessir," I faltered, "but I don't know about holding it. Suppose they should counterattack?" But I knew as I said it that the possibility was remote. The disintegrated enemy had long since displayed insufficient force to counterattack, but it was a possibility that was difficult to forget after my harrowing indoctrination in the Siegfried Line.

"I told regiment I thought you could do it," Colonel Smith continued. *Well, thanks, old man, we're a great little outfit, but, really*—"As soon as you're on position, have the rest of your company join you there to help defend it."

"Roger," I said, thoughtfully.

I radioed the information to Barnes, and I saw the men of his platoon rise reluctantly from the ground where they had been resting during the shelling. I told him we would continue to fire until we saw him nearing the gun positions. The platoon moved out.

I watched them anxiously from the upstairs window. They were a ridiculously small force to send against his formidable objective, but it did seem almost impossible now that the area would be defended. We had seen the enemy retreating.

The men moved quickly through the cluster of barracks beside the highway, and I could see them with my field glasses nearing the big guns. I told Captain Graniss to lift his fire. A final volley thundered upon the positions.

I followed the moving figures with my glasses, expecting at any moment to see them hit the ground at the sound of small-arms fire. But the men disappeared in the maze of fortifications around the big guns, and I heard no fire. I motioned to my CP group, and we moved from the house and up the road toward the objective.

When we passed the first group of barracks, I was surprised to see two 88mm flak guns that had been hidden from our view by the barracks. This was evidently what the 3d Battalion had thought was holding them up.

Two men from the 3d Platoon met us, marching a platoon of Germans before them, their hands laced on top of their heads.

"Got more prisoners than we had men to take 'em," one of the guards said. "There're twenty-four flak guns. We got sixty Kraut sol'jers and two women."

He winked at me and made a clucking noise between his teeth.

The news of the capture of the flak guns evidently spread quickly through the surrounding towns. German civilians and slave laborers flooded the area looking for salvageable articles left behind by the German garrison.

The 3d Platoon medic, sleeping with his shoes off in the bright sunlight, became a victim of their search when a slave laborer ran off with his shoes. We had to borrow a pair for him from the kitchen force.

I tried to get some sleep on a straw mattress inside one of the lesser damaged barracks, but I had no sooner fallen asleep than Colonel Smith and Captain Byrd arrived with information on the next attack. We would jump off again as soon as it was dark. *But, Colonel, don't you remember? This was my forty-eighth mission. I'm due for thirty days in the States.*

We moved back into Wallendorf at dusk and formed behind F Company on the highway leading out of town to the east. The plan of attack called for us to follow F Company to the first town of Zoschen. While they were clearing out the town, we would pass through them to take the second town. At that point we would take separate roads, G Company going to the left until we reached the small town of Klein Liebenau, five miles to the east. That would place us near the outskirts of Leipzig.

The men in the company could not understand why we had been chosen again as one of the assault companies, and I was inclined to wonder with them. The 3d Platoon was particularly adamant in their denunciation of the order. We had been the reserve company only once since I had been with the battalion, and the men said that the same condition had existed before I came.

"Guess they just figure G Company can do it, no matter what it is," one soldier suggested.

I smiled to myself. The words had a familiar ring. I had heard them time after time with I Company, and even now the company whose position we were envying probably thought themselves no more fortunate than we.

Darkness fell, and the head of the column moved forward. F Company moved almost as quickly as had E Company the night before, and I found myself perspiring freely in my efforts to keep up with the tail of the company ahead of us. They entered Zoschen. Only a furiously barking dog that I thought would surely arouse the countryside showed any sign of resistance.

We passed through F Company, and I dropped back to the rear of the lead platoon with my CP group. The lack of enemy resistance the previous night had made me less cautious, and I decided it was not necessary to keep one squad in the fields on either side of the highway.

The night was bright with a half-moon, and I saw the outline of the buildings in Gohren, our first objective. The lead platoon moved in quickly and made a search of the buildings, breaking down doors when the occupants did not respond quickly enough. A group of dogs barked furiously.

The platoons reassembled on the north edge of town, and we moved down the road again, following a small canal, and curved back to the east into Zweimen, the second objective, a little town built around a pond that glimmered in the moonlight. Dogs announced our coming as usual.

The 1st Platoon took five prisoners who said they had been in the group which fled the flak guns that morning. I went inside a house to check over my map, and Harms talked with the civilians. They said there were no German soldiers anywhere near, they had all withdrawn that morning to the east to join an antiaircraft garrison nearer Leipzig.

I knew that the information from the civilians was not trustworthy, but I worried over the possibility of finding ourselves face to face with another flak gun position. Battalion had not told us that we might meet up with such positions, but then battalion had not warned us of the first flak guns we had encountered. I wondered again what had become of the Polish civilian who had joined us in Schotterey with knowledge of the gun locations.

The platoons completed searching the town and waited for me outside. I joined them and we moved out again to the east.

Our march to the next town of Dolkau was unimpeded. Two streets ran through the town to join into one road at the entrance to a woods to the east, so I sent one platoon down either road, and they reassembled at the road junction. One soldier had entered a bakery in his search for the enemy and had found none, but would I care for a piece of cake?

According to my map, the next town lay immediately beyond the woods before us. Fearing an ambush in the woods, I directed both the 1st and 2d Platoons forward, one squad from each platoon keeping inside the edge of the woods.

The men sounded like cattle thrashing through the underbrush in the darkness. The platoon leaders anticipated my decision to pull the squads back to the road, and the column moved on swiftly and announced they had entered the objective, Harburg. I followed and stepped inside a house to look at my map. An old man and his wife watched the proceedings with interest, complaining because we had broken the lock rather than waiting for them to open the door. I told Harms to ask them if they knew anything about any flak guns in the area.

They expressed complete ignorance of any enemy guns. I decided from looking at my map that the open field beyond Harburg was the only possible location before we reached our final objective. I also noted that we would pass an underpass beneath an *Autobahn* before reaching Klein Liebenau, and it was a likely spot for an enemy delaying force. I warned the platoon leaders about the underpass, and the column moved forward, both the 1st and 2d Platoons in the assault formation.

The moon disappeared, and we were upon the *Autobahn* before I knew it. We passed and approached the final objective. I heard voices in a streak of woods fifty yards to our left, but the lead platoons had already passed. I warned the 3d Platoon behind me to be on the alert, but no resistance developed.

The lead platoons cleared Klein Liebenau quickly, and I assigned them their defensive sectors over the platoon radio. Harms and Lieutenant Loberg picked out the town *Gasthaus* as a CP and I went inside. Someone pressed an electric light switch and the room was flooded with light.

Fulton raised his hands high and solemnly bowed three times to the floor. It was our first electricity in weeks.

Strains of music and sounds of laughter downstairs awoke me shortly before noon, and I went out into the warm sunlight in the courtyard behind the house to wash and shave. A group of Poles and Russians were holding a dance in the room of the *Gasthaus* where my kitchen had been set up. One of the Russians played an accordion, and it brought gales of laughter when one of the GIs tried to join in the intricate steps of the folk dances.

A jeep driver from battalion came for me after lunch and drove me to the town occupied by battalion headquarters, where Colonel Smith gave me the plans for the continuation of the attack.

"We're approaching Leipzig," he said, "and the Colonel's a little afraid of these night attacks. We might run up against a main line of defense around the city. To avoid that I want you to send out one platoon immediately as a patrol and follow with the remainder of your company at six o'clock this afternoon."

"F Company will meet you in Gundorf," he continued, pointing to his map, "and you'll enter the city together. If your patrol runs up against any semblance of a main line, we'll hold up and wait for daylight tomorrow to attack."

I alerted the 3d Platoon by radio to move and hurried back to the company to give Sergeant Barnes the order. According to the map, the road from Klein Liebenau curved back and forth through a dense woods until it reached an open area on the edge of Gundorf. The next town, not over six hundred yards from Gundorf, was Bohlitz-Ehrenburg, which appeared to be a suburb of Leipzig, extending to the Pleisse-Elster Canal which separated the suburb from the main section of the city.

Sergeant Barnes moved forward equipped with a 300 radio for communication with my CP. He found no opposition until he reached a house and beer garden in a small clearing half-way through the woods.

"A couple o' Germans ran in the house when they saw us coming," he radioed. "They're firing at us, but it looks pretty simple."

It was nearing six o'clock when I dispatched messengers to the other platoons, and they formed on the eastern edge of the town to move forward. Barnes reported that his platoon had overcome the resistance at the clearing, wounding the three Germans who were firing at them, and were continuing forward leaving a guard with the Germans. He was pleased to hear I was following now with the rest of the company. He didn't like going through the woods alone.

The distance between us and the lead patrol narrowed until I saw the tail of Barnes' platoon entering Gundorf as we came to the edge of the woods. I picked up the pace, and the platoon fanned out to search the houses. I moved to the center of the town with my CP group and waited where three main streets joined to form a small village square.

Harms talked with the civilians while we waited for the rifle platoons to reassemble. "They say the Germans are dug in half-way between here and the next town," he told me.

I saw that the sun was setting in the west and dusk was

approaching. In a few minutes we would be unable to see the buildings in the next town. "Get one of the civilians to come with you and follow me," I said to Harms.

I moved down the street to the east, keeping close to the buildings in case some unseen enemy to the front might have the street covered with fire. I moved cautiously around a small lone house on the right side of the street and looked around the corner. The area on the right of the road was a flat open field, extending six hundred yards to a high brick wall which seemed to surround a small factory, the open field broken only by a brick cistern midway across the field. On the left of the highway a brick wall ran parallel to the road for one hundred yards before it stopped opposite the cistern. An open field stretched from the end of the wall to a group of houses across the street from the factory. Trees lined the short stretch of open highway.

The German civilian pointed to the brick cistern and spoke excitedly in German.

"He says the Germans are dug in around the cistern and the wall around the factory," Harms said.

I moved back and sent Lieutenant Speed forward with a mortar squad to place fire around the cistern and along the factory wall. Lieutenant Reed set up his artillery radio ready to fire at the factory.

I told battalion that with the situation as it was I would prefer waiting until morning to attack, but Colonel Smith insisted that we get going. "Get a patrol started forward right away," he said. "F Company is on the way to Gundorf now, and they'll take over the right side of the highway from you. Get moving before it gets any darker."

I reluctantly sent the 2d Platoon forward as a patrol with Shepherd accompanying them with the spare 300 radio. They went behind the wall on the left of the highway and ran across the remaining open space to the houses on the left.

"No fight," Whitman radioed, "but it's getting dark as hell."

I sent the 1st Platoon forward to join the 2d.

Captain Calhoun arrived with F Company. When he learned the situation, he was as reluctant as I to continue until daylight. Our maps showed a continuous stretch of buildings all the way from Bohlitz-Ehrenburg to the

Pleisse-Elster Canal, and night fighting in the cities was not to our liking. He radioed battalion, but the Colonel was insistent. "The farther we go tonight, the less we'll have to do tomorrow," he said.

Lieutenant Whitman called over the radio.

"The 1st Platoon is here, and I'm across in the factory," he said. "There's no fight, but I've got a crew of Kraut trapped in the basement of the factory and the sonofabitches won't give up."

I decided to go forward with the remainder of the company. F Company was going up on the right of the highway. Wesmiller, carrying the 300 radio, Townsend, with the 536 radio, and Lieutenant Reed and his two artillery assistants and I moved up on the left. The 3d Platoon followed closely behind us.

Lieutenant Whitman called suddenly over the radio, and I knew by the excitement in his voice that something had either happened or was about to happen. "You'd better get somebody else up here to help us out. Sounds like a whole regiment of Kraut coming up the highway."

We reached the end of the brick wall on our left, and I moved quickly into the open field. I told Whitman that F Company was on the way up on the right and I was about three hundred yards from the houses on the left with the 3d Platoon. We would be with them in a matter of minutes.

Before Whitman could reply a burst of small-arms fire chattered to our front. I dropped to the ground. There was no ditch beside the highway, and the roadbed, two feet higher than the field, provided cover only from fire from the right of the highway. I motioned the men behind me to continue forward, and I ran ahead, crouching beside the raised roadbed.

A shell from a *Panzerfaust* burst in the center of the highway ahead of me. Fragments sprayed the trees on either side of the road, and I dropped face-down to the ground. Another flurry of small-arms fire came from the houses in front of us, and tracer bullets skimmed the ground on either side of the highway. The raised roadbed was scant protection now. A flare burst high in the air above the buildings, bathing the entire area in a white, incandescent light that blinded me for a moment.

The flare seemed to be a signal for another burst of

machine-gun and rifle fire. Tracer bullets criss-crossed the open fields on either side of the road. Another *Panzerfaust* shell exploded in the midst of the F Company platoons.

The flare died down, but the fire continued. I heard the trampling of many feet and the rattle of equipment on the other side of the highway. I saw the sparks from another ascending flare, and it burst in the air immediately above us. I blinked my eyes to erase the temporary blindness and looked across the highway. The men from F Company were running rapidly to the rear. I looked behind me. I was alone with my forward CP group. The men from my 3d Platoon had turned and were streaking toward the rear.

I sprang to my knees.

"Good God, Barnes! Get those men stopped!" I yelled.

My cry was lost in another flurry of machine-gun fire. Wesmiller pulled me to the ground, and tracer bullets whistled inches above our heads.

The radio sputtered. "Hello, G six, this is Whit. For God's sake get somebody up here to help us. There's Germans all over the goddamned place."

I grasped the speaker from Wesmiller's outstretched hand. "Whit, this is Mac," I said. "They caught us halfway across this open field. The men have taken off. I'll have to go back and get them to come up. Over."

"For God's sake, get us some help quick." He was frantic. "We're completely surrounded. Roger. Out."

We turned toward the road and crawled on our hands and knees. Another flare exploded above us, and we flattened ourselves on the ground. The Germans started firing again. The raised roadbed was no protection with the fire on both sides of the road.

The flare died out, and we crawled again toward the rear, squirming forward slowly on our bellies beneath a low curtain of small-arms fire. Another *Panzerfaust* shell exploded on the highway. We crawled faster. A wooden paling fence that joined the end of the brick wall beside the road loomed ahead of us, a shallow depression that could hardly be called a ditch running along the fence. I crawled into it and pushed forward to allow room for the men behind me to move single file into the shallow depression.

Another flare went up. I wondered if they could see the

big radio strapped to Wesmiller's back above the green shoots of grain that waved back and forth in the breeze. I raised my head high enough to look over the low grain toward the houses beyond the field. I could see black figures running back and forth along the walls of the houses. I suddenly realized that there was no one between us and the Germans. If this was a counterattack, they might not stop until they had smashed into Gundorf.

One of the artillerymen pried loose the bottom crossboard of the wooden fence, and we crawled through quickly. We waited for a lull in the firing and then sprang to our feet and ran toward the rear. The fenced area was a garden, and we came to a lone house in the center and halted behind the cover of the house.

Captain Calhoun was explaining the situation over the radio to Colonel Smith. I thought they would never stop talking. I wanted desperately to talk to Whitman again to find out the situation. Townsend tried to get Lieutenant Bagby on the platoon radio, but with no success. He contacted Sergeant Barnes, and I told him to join us in the garden with his platoon and the Weapons Platoon.

The battalion radio was silent. I called for Lieutenant Whitman, and his voice came through weakly, as though he were speaking in a stage whisper. "I'm back on the left side of the highway," he said, "in a house. I've got nine men with me. Germans are running around all over the place. I lost track of all the other men . . . heard some of them surrendering. Get us some help quick or they'll find us when they start searching the houses."

My own support platoon seemed pitifully inadequate to counterattack against an enemy force which must be as large as a company. My mind was already filled with thoughts of the pitiful remnants of the 1st and 2d Platoons we might eventually extract from the buildings, and I did not want to see any more of my company annihilated. If battalion would order F Company to counterattack—none of their men had reached the buildings on the right, and they must have gotten out intact.

But Colonel Smith refused my suggestion. Committing F Company would leave Gundorf undefended except for my one rifle platoon and my Weapons Platoon. I told him I thought a counterattack with my one platoon would be foolish.

"Put your platoon in the defense on the left of the road," he decided, "And I'll have Fox dig in on the right. I'm coming right up with Easy Company, and we'll work up a counterattack some way."

I asked Whitman if he had heard the conversation. He said he had.

"There's only one thing to do then," he continued. "If we have to wait that long, they're sure to find us. We'll go down to the cellar and you start plastering us with artillery fire. We're inside, and the Kraut are out in the open. We'll help you direct the fire from here."

I knew his decision called for a generous amount of fortitude, even though he would be partially protected in the cellar. Lieutenant Reed set up his artillery radio, and artillery gave us a priority mission.

Sergeant Barnes arrived with his platoon and the machine-gun section. I sent them into position along with a platoon of heavy machine guns from H Company.

"To hell with the ammunition," I said. "We'll get more from somewhere. Spray hell out of the whole area."

The machine guns opened up, and artillery whistled overhead, thundering into the open field dangerously close to the paling fence at the end of the garden.

"Three hundred short!" Lieutenant Reed yelled into his radio. "Three hundred short!"

The artillery whistled overhead again and plummeted into the houses beyond us with a terrific roar. Orange flames lit the darkness like flashes of lightning.

"That's right on top of us!" Whitman cried, delighted. "Let 'er go again! We can hear Germans running all over the place outside."

Lieutenant Reed called for barrage after barrage, and the big shells roared into the objective. The Germans made feeble efforts at retaliation with their machine guns, but the shots died away in the explosion of the big artillery shells. A direct hit transformed a house into a mass of roaring flames.

"Is that your house?" I asked Whitman, half fearfully.

"No. . . . seems to be on our left," he answered. "Give us another volley in the same place. Sounds like a tank or some kind of armored car pulled up."

Lieutenant Reed called for a repeat volley.

"That hit just right," Whitman said. His voice was

scarcely audible over the radio. I wondered what had happened to his radio and was afraid that perhaps the batteries were going dead, and we would lose our only means of communication.

"I can't talk loud," he said. "I've got fifteen Kraut prisoners down here in the cellar with me, and some Germans have come in upstairs. We can hear them walking around. If one of these prisoners so much as opens his mouth, I'll plug him."

25

"WANT TO CAPTURE LEIPZIG?"

I held my breath awaiting Whitman's next transmission. I could visualize enemy soldiers tossing hand grenades upon the frightened little group in the cellar. Perhaps there would be no next transmission. Perhaps one of the prisoners would cry out and reveal their location to their comrades in the house above them. The nine frightened men were all I had left of two platoons. *Dear God, don't let them get them too.*

But Whitman did radio again. "They've gone," he said, and I was alive with relief. "We held our guns on the prisoners and told them if they made a sound, we'd let them have it right through the heads."

A slow, drizzling rain began to fall, adding to the night chill and making me shiver. I knew the men in the defensive position along the paling fence must be miserable.

A lieutenant stepped from the darkness, and I recognized Lieutenant Bagby. I felt as if I had seen a ghost. For all I knew he was dead or taken prisoner in the mêlée around the factory.

"I couldn't reach you with my platoon radio, and I lost Whit," he said. "I was heading back with my radio operator to contact you when the Kraut opened up. I was half-way across the field and couldn't get back, so I came out with F Company."

He did not know what had happened to his platoon. I prayed that some miracle might have happened, but I could not convince myself that they were not all casualties or prisoners.

Colonel Smith arrived in Gundorf and radioed for me to keep up the artillery and machine-gun fire. K Company was arriving to take over the defense of Gundorf, and when they arrived, E and F Companies would counter-attack and continue the drive into the city. That should be around three o'clock.

Lieutenant Reed tirelessly continued to direct artillery against the houses and the factory, one round at a time now to conserve ammunition and keep up continuous fire until time for the counterattack. The machine guns fired sporadically.

I was drenched to the skin by the rain and trembling from the cold, and I thought three o'clock would never come. The minutes dragged into hours, and the hours dragged on until it was at last three o'clock and E and F were ready to move out, and I should lift my artillery fire, and I would soon know what was left of my company.

I waited breathlessly while the two companies moved across the open ground around the flank, coming in on the objective from the north, but the situation was strangely quiet. The artillery and machine-gun fire had evidently driven the Germans away.

Lieutenant Heitzman's voice came over the battalion radio like music to my ears. "We've got Lieutenant Whit-man out, and we found Sergeant Campbell from George Company's 1st Platoon in another cellar with thirty men. They're heading back to Gundorf now."

Sergeant Campbell and thirty men! With Lieutenant Whitman and the nine men with him, and Lieutenant Bagby and his radio oprator, that would make forty-three. I tried to remember how many men we had had in the two platoons, but I only knew that their number was approximately fifty. Or was it more? But I could hope that the others would turn up later somehow. There was no time for worry now. I had forty-three more men than I had thought vaguely possible.

We moved back into Gundorf and the men went to sleep in houses for the remaining hour until daylight. I was suddenly aware that I was ravenously hungry, but there was no food available. I tried to catch a few min-utes sleep, but a call came for me from Colonel Smith.

"Heitzman and Calhoun are moving on in at dawn," the Colonel said. "They'll jump off at six. I want you to be ready to follow them at six-thirty. Forget about breakfast. We'll get it up at the first halt."

Eight more men arrived from the 2d Platoon. They had

been in the factory but had made it out with F Company.
I tried again to determine how many men were missing,
and with the help of Sergeant Quinn, narrowed the number down to six.

It was not long until dawn. I decided not to try to sleep
again. It would be more difficult to wake up after sleeping
for a few minutes than to stay awake. Fatigue gnawed
at every muscle of my body, and I was hungry.

A platoon of tanks clattered down the highway to join
the two assault companies.

I formed the company at 6:30 and moved down the
highway. The surroundings looked unfamiliar in the light
of day. The street was littered with fallen wires and
broken branches from the freshly-green trees. The fire
from the house which had burned still smoldered. The
windows in the houses stared back at me blankly with
shattered eyes that had been window-panes.

The buildings along the street grew in height and densi-
ty until we knew that at last we were in the outskirts of
Leipzig. Civilians formed in thick bunches as if to watch
a parade.

A voice beckoned me from an open window, and I
recognized a soldier from battalion headquarters. The
Colonel was inside and wanted to see me. I halted the
column, and the men sat down on the edges of the sidewalks, unperturbed by the unabashed stares of the curious
civilians.

Inside the building the Colonel and the battalion staff
were eating breakfast. The sight startled me at first and I
said a bad word to myself. The pursuit of the war could
not wait long enough for the rifle companies to eat, but
there was time for battalion headquarters to breakfast in
the luxury of a house that the sweat of the rifle companies had taken. I passed it off as another of the injus-
tices to which we had become accustomed.

"I've got good news for you first," the Colonel said. "F
Company found three of your men in a German hospital
across the street this morning . . . only slightly wounded.
The Krauts took them prisoner last night."

That would leave only three men missing, I figured
quickly. I was half-overcome with happiness, but I
strangely wanted to cry.

"These men say the Germans took three other men

prisoner at the same time," the Colonel continued, "but the other three weren't wounded, and they lost track of them when they were left here in the hospital."

I looked down so the Colonel would not see the tears forming in my eyes. The strain and lack of sleep had left me strangely emotional, and the news of the men whom I had at one time given up for lost filled me with a warm foolish feeling that bubbled up inside.

The Colonel took out his map. "E and F Companies are approximately here now," he said, pointing. "I want you to continue down the street until it crosses a hodge-podge of railroad tracks. Take the street to the northeast to the point where the street joins this boulevard. Hold your company there and send a patrol forward to secure the three railroad bridges across two small canals and the main canal. Our orders are to secure all bridges and hold up at the main canal while another division comes up from the south and takes the main part of the city."

I judged from the map that the route to the northeast separated us at least a mile from the remainder of the battalion, and the area from the boulevard to the bridges was dense woods. I did not like the plan, and the Colonel agreed that he did not like to commit us that far from the remainder of the battalion, but there was no alternative.

I rejoined the company outside and moved down the street, passing a dead German soldier on a street corner beside his overturned motorcycle. We moved faster than the assault elements, and I could see the tail of the forward companies as we reached the railroad tracks and took the turn to the left.

The 2d and 3d Platoons fanned out into an approach-march formation on either side of the side street, and we reached the boulevard. I dispatched the 3d Platoon up the railroad track as a patrol to secure the bridges. The raised tracks ran like a giant double steel arrow through the woods, now green and heavy with spring foliage. The other platoons began to search the impressive villas on the right of the tracks for stray Germans. I watched anxiously as the 3d Platoon moved toward the first bridge a quarter of a mile away.

Barnes radioed that he had reached the first bridge, and there was no opposition. His men were beginning to cross. Then I heard the sound of small-arms fire to the front, and the tiny figures that were the last of Barnes' men scurried from the tracks to the concealment of the woods on either side.

"There's a group o' buildings a hundred yards past the bridge," he radioed. "Seem to be a few Germans inside, and they opened fire when we started across the bridge. We're movin' on in."

An occasional shot sounded from far up the tracks. I wanted to ask again what was going on, but I knew continual chatter over the radio was maddening when engaged in a fire fight. If anything serious developed, Barnes would call me.

Captain Byrd radioed a change of orders. "We're to cross the canal now and hold up there," he said. "Fox has a patrol down at the main bridge but has run into trouble. Take your entire company on across the canal."

I alerted the remainder of the company and led them into the woods.

Barnes reported again over the platoon radio. "We chased the Kraut outa the buildin's," he drawled. "We're now on a little hill that looks like a garbage dump about fifty yards beyond the buildin's."

"Roger," I answered. "Hold up there until we reach the first canal. We're coming up behind you, and there's no need of your getting too far out front."

We reached the banks of the small canal, and I saw that the area to our front was open on the left of the tracks except for two small concrete buildings and a white knoll twenty feet high beyond them. The knoll had evidently been formed by years of dumping a big city's garbage and ashes. The woods continued in a mass of dense green undergrowth on the right.

I talked with Barnes again on the radio. He said he could see the second railroad bridge not over seventy-five yards beyond the white knoll and the third bridge over the main canal two hundred yards beyond the second. "But if anybody moves across the railroad tracks, they get shot at from the second bridge," he said.

I decided to commit but one platoon until the enemy's strength beyond the second bridge was determined, so I ordered Barnes to continue forward. We fired several volleys of artillery beyond the second bridge before he

moved out. The big shells whistled overhead and exploded to the front, and I saw the riflemen rise and start
forward.

Then I heard a flurry of small-arms fire when the platoon crossed the crest of the dump, and stray bullets
whined across the canal. I heard Barnes' men open fire.
The small-arms fire grew in intensity, and then all was
quiet again, broken only by the sound of an occasional
shot or a short burst of automatic fire.

"There's a garden or something near the last bridge,"
Barnes reported. "We can't pick up the damned Krauts for
the bushes. I'm at the foot of the dump pile on the other
side, but we can't get any farther. I've got two men
wounded. One can walk, but I'll need a litter for the other
one."

There seemed only one thing to do now, commit at
least one other platoon. I sent the 2d across the canal on
the right of the bridge to come up abreast of the 3d
through the cover of the woods. I led the other two platoons under the bridge and across the shallow canal on
stepping-stones of rocks, telling Lieutenant Bagby to place
his platoon in position atop the dump to protect our left
flank. I reported our situation to battalion.

"I've contacted regiment," Colonel Smith replied.
"They're sending K Company up to hold in the woods
around the first bridge to protect your rear."

I was relieved by the news. Strangely, I was not particularly worried about the enemy situation to our front
—the whole thing seemed lazy and unexciting—but the
possibility of enemy forces approaching unseen through
the woods to our rear was of great concern. I thought we
could take care of the resistance to our front in a matter
of time; from the sound of the firing, it appeared to be
only a few snipers and one automatic weapon.

I saw the 2d Platoon move into position along the forward edge of the underbrush on the right of the tracks,
the riflemen firing occasional shots to their front. Enemy
bullets whined through the area at intervals to attest to
the fact that it was unsafe to venture across the open
tracks.

Sergeant Barnes shuffled slowly across the crest of the
dump. Beside him the platoon aid man walked, half-

supporting another soldier who had a bandage strapped to his right side. Sniper bullets whined around them, but this did not seem to alter their pace.

I moved forward and met them on the reverse slope of the dump. "I called battalion for a litter," I told him, "but so far it hasn't come. Two of the Weapons Platoon men can take him back to the edge of town. Our jeeps can take him from there."

We moved to the crest of the dump heap, and I could see the area to our front clearly, but there was no sign of the enemy. I saw the narrow ribbon of water that was the first canal and the wooden railway trestle across it. The area beyond was open except for many clusters of small bushes and the garden on the right of the tracks. I could not see the water in the second, and larger, canal, but there was another bridge, and beyond the banks of the canal on the left was an orchard. On the right was a sports park with the back of a wooden grandstand facing us. The area on the right between the canals was open for six hundred yards before the canals joined and became one. The woods began again on the other side of the larger canal.

The obvious solution to being unable to advance frontally against the unseen enemy was to send a flanking platoon around the right, having them enter the woods and come in on the defenders from the flank and rear, but I balked at the thought of sending one platoon such a great distance, when, for all I knew, the woods beyond the canals might be thick with enemy. I decided to cover our front with artillery and have two platoons try to advance frontally, and I notified the 2d and 3d Platoons to be ready to move forward under cover of the artillery barrage.

But the enemy came suddenly to life when the riflemen rose to go forward and repulsed three efforts to advance.

I could discern that the lead platoons were not exerting their greatest efforts to advance; at least, they were not going forward recklessly. If they had tried as they had in the past, they could have advanced even without artillery support against this small resistance, but there would have been casualties, and I knew the men were tired and sleepy and hungry. Battalion was exerting no particular pressure on us to hurry our advance, so I was content to let the afternoon pass slowly and quietly for the moment.

One volley of artillery was over the target and crashed into the grandstand in the sports park beyond the farthest canal. An ear-splitting explosion shook the dump heap, and the wind whipped the dust into our faces. I wiped my eyes and saw that a huge black curl of smoke was billowing skyward above the sports park. Another deafening explosion shook the little man-made hill and another cloud of smoke billowed skyward. We decided that the Germans must have some type of explosives stored in the sports park.

The afternoon wore on, and I became more and more conscious of the gnawing hunger deep in my stomach. I knew the men must be famished, but at least we were resting, even if it was under fire.

Then battalion began to call. The other two companies were making progress against the main bridge. Did I think we could move forward?

The sun was beginning to slide gently toward the horizon in rear of us, and I knew I had to do something. Our orders were to cross the large canal before night. I would have to send a platoon around the flank to come in through the woods in the enemy's rear.

I sent Whitman the spare 300 radio and ordered him across the canal. He moved out quickly, and far to the right I could see his men emerge from the woods and wade across the first canal, the water coming to the necks of the shorter man. My fear of a larger enemy force in the woods overcame my fear for the safety of our left flank, and I ordered Lieutenant Bagby's platoon to follow the flanking force.

We could see the little dots that were Whitman's men emerge from the woods and double-time toward the garden. Lieutenant Reed stopped the artillery fire. The 3d Platoon to my front began to advance, and I knew it was only a matter of minutes until the objective would be ours.

I signalled the CP group, and we moved to the railroad tracks and on toward the bridge, past three wounded Germans lying helplessly in the gulley beside the tracks where Barnes' men had evidently shot them early in the day.

The enemy automatic weapon suddenly opened up again at the 3d Platoon, but the men were close enough now to pick up the bush from which it was firing. They fired round after round into the clump of bushes, and the weapon was silent.

The platoons had completed wiping out the delaying force and were lying around resting when I arrived at the last bridge. The men from the 1st and 2d Platoons were soaked from wading the smaller canal.

With my CP group I moved past the sports park in the direction of the woods and a house that showed on my map. In the sports park we saw that our artillery had set off two five-hundred-pound bombs, part of a large collection of unexploded bombs that had evidently been dropped on the city by our air forces.

The woods turned out to be a park, a paved road winding gracefully in and out of the trees.

The house, which I decided would house the mortar section and the CP group, turned out to have electricity and two bathrooms. I wanted to call Lieutenant Bagby and ask him if he had a bathroom, but I could not bring myself to do it, since I knew the 1st Platoon would be sleeping in the open that night.

One company jeep and the artillery jeep arrived over a trail through the woods from the direction of the main bridge across the Pleisse-Elster Canal. Colonel Smith came up later to check our position, the battalion wire section laid a telephone wire, and the kitchen jeep arrived with a hot supper.

Dusk was gathering and I had finished eating when Lieutenant Whitman and Staff Sergeant Joe Weylandt, who as a Pfc. had given me my first German pistol in Heimbach, arrived with the kitchen jeep on its return trip. They called me outside, and I saw that they had a German lieutenant with them, but I was surprised to see that the lieutenant still carried his pistol.

"What gives?" I asked.

Whitman was aglow with suppressed excitement, and his shining boyish face glowed pleasantly. Weylandt was none the less excited. I knew that something insane must be about to happen, but I was hardly prepared for Whitman's question.

"Want to capture Leipzig?" he asked.

"Do I want to what?" I asked incredulously.

"Just what I said," Whitman continued. "This is an *Oberleutnant* from Leipzig . . ."—the German bowed and smiled stupidly at the reference—". . . and his CG wants to surrender the city . . . without a fight!"

The men from company headquarters and the Weapons Platoon were gathered around, straining for every word. They suddenly broke out with a chorus of enthusiasm for the prospects of this crazy scheme.

I motioned for them to be quiet, and Whitman continued: "You know those big buildings that rise up out of the orchard about a mile in front of my platoon? Well, civilians began to stream down the road toward us while we were eating supper. They gathered around and started jabbering away, wanting us to go back into town with them. They said this German major there wanted to surrender with six-hundred men.

"Well, Weylandt and I walked back into town with a bunch of them, and they took us to the police station. We talked to the major. He not only wanted to surrender his six hundred men, but he said his commanding general would surrender the whole goddamned city if I'd go back and get my CO."

There seemed to be no doubt among the CP group that I would go, even at this embryonic stage of the proceedings. They talked excitedly and clamored to be included in the group that would go with me.

"Now wait a minute," I said. "Does he know I'm just a captain? Will he surrender to a captain?"

"Yeah, we told him that," Whitman said, "but he said it doesn't matter. A captain's good enough. The *Oberleutnant* here came along so you'd believe us. He'll tell you." He spoke to the German officer in German mixed with gestures, mostly gestures, and the *Oberleutnant* looked at me and smiled widely, shaking his head up and down and saying, *"Jawohl! Jawohl! Ist gut! Ist gut!"*

It was hard to resist. My decision seemed to have been made already by the men around me. I was tired and sleepy, and I had no desire to go wandering around in cities that hadn't been captured—particularly not at this time of night. Someone said, "It might look good in the papers." I fell victim to the spontaneous excitement of the men around me, and, against my better judgment, I nodded my assent.

"I'll go," I said, "but I'll have to get an OK from battalion first."

I went inside the house to telephone Colonel Smith, and Whitman followed me.

"I'll talk to him if he says 'no,'" Whitman said. "You've just gotta go, Cap'n. It's on the level. I swear it is. I can tell by the way the whole set-up looks. You've got to go."

The Colonel was not in at battalion. I talked with Major Joseph. He thought I was joking at first, but I finally convinced him. I'll have to talk to regiment," he said.

We waited a few minutes while he called regiment, and Whitman told me more details about the adventure. We grew impatient. Darkness was falling fast. I called battalion again.

"The Colonel's out at regiment," Major Joseph said, "but they've called division. Regiment will call me back in a few minutes."

We hung up. The men around me were impatient and were already deciding where they were going to sit in the jeep that would take us in. I said I would take both our company jeep and the artillery jeep and a 300 radio for communication to my CP. They could transmit the messages to battalion.

I called battalion again.

"Regiment hasn't heard from division," Major Joseph said. "I think they called corps for a decision. Wait a minute and I'll call regiment again. You can talk to the exec."

I waited while the operator got the regimental executive officer on the phone. I knew I would have to do some fancy talking, particularly since this thing was already up to corps headquarters. I wondered what General Eisenhower would say if he heard about it.

I explained the situation to the regimental exec. ". . . and we can't wait much longer, sir. It's getting almost too dark now."

"All right," the executive officer said. "Keep in touch with your battalion and go ahead. Let us know how you come out."

I gulped. Now that I had the necessary authority I almost wished they had refused. But there would be no refusing the excited soldiers around me. They rushed to get seats on the two jeeps.

I told Harms to come with me as interpreter and Wesmiller to carry the 300 radio. I had to tell the majority of the other men that they would be left behind. The jeeps were too crowded. Lieutenant Whitman and Lieutenant Reed came with me, and the German *Oberleutnant* took a seat in full view on the right front fender of the lead jeep.

We debated whether we should carry a white flag, and then decided that would look as if *we* were surrendering, which we most certainly were *not*.

I took my place and signalled for the other jeep to follow. The men from the rifle platoons waved and cheered us as we passed.

I was not afraid, but I was tremendously excited. I was about to accept the surrender of Germany's fifth largest city and one of the most important prizes left to American forces in Europe. I was staggered with the import of our mission.

Pardon me, Herr General, but even now the forces of Company G lay siege to your fortress city. Would you care to surrender, please?

26

I DO NOT CAPTURE LEIPZIG

The buildings rose abruptly from the far end of the orchard: tall, straight, closely-knit apartment houses rising against a rapidly darkening sky. The road was lined with curious civilians streaming toward the railroad bridge to see the fabled Americans, forcing our jeep to progress at a snail-like pace along the narrow road.

The narrow chasm formed by the towering buildings was darker than the open orchard, and the early evening wind whistled around us. The streets seemed deserted compared to the mass of people who had lined the road through the orchard, but here and there a group of civilians stopped to stare at us, and some to wave cheerfully. I was relieved to see them for we had come to know that where there were civilians there was usually no opposition.

Whitman directed the jeep driver to the police station, an imposing three-story public building which, with its surrounding grounds, occupied an entire block at the end of the street. A tall iron grill fence enclosed the grounds, and we drew up to a gate in the fence where two Germans in uniform stood guard.

Civilians appeared from every direction and crowded around us, jabbering excitedly and curiously and examining the jeeps and our equipment as if we had been men from Mars. The news that the Americans had come and the city was to be surrendered seemed to be spreading quickly. German soldiers who passed on the sidewalks, their weapons slung over their shoulders or about their waists, would stop abruptly at the sight of civilians gathered around the two jeeps, their mouths dropping open in astonishment at the sight of our OD uniforms.

They would stare for a moment and casually shrug their shoulders and walk on, as if to say, "What a hell of a war."

Another group of Americans joined the circle of civilians around the jeeps. Their faces were so pale that I wondered if there was any blood in them at all. Their bodies were thin as though they had done without proper food for many months. All seven walked on crutches. Some had bandages around their feet or legs. Others were amputees. Their comrades were twenty Britishers and Frenchmen in much the same condition. Tears streamed down their faces as our GIs smothered them with cigarettes and K-rations. They had been prisoners of war, some of them since the breakthrough in the Ardennes.

"We're in the hospital across the street," one of them said. "They moved everybody who could walk two days ago, but they left us behind."

Whitman and Sergeant Weylandt took command of the situation at the gate, and the smiling, smartly-uniformed guards opened the gates when Whitman's broken German told them that *"Der Kommandant"* had arrived to effect the surrender. I told Harms to come with me, and the other men remained with the vehicles.

We passed through the gate and to the rear of the building, past uniformed Germans who smiled insipid smiles at us as we passed. As we neared the entrance to the building, three German officers walked stiffly toward us.

"The tall one . . . that's the major," Whitman said. "He's the one who says they'll surrender."

The officers were immaculately groomed, their uniforms stiffly pressed and their boots brilliantly shined. The jaunty officer caps sat erectly on their heads, their smoothly shaven faces shining beneath them. I was suddenly conscious of my own shabby appearance. I felt my beard, unshaven in at least a week, my face and hands unwashed for two days, my uniform a dirty, ill-fitting combination, and my combat boots covered with the dust of the city dump.

I wondered whether I should salute. I could remember nothing in the Army manuals that had described the decorum of accepting a formal enemy surrender, particularly in the stronghold of the enemy. I decided that it would

be best to salute anything that closely resembled an officer. I stopped a few paces from the major, tried my best
to make my rough heels click and found myself imitating
the stiff stance of the Germans and flinging a sharp, high
salute that I hoped showed no element of subservience.

The German major returned the salute and proffered
his hand. The move startled me, and he must have seen
my discomposure. I had no desire to shake hands with a
German officer, but I tried to recover quickly and grasped
his hand firmly, if not warmly. He said a few words in
German and motioned toward the entrance of the building. I swung into step beside him, and the two lesser
officers joined the group that was with me. I found myself
unconsciously imitating the stiff military bearing of the
Germans, but my shabby appearance must have belied my
efforts.

The major led us upstairs. He opened a door on the
second floor and motioned for me to enter. I went inside.
The room was small but luxuriously furnished with up-
holstered chairs and a deep rug. An attractive girl and
another group of officers rose when I entered. The major
began to introduce me to the officers, pausing for me to
say my name. I smiled profusely as a substitute for saluting, which I decided would be out of place inside, but I
tried to imitate the smart clicking of heels and slight bow
of the Germans when they were introduced.

We sat down, and the room became a confused jumble
of mixed languages. The major tried to talk to me in
German, and when I said *"nicht verstehe,"* he called the
girl to translate for him. Her English was weak, so I sum-
moned Harms. Whitman was not content to be excluded
from the conversation, and he broke in at intervals with
scrambled German and English that made the Germans
roar with laughter. His shining face and boyish laughter
were infectious, and he had evidently made quite an im-
pression on his first visit. Whitman, to these Germans at
least, was a card.

The scrambled conversation was getting us no place, so
I cautioned Whitman to be quiet. I made out the German major's story from the mixed translations of Harms
and the German girl.

He and his men, he said, were not German soldiers,
even though their uniforms, military customs and weapons

were practically identical. They were policemen of the Leipzig police force, 2,500 strong, with six hundred quartered at this particular station, the Gohlis section of Leipzig. The city was filled with displaced persons and German civilians, and they wanted to avoid any fighting, if possible. He knew that Germany was *kaput* and nothing was to be gained by making a battleground of the city.

The Commanding General of the police force was of the same opinion and was willing to guarantee that there would be no fighting by the policemen and civilians, if we would assure them there would be no shooting on our part and the policemen would retain control of the civilians even after our entry.

I began to think that this man was a bit absurd, if he and his superiors only controlled the civilians and the police. There was no guarantee about the *Wehrmacht*.

The commanding general had absolutely no control over the *Wehrmacht*, I ascertained when I questioned the major. But most of the soldiers had left the city that morning. He did not think we would have much to worry about in the soldiers. But he could not promise anything.

I saw my dreams of newspaper headlines fading, and I knew General Eisenhower would be very disappointed in me. These Germans wanted us to say that we would not shoot, but they could not assure us that the German soldiers would not fight. The people were insane!

But I was not willing to give up. We argued back and forth for what seemed like hours. Finally, the major offered a suggestion.

"I will take you to see the general," Harms translated.

He called for an orderly and sent a message for his car, dispatching a second orderly for cognac. The orderly returned with cocktail glasses on a silver tray, and the major poured drinks around. I decided that I must be quite mad. My wildest dreams had never envisioned a social hour with a group of German officers—and certainly not with the Germans as hosts.

The orderly returned shortly with the information that the car awaited us outside. I told Whitman to take charge of the group remaining at the police station until I should return, and we went outside where the chauffeur waited with a luxurious Mercedes-Benz. I climbed into the back seat with Harms and a German lieutenant, and the major sat up front with the chauffeur. The big car rolled easily across the grounds and out a back gate and around to the front of the police station.

The major turned around and spoke to me in German, pointing to windows high up in the apartment buildings. Civilians were turning on their lights without blackout curtains. The word of the surrender was spreading, for better or for worse. Now the war was surely over for Leipzig. I found myself forgetting my earlier disappointment when I had found that only the police were ready to surrender. Perhaps something could be made of the situation, after all.

"*Ist gut! Ist gut!*" the major exclaimed, laughing and pointing to the lighted windows.

"*Ja,*" I answered, running the gamut of my German vocabulary. "*Ist gut. Ist gut.*"

The big car rolled easily on as the chauffeur pressed on the gas. Darkness had completely fallen.

I had not the slightest idea where we were going, except that I was to confer with the commanding general near the center of the city. I wondered if we had to pass through any German Army defenses to reach our destination, but I was not particularly afraid of trouble with German sentries. The police officers evidently commanded the same respect as regular *Wehrmacht* officers, and I felt relatively safe from the *Wehrmacht* while in their company.

I involuntarily sank lower in the deep back seat, however, when a German sentry stopped us in the middle of the dark street. I wondered what would be his reaction should he see two Americans in the back of the automobile, but he asked no questions. He wanted to tell us that it was impossible to go up the street we were following. The Americans were firing artillery. We could not reach the center of town by this route.

The driver turned the big car around and retraced our route toward the Gohlis police station.

"Perhaps the telephone lines are not out, and we can telephone the general," the major said, and Harms translated for me. Perhaps I could contact American headquarters on my radio and have them stop the artillery fire?

From what little I had been able to determine about

the direction in which we had been travelling, we had been driving toward the southeast. That would be the 69th Division sector. Getting artillery fire stopped there would necessitate contacting corps headquarters. I talked with Wesmiller when we stopped again at the police station, however, but he had been unable to reach battalion. First Lieutenant George W. Payne, of Indianapolis, Ind., the battalion intelligence officer, had come into town in another jeep, and he volunteered to return to battalion headquarters to get a stronger radio.

We went inside to a large room on the first floor where the major said we should wait while he telephoned the General. Lieutenant Whitman was entertaining a group of German enlisted men from the police force and had evidently not been idle while I was gone. Someone's cognac bottle had suffered.

The Germans were fascinated by the Indianhead on our 2d Division shoulder patches. Whitman found a blanket to wrap around his body, and placing his fingers behind his head to indicate feathers, he did a war dance around the room.

"Me Indian!" he cried. "Me Indian! Woo—woo—woo —woo—woo!"

The Germans loved it. They laughed uproariously and produced another cognac bottle as if by magic and poured drinks for all of us. Whitman downed his drink in one quick gulp and extended his glass again. The German laughingly obliged.

I took out a package of cigarettes and offered one to the officers. They accepted like children accepting candy from a stranger . . . they felt they really shouldn't but they wanted to so badly. I could not ignore the hungry looks on the faces of the other Germans in the room, and I remembered that I was in an enemy stronghold and perhaps it would be best to court their favor in every possible way. I passed the cigarettes around, hoping perhaps a few would refuse, since the package was almost empty, but there were no refusals. My cigarettes were gone.

Sergeant Weylandt brought in three K-rations from the jeep. The Germans watched in wide-eyed amazement as he and Whitman opened the K-rations and began to eat. Whitman noticed their interest and tossed the extra box to one of the Germans. The others gathered around, chattering wildly. They found a can of chopped ham and eggs and a bar of chocolate in the package. They were wild with delight.

Whitman said, "A prize in every package!"

The major finally completed his telephone call, and Harms and I followed him outside again to the waiting car. I had not the slightest idea how he intended getting past the artillery fire, but he seemed to know what he was doing, and I did not think I was exactly in a position to question his actions. I settled back in the deep rear seat and marvelled at the oddity of the trip—two American soldiers riding unmolested through the streets of Leipzig in a Mercedes-Benz driven by a German chauffeur and with two German officers as travelling companions, their jaunty caps silhouetted against the dark windshield.

The car rolled slowly down the dark deserted streets, past a section of town with bomb-gutted buildings and wrecked trolley cars. Debris filled the streets, and the chauffeur drove slowly to avoid large bomb craters in the street. We passed the gutted area, and the buildings thinned out, and I realized we had entered a park. The dense trees growing on either side of the curving road reminded me of the park where my company CP occupied the lone house.

I heard a sudden command of "Halt!" and saw a soldier standing beside the car, rifle at the ready position. The chauffeur jammed on the brakes. For a moment I tried to push deeper into the recesses of the back seat to avoid being seen. Then I saw the shape of the soldier's helmet, and a glint of moonlight revealed the uniform he was wearing. *These crazy Krauts have driven us smack into our own lines!*

The soldier sentry was saying something about dismount, and I flung open the back door and jumped out to face the muzzle of an M1 rifle pointed at my stomach.

"I'm Captain MacDonald, G Company," I said quickly, the words rolling off my tongue in an effort to identify myself before the soldier should shoot. "That's 23d Infantry. I'm with these German officers to try to get the city to surrender. This is my interpreter with me. For God's sake, don't shoot!" I talked on until the soldier seemed convinced.

"This is E Company, Cap'n," he said, finally, dropping

his rifle to his side. "They told us at the company CP that you might be through tonight, but I just had to make sure."

"Thank gosh for that," I said. "I don't know what possessed these crazy people to come through our lines. We're headed for the center of the city."

"I'd suggest you drive slow, Cap'n," the soldier said. "We've got guards all along this road. F Company is in some buildings just beyond us."

I told Harms to ride on the fender of the car. Perhaps that would identify us before someone should shoot. The major suggested that the German lieutenant ride on the other fender and carry a white flag. I agreed. We climbed back into the car and moved again down the curving street, more slowly than before, expecting at any moment to hear the bark of another sentry.

My imagination began to run wild, and I wondered if all the sentries would wait to challenge. BARs and M1 rifles could be deadly weapons. I wondered if we had to pass the Negro platoon from F Company. The memory of what they had done to the German staff car in Hameln beside the Weser River made me shudder.

Another sentry on the right of the road yelled, "Halt!" and I wondered how a man could put so much menace and foreboding into one word. Harms jumped from the fender and was explaining our presence before I could open the back door to join him. The soldier seemed convinced, and began to lower his rifle, but another soldier ran from the darkness to join him.

"Wait a minute," the new arrival said. "What the hell! This might be a trick. You'd better make damned sure who this is."

I broke into another hurried explanation of who I was and what I was doing. I mentioned the name of every officer in battalion headquarters and E Company. That convinced them, and we climbed back in and on the car and moved slowly forward again.

The park changed into another residential district with tall apartment houses, and I knew we must be in F Company's sector. I shuddered again at the thought of what the Negro platoon might do and waited expectantly to be challenged again, but not a sound except the steady hum of our motor broke the night stillness. I saw a tank destroyer hunched beside the buildings on the right of the street, its muzzle pointed in the direction we were going. I motioned for the driver to go even more slowly. I didn't want to have trouble with this baby.

I held my breath, but no sound came from the TD, and we passed. The car rolled on through the darkness and began to pick up speed again. I exhaled my breath in a long sigh. Strangely, I felt better. We were back in German territory again.

The driver turned up a street to the southeast, and the apartment buildings gave way to fire-gutted public buildings. The major spoke, and I gathered from occasional words and motions of his hands that we were approaching the heart of the city. Almost all of it had been destroyed by American incendiary bombs. We would soon be at the general's office.

The chauffeur turned to the right up a narrow side street, and we found ourselves beneath an arched roof lit by a dim blue blackout light. A uniformed German sentry snapped to attention and raised his right hand in the Nazi salute.

"Heil Hitler!"

He opened the door of the car stiffly, and the major alighted and returned the salute. He indicated the rear door. The orderly opened the door as stiffly as before, and I stepped out. The major said a few words in German, and the sentry bowed from the waist and opened a door leading into the building on our right. I followed with Harms and the other German officer.

We found ourselves in a well lighted corridor. Guards, stationed at intervals along the walls, snapped to attention as we passed, giving stiff *"Heil Hitler"* salutes. The major and the lieutenant returned the salutes without stopping. I wondered what the guards thought of the appearance of the two disheveled Americans, but the stony expressions on their faces told me nothing.

A stiff guard at the end of the corridor gave the Nazi salute and indicated that we should follow him, as if he had been specially stationed there to wait for us. He led us up a gracefully curving marble staircase into a room on the second floor.

I took in the room at a glance. It was elaborately furnished with a rounded oblong mahogany conference table in the center surrounded by cushioned mahogany chairs. The paneled ceiling was high, and the walls were decoratively and elaborately paneled. The floor, again, was marble.

The major spoke to Harms in German and indicated that we should have a seat. "He says the general will be with us shortly," Harms told me.

I talked with Harms, and the Germans conversed with an orderly. Harms and I shook our heads. If we ever got out of this situation, the others in the company would probably never believe it.

The major barked a command that must have said "Attention," and the general entered. The two officers and the orderly stood stiffly at attention. Harms and I rose quickly. I found myself imitating their stiff military stance without intention. The general gave some command, which must have been "at ease," and entered the room.

I was suddenly conscious of my appearance again. The general was even more immaculately dressed than the others, a long row of military decorations across his chest. His face was round and red and cleanly shaven. A monocle in his right eye gave him an appearance that made me want to congratulate Hollywood on its movie interpretations of high-ranking Nazis.

I wondered if I should salute, but the general's outstretched hand told me differently. I shook his hand and mumbled my name. He indicated three other officers and a brown-suited civilian who entered with him. I shook hands around. The civilian, a slim, elderly grey-haired man who looked like a typical American businessman, explained in English that he was the general's interpreter.

"Before the war I studied at the University of Chicago," he said in impeccable English that bore only a trace of an accent. "When the war began, I was professor of English at the University of Bern, Switzerland."

The general motioned us to have seats. Harms and I sat on the right of the table with the German major and lieutenant who had come with us from Gohlis. The general took his seat at the head of the table, the civilian interpreter on his left, and the other three officers, whom I took to be ranking members of the general's staff, to the left of the interpreter.

The general spoke to the waiting orderly, and I caught

the word "cognac." The orderly clicked his heels sharply and left the room.

I thought the Germans were staring at our shabby appearance, so I told Harms to explain that we were combat soldiers and had had no opportunity to dress for the occasion. The general smiled at the statement, and the civilian interpreter informed me that the general had only been noticing that I was quite young to be a captain. I told him, yes, I was a bit young, but age made no great difference in the American Army, and mentally marked one up for Democracy.

A pretty girl in a stiffly starched white dress entered with a tray loaded with delicate cocktail glasses filled with cognac. My eyes wandered irresisitibly toward her, and the general laughed and spoke to his interpreter.

"You like the *fräulein*, no?" the civilian asked.

The girl smiled shyly and completed placing the cognac before us.

The general stood and raised his glass, proposing a toast in German. We all stood and drank. I wondered if I was drinking to long life for Adolf or what, but I drank.

The conference settled down to its purpose, and the general talked long and rapidly. The civilian interpreter had to break in at intervals to explain to me what the general was saying.

His story proved to be relatively the same as that told me by the major earlier in the evening. He was concerned that there would be no adequate police to control the thousands of displaced persons in Leipzig after the Americans entered, unless we kept his 2,500 policemen in control. He was willing to guarantee that the police and the civilians would not fight, if the Americans would enter the city peacefully, leaving the police with their arms and control of the civilians.

Again my hopes of the city's surrender fell rapidly. What about the *Wehrmacht?*

I told him I was willing to leave my men who were at the Gohlis police station there overnight, if several high German officers would return with me to my battalion headquarters for the night. We would re-enter the city peacefully the next morning, but—he must guarantee that there would be no resistance from the *Wehrmacht* as well as the policemen and civilians.

The general shook his head. It was impossible. He had absolutely no control over the *Wehrmacht* and at this moment did not know where to contact the commanding officer of the soldiers. He did not think there would be any fighting, however, he added quickly. Most of the German soldiers had already evacuated the city.

The conversation went around and around, always returning to the fact that the general could not guarantee there would be no fight from the German Army in Leipzig. His situation became quite clear—he was anxious to keep his police in control, but he had attempted negotiations too early. He should have waited until our forces actually captured the city and then contacted our military government officials.

I looked at my watch and was surprised to see that it was almost midnight. I wondered if my men at the Gohlis police station had given me up. No doubt battalion and regiment—and maybe General Eisenhower?—considered me lost. I had had no communication with them since we first entered the city at dusk.

I wanted to tell the general that the situation was hopeless, but I declined to admit defeat. Also, they might refuse to allow us to return if we said there was nothing we could do about the negotiations. I suggested that he and his staff come with me to my battalion headquarters to contact my commanding officer—the Colonel. The word "colonel" seemed magical, and they rose from the table quickly, ready to go.

We went back down the curving staircase, past the chant of "Heil Hitlers" from the guards in the corridor, to the outside. The general's open-top car was waiting. He indicated the front seat for me, and an orderly opened the door. The general would drive. The civilian interpreter and one of the staff officers rode in the back of the car, and Harms and the German lieutenant took their places on the fenders of the lead auto.

We retraced our route toward F Company's positions. I shuddered again at the thought of what might happen should we run into the Negro platoon, but the prospect of driving head-on into the waiting cannon of the tank destroyer frightened me even more.

When we reached especially dark sections of the street, the general would turn on his headlights briefly to get his bearings. I finally could stand this no longer, and I told the civilian interpreter to tell the general that I thought it best not to turn on the lights. The general complied.

We were upon the TD almost before I realized we were nearing the F Company positions, but I heard no challenge. We turned off the street onto a four-lane drive which I knew must be Frankfurter Street, and we reached the Zeppelin Bridge, across the Pleisse-Elster Canal. Still there was no challenge. We crossed the bridge, past an overturned trolley car which the Germans had used to defend the bridge and into the sector of the city that lay west of the canal.

We were not challenged until we dismounted and reached the door of the battalion CP. The guard recognized me but was amazed to see me in company with the German officers. I left the officers in the entrance downstairs while I went upstairs to look for Colonel Smith, wondering the while if it would be as simple for a German task force to reach the CP without being challenged as it had been for us.

The Colonel was asleep. Major Joseph was on duty and did not want to awaken him. I told him my story and added that I did not think anything was going to come of the surrender negotiations. It appeared that my night's adventure had been for naught.

"I'll go down and talk with them," Major Joseph said. "I've got radio communication with your men in Gohlis now, so call them and have them come on out of the city. If the general wants, I'll send him back to Corps Military Government. They're the only people to handle his case."

I radioed the message for Lieutenant Whitman to bring his men back to our lines. Wesmiller was on the radio. He seemed irritated that they had to pull out. They were all bedded down comfortably for the night in the police station.

I lay down on a sofa upstairs and went to sleep while the major discussed the situation with the Germans downstairs. It seemed that I had no sooner closed my eyes than Major Joseph awakened me.

"I'm keeping the general, the civilian and the staff officers here tonight and sending them on to Corps Military

Government in the morning," he said, "but the general wants you to lead the major and the lieutenant back through our lines so they can telephone the general's office to let them know what became of the old man."

We secured a jeep from battalion and preceded the Mercedes-Benz back across the Zeppelin Bridge and through F Company's sector. The E Company guards challenged us again in the park, but I felt safer this time since the jeep was easily recognizable, and they were more easily convinced who I was. I led the officers back to the bombed sector which we had passed earlier and left them there. The jeep driver carried Harms and me back to my company CP in the edge of the park.

The two bathrooms in my CP were still being overworked when I returned, despite the fact that it was four o'clock in the morning. The men who had been at the police station had returned, and I talked with Wesmiller.

"We were pretty worried about you, Cap'n," he said. "We thought maybe you had run into trouble."

But from his story, I could not see how they had found much time for worry. The Germans had invited them all in for a cognac party in the police station, and except for guards on the jeeps, they had accepted. Whitman had become quite intoxicated and began to insist that it was time for every one to go to bed, and that the German girl who spoke English should sleep with him.

"*Fräulein schlafen mit der Leutnant*," he insisted over and over, ignoring the *fräulein's* emphatic "*nein.*" Wesmiller and the other men became alarmed. They knew that the *fräulein* was the German major's girl, and the situation could become quite hostile.

One of the other German officers broke the tenseness when he suddenly ordered the *fräulein* to "*schaf mit dem Leutnant.*" She seemed to take the order as final and went into a bedroom with Whitman to comply without further protestation.

Whereupon, Whitman passed out immediately.

I crawled into my sleeping bag after a shave and a bath. The events of the night seemed ridiculous and unreal, and I wondered how they could have really happened.

I saw the headlines which I had envisioned when we first started out on the zany mission fading away into nothing. My eyes closed and I was sinking into delightful sleep.

Perhaps later in the day we would attack the city and enter like civilized soldiers, not like fugitives from a lunatic asylum.

The German police general, I have learned since the war, was a most sincere man. His name was General-major der Polizei Wilhelm von Grolmann. For weeks before our arrival in Leipzig, Grolmann had been impressed with the futility of trying to defend the city. The only troops available for defense were the flak troops manning the antiaircraft guns to the west, two battalions of an infantry regiment totalling about a thousand men, a smattering of Volkstrum—*People's Army—units, and Grolmann's own policemen. They obviously were incapable of a strong defense, but every effort that Grolmann made to convince the army commander in the city, a Colonel von Poncet, met rebuff. The only concession Poncet would grant was to refrain from demolishing the bridges over the Pleisse-Elster Canal. This he agreed to in order to keep the western section of the city supplied with water, electricity, and gas.*

On the day before we arrived at the canal, General Grolmann called on Colonel Poncet and made a last effort to prevent a fight. Poncet again refused. That evening Grolmann saw the mayor, Dr. Freyberg, and spent several hours trying to talk the mayor out of taking his own life. In vain. The mayor, and his wife, and their 17-year-old daughter, took poison during the night.

The police major with whom Lieutenant Whitman made contact in the Gohlis sector had, in reality, been authorized by Grolmann to make a surrender offer to the American commander. After the major telephoned Grolmann from the Gohlis station, Grolmann telephoned Colonel Poncet and once again tried to talk him into surrender. Again Poncet refused. He had moved his command post into a vault under the Battle of the Nations monument, a memorial to the end of Napoleonic despotism, and from there, with about 200 men, he conducted the only real combat to take place in Leipzig.

Thus when Grolmann talked with me at police head-

quarters, he was genuinely unable to surrender the whole city, though he fully believed there would be no real fight.

I might add that my interpreter, Pfc. Harms, would, I am sure, be pleased to know that the general believed he was talking to, not one, but two U.S. Army captains.

27

TWO THOUSAND CASES
OF CHAMPAGNE

I slept until noon when I was awakened to talk with a major from the 69th Division. He was on reconnaissance to determine the exact front lines of our division, and I pointed out the dispositions of my company on his map.

"We had quite a scrap this morning," the major volunteered, "over around the city hall. Had three tanks knocked out."

I said, "I was there about midnight last night."

The major was amazed.

Colonel Smith called at three o'clock and said that orders had been changed and we would continue into the city. Our battalion would occupy the Gohlis section, and my company would set up around the police station where we had first contacted the German policemen.

I alerted the platoons and rode with Lieutenant Reed in the artillery jeep to the railroad bridge across the canal. The rifle platoons were forming there to continue into the city. I assigned sectors around the police station for their occupation and asked Whitman, "How was the *fräulein?*" He grinned sheepishly.

The 1st and 2d Platoons preceded us into town, a single column of men on either side of the narrow road. We hugged the sides of the buildings when we came once again to the narrow chasm that was the street leading to the police station, wary lest we run into defenses prepared during the day. But there were no signs of resistance and the presence of civilians in the streets indicated that there would be none. They seemed less interested in us now than they had been the night before. Evidently, they still believed that the city had surrendered last night, and our entrance was anticlimactic.

I paused on the street corner outside the building which served as a hospital and talked with the GI PWs whom we had rescued the night before, only to leave again when we pulled out in the early hours of the morning. I apologized for having to leave them, but they said they knew we would be back.

The platoons disappeared into the sectors assigned them, and Harms and Lieutenant Loberg began their search for a CP. The jeeps arrived, and I solicited a ride with Lieutenant Reed and his artillerymen to visit the platoon areas.

The 2d Platoon was to go into position to the south of the police station, but I could find no sign of the riflemen, so we drove warily on. An underpass beneath a railroad track loomed ahead of us, two mammoth German railroad guns on the tracks above it. This was supposed to have been the limiting point of my company's advance, but I saw a group of GIs beyond the tracks. They were from the 2d Platoon.

We rode up beside them, and I recognized Technical Sergeant Wesley I. Phillips, of Edna, Kansas, the platoon sergeant. "I thought you knew not to go past the railroad tracks," I said. "Where's Lieutenant Whitman?"

"I know, Cap'n," Sergeant Phillips replied, "but the lieutenant saw all these nice buildings over here and decided to have a look at them. He's gone over to the left to some German barracks or something."

I saw Whitman and Sergeant Weylandt approaching down the street to the left. Something told me I was in for another crazy scheme of some sort, but I steeled myself against becoming a party to it. Whitman spoke before I could begin dressing him down for crossing the railroad.

"There's sixty Germans and a lieutenant over there who want to surrender. There's a whole big German garrison area . . . beaucoup weapons and supplies."

I sighed. There was no use pretending. I would end up eventually going over to accept the surrender. I would save time if I gave in without further ado.

"The lieutenant says they've been waiting to surrender

ever since we came in last night," Whitman continued, "and he's getting damned tired of waiting. But he wants to surrender to at least a captain."

"Climb on," I said, resigning myself to the fate that had given me two such zany characters in my company. "Tell us where to go."

The street ended two blocks away at the German garrison area. A sentry whom I knew this time to be a member of the German Army stood guard at a massive iron gate leading into the grounds around a group of large three-story stone barracks and warehouses. Whitman said something to the guard in German, and the soldier clicked his heels, bowed slightly from the waist and held out the keys of the gate to me.

I took the keys and opened the gate. A group of Germans, led by a stiff lieutenant resplendent in a neatly pressed uniform and shined boots, emerged from the nearest barracks. The lieutenant stopped and clicked his heels, saluting smartly, as we approached. He nodded his head toward Whitman to indicate that he remembered him.

I decided to waste no time in this surrender. Either they did or they didn't. Standing in the open area surrounded by hostile barracks on three sides was not to my liking.

"Tell him to bring all his weapons and pile them here at the gate," I told Whitman. "Then he can line up his men, and we'll take them on in."

The lieutenant acknowledged the order and repeated it to his noncommissioned officers. They saluted smartly and disappeared into the two nearest barracks. A single file of German soldiers carrying rifles, machine guns, *Panzerfausts* and pistols began to emerge from the buildings. They piled the weapons near the gate, and the five men from Whitman's platoon began to break them up against the tree trunks, quickly confiscating the treasured pistols.

Soon the task was completed. The Germans lined up in platoon formation with their baggage, and the officer took over from the noncoms. I moved over to stand behind the German officer as he addressed his men, their heads bowed slightly toward the ground, but their bodies stiffly at attention.

The lieutenant spoke to them in German, but I could discern from occasional words that he was telling them the war was over for them and they were making an honorable surrender. At his command they should give one last *"Heil Hitler."*

The officer barked the command. Their heads snapped quickly to attention, and they shouted in unison, *"Heil Hitler!"*

The officer did an about face and saluted me. He indicated by a nod of his head that I should remove the pistol from about his waist. I did not like the idea of being told how to conduct the surrender, when I was the one supposedly conducting it, but I did not feel inclined to disagree. For all I knew, the other barracks might be filled with Germans, their rifles trained upon us. Also, I wanted the pistol.

The men from the 2d Platoon took charge of the Germans, and an orderly placed the officer's bag on the artillery jeep. We climbed aboard and returned to the police station.

An order from battalion had prompted Lieutenant Loberg to lock the gates of the police station and put GI guards around the iron fence. The station was now the battalion PW enclosure, and the six hundred policemen found themselves prisoners of war. I saw the police major as I deposited the German lieutenant at the enclosure and nodded toward him. He seemed to recognize me, but he was none too cheerful.

Two war correspondents were on hand when I returned to my CP. One was an attractive blonde girl whose clear American voice sounded good in the strange surroundings.

"I heard that you had quite an experience last night," she said. "Also I'd like to get stories on these boys you've rescued here in the hospital."

I invited them to spend the night with us, and Harms cleared another floor of German civilians in the apartment house which Lieutenant Loberg had taken over as a CP. I decided that we were one of the few rifle companies in the US Army who could boast of having an American girl spend the night in its CP in such forward positions. She was Lee Miller of *Vogue* magazine.

Darkness was falling rapidly, so we went across the street to a restaurant which our kitchen had requisitioned. The long line of GIs had already formed for chow, and inside the cooks were serving meals to the seven GIs and the British and French who had been prisoners of war in the hospital. I warned them not to eat too heavily for their first meal, but they were too overjoyed at the sight of the food to comply. Almost all of them ended up outside with upset stomachs.

As we ate I heard the approach of hundreds of hobnailed marching feet on the pavement outside. Those hobnailed boots could mean only one thing—Germans. I went outside. A group of GIs were approaching with over two hundred German prisoners in marching formation.

"We're from K Company," one of the guards said, when I asked. "We're on your left. Got these Kraut out of a garrison area across the railroad tracks."

I shuddered. So these two hundred Germans had been watching when I had so unwittingly accepted the surrender of the German lieutenant and his sixty men. Thank God, we hadn't been rough with them, I thought.

I told the story inside.

"That's nothing, Cap'n," Whitman said. "Right after you left we found sump'n sitting right around the corner of one of one of the barracks that sure made us feel silly . . . a brand new German tank ready for action."

"Whitman," I said, slowly and forcefully, " if you ever decide to accept the surrender of any more Germans, you're going to do so entirely on your own. Is that clear? I've had quite enough."[1]

I found three more hungry former PWs waiting for me at my CP when I returned. A 69th Division jeep had deposited the three men from the 1st Platoon who had been captured the night the 1st and 2d Platoons were surrounded in Bohlitz-Ehrenburg. They had been recaptured in the fighting in the southern part of the city that morning.

The men were none the worse for their capture, except for the lack of food, but the Germans had given them the same food which they themselves received, they said. They did not disturb their watches or other personal belongings, but they had reconfiscated their German pistols. They

---

[1]As far as I have been able to determine since the war, these troops and the ones we took earlier from the barracks were part of the two battalions of the *107th Infantry Regiment*, the only bona fide German army unit in Leipzig.

agreed that the behavior of their captors was a far cry from the days of the Ardennes when the German nation had not known its defeat.

I was called to battalion the next morning to go on reconnaissance, and with a convoy of four jeeps we traveled over fifty dusty miles to the southeast to a little town on the banks of the Mulde River, a tributary of the Elbe. The Mulde was to be the limit of advance for American forces in our sector. We would relieve elements of the 9th Armored Division and awaited contact with the Russians driving toward the west.

I returned to the company in Leipzig at dusk and found the entire company in a state of hilarity from the discovery of over two thousand cases of champagne in the warehouses of the German garrison across the railroad tracks. Sergeant Quinn had found the huge store of champagne and two new Ford trucks. The men from the company had transported what champagne they could by hand, and the two trucks were loaded.

To the casual observer walking through the streets that night, the Gohlis section of Leipzig might have been a dead city, but I knew that behind those blackout curtains a host of GIs were having riotous celebrations. Hundreds of displaced persons had been welcomed into the luxurious apartment houses, cleared of German civilians, and the more attractive *fräuleins* had found that it was not necessary for them to evacuate. Non-fraternization rules were forgotten behind the anonymity of the blackout curtains. Every GI was a king for a night, and his kingdom consisted of girls and champagne and wonderful soft beds and a roof over his head.

One man slept with a German opera singer.

We moved the next morning and arrived at the little town of Kleinbothern on the Mulde River in mid-afternoon. The 9th Armored had had virtually no enemy contact since reaching the area, and we settled down to a period of watchful waiting—less watchful for Germans than for Russians.

Regiment sent out detailed information on markings of Russian armored vehicles. Supply issued special pyrotechnics to use in the event of appearance of Russian troops. No artillery could be fired without clearance through regiment. A host of war correspondents camped at the regimental CP awaiting the event.

Rumors spread constantly. A request by the supply section for sizes of dress uniforms brought the widespread speculation that our division had seen its last combat and would be returned to the US to parade down Fifth Avenue on July 4. An artillery Cub observation plane had spotted a column of troops approaching that were without doubt Russians. They were not over five miles away. That news was a rumor, but for truth, a Cub plane had spotted Russian tanks ten miles away. The Russians would arrive any day.

Lieutenant Bagby went to the aid station to have his ear treated and was evacuated. Lieutenant Speed was one of two officers from the regiment to return to the States on rotation. That left Sergeant Campbell and Technical Sergeant Raymond D. Yardley, of Dallas, Texas, in command of the two platoons. Citrone was transferred to battalion, and Townsend became my runner and 536 radio operator.

Close-order drill in the open field behind Kleinbothern fanned the rumor of a New York parade from a spark into a flame. Almost every man hoped secretly that the Germans across the river would throw a few rounds of artillery into the area to stop this close-order drill, but we heard no sound of enemy fire.

When the Russians did not appear and rumors were rife that a meeting was coming farther north, regiment sent out motorized patrols far to the front in an effort to contact the Soviet forces. The third patrol brought disaster and an end to the patrolling when a lieutenant colonel in command of the suporting artillery battalion, who went along voluntarily on the patrol, was killed when he fired at a group of fleeing Germans with his .45 pistol. The covey of war correspondents forsook the regiment to move to the north where the 69th Division eventually made contact with the Russians.

Out stock of champagne from Leipzig was quickly depleted, but Sergeant Quinn held out a keg of cognac which he had rifled from the German warehouses. This was set aside specifically as V-E Day material.

The rumors of no more combat came to a sudden end on April 30 when battalion called for a billeting guide. We were being transferred to the Third Army for a drive into Czechoslovakia. We cursed and swore. We knew that a number of divisions had seen no combat since the breakout beyond the Rhine River, and we could not understand why they were not called upon for this mission, but all to no avail. We left by truck convoy on a three-hundred-mile journey to the Czechoslovakian border the next morning, May 1.

The ride was harrowing after leaving the north-south *Autobahn* at dark and moving to the twisting, narrow mountain roads of Eastern Bavaria. To our amazement it began to snow, and we shivered from the cold in the open trucks.

Vehicular accidents and the snow-covered roads delayed the column for hours at a time. The villages we passed were cold and deserted under a blanket of snow, and I was reminded of the sleepy little Belgian villages during the winter campaign in the Ardennes.

Dawn was breaking when we finally reached our destination, the little "cow town" of Burkhardtsreith four miles from the border.

I was called to battalion for reconnaissance immediately after breakfast. The falling snow had turned into a needlesharp rain, and the snow that covered the ground began

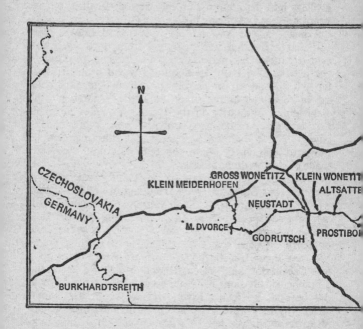

to melt. The little country trails were almost impassable with ice and slush.

Colonel Smith explained that our regiment was to relieve elements of the 97th Division a few miles inside Czechoslovakia the next day. Their defenses were concentrated in a series of farming towns, and the sector was almost as quiet as the one which we had left on the Mulde River. The 97th had been making limited-objective attacks and found resistance only in the towns, except for heavily mined roadblocks in the extensive woods that were generally undefended. Only one main highway ran through the area and that along the left flank of our prospective positions. The highway led to Pilsen.

Reconnaissance revealed that our defenses lay in a broad valley dotted here and there by clusters of white houses with red roofs. A north-south dirt road was the general front-line marker, running parallel almost three-fourths of a mile from a tree-covered ridge which marked

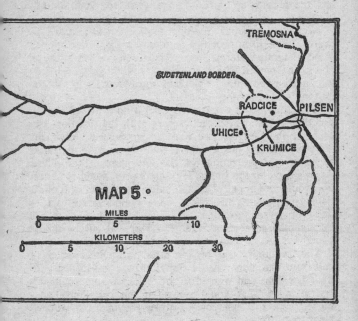

the end of the valley. My company, on the left flank, would occupy two picturesque little villages a quarter-mile apart, and F Company on our right would be a mile away.

The company commander of the unit I was to relieve revealed that he had had three men killed that morning on a patrol against the wooded ridge to the east. There had been no enemy artillery or mortar fire, however, and the road along the front line could be used without danger even by truck convoys. A small church atop a hill between his positions and a German-held town at the edge of the woods to the right front was unoccupied, but a patrol had drawn fire there from the German-held town.

The towns were clusters of white and pale blue stone houses joined by high stone walls and facing on a town square with a small duck pond and chapel. I decided to place my 2d Platoon and a platoon of H Company machine guns in the town on the left, Klein Meiderhofen, and the remainder of the company on the right in M. Dvorce.

We moved by trucks the next morning, a total move of twelve miles. In answer to numerous queries, the Colonel eased the non-fraternization restrictions, allowing us to live in the houses with the civilians, although we were in the Sudetenland, and the civilians were German in speech, customs and sympathy.

We settled down comfortably, but a bit crowded, in the two little towns. I was well pleased with the situation, except for the fact that we were so spread out. Regiment did not seem anxious to attack, and our mission appeared to be merely protection for the left flank of the Third Army's drive to the south. My only worry was that battalion would order patrols, and such a step seemed foolish, risking men's lives needlessly when radio reports told us daily of fresh surrender of masses of German troops throughout the combat area. The war was surely almost over.

The tranquility was broken after dark, however, by a call from battalion. The 3d Battalion was dissatisfied with their positions and wanted to move forward approximately two miles. That would necessitate our battalion attacking to take the first row of towns beyond the wooded ridge to our front.

I must send out a patrol at daylight the next morning to find a route through the woods to our front.

I chose the 1st Platoon to furnish the patrol, and Sergeant Campbell and Staff Sergeant Mathew P. Butwina, of Cleveland, Ohio, the squad leader of the squad Campbell had chosen, reported to my CP.

The patrol's mission was to investigate a trail which the map showed to run through the woods from a point almost halfway between our location and the town occupied by the 2d Platoon. Accomplishing the mission would probably be simple once the men had crossed the wide-open space to the woods line, but crossing that open space was the problem.

The patrol would leave the next morning at four o'clock, thus providing a cover of darkness to reach the woods. I told Campbell to provide the squad with one 536 radio, and he could maintain an outpost in a small, round patch of firs between the town and the main woods with another 536 radio and the light machine guns to provide supporting fire, if necessary. Lieutenant Reed gave the patrol leader an overlay of artillery concentrations he had plotted by firing during the afternoon.

I left instructions with the man on telephone guard to awaken me when the patrol was ready to start out the next morning.

It was cold when Fulton awakened me, but the rain had stopped and a half-moon was shining dully through rapidly vanishing clouds in the sky. The patrol waited outside the house. Fulton would operate a 536 radio at the CP to keep in contact with the outpost in the patch of fir trees.

I wished the men good luck, and they moved out into the dark. Fulton warmed me a cup of coffee. Campbell reported all clear from the patch of firs. The patrol squad was moving on.

Campbell described the squad's route to the woods line as a shallow, open draw extending almost to the woods. He said it was beginning to get light.

It was almost daylight when I heard the first sound of small-arms fire in the distance. I had been unconsciously listening for it through the long minutes of waiting, but when it came I was startled by the suddenness of it, and its dread portent.

Fulton contacted Campbell on the radio, but the transmission came through weakly. He ran from the house to the edge of town, and I opened up a fourth 536 to receive his relayed message.

"The patrol has hit small-arms fire from the edge of the woods," he relayed, "but the enemy disappeared across a low rise, and Campbell can't see 'em. He's lost contact by radio."

I thought perhaps the weakness of the batteries in Campbell's radio made him unable to reach the patrol, but Fulton ran forward to exchange radios. He still could not contact Sergeant Butwina.

Only an occasional burst of distant automatic fire broke the morning stillness. There seemed to be nothing to do but wait. Perhaps Butwina could send a messenger back to the outpost. That would seem to be easier than trying to send a messenger to reach him when we did not know his position.

An hour passed slowly. I called Sergeant Campbell again and again for information, but he had none. I could picture the men in the patrol squad hugging the damp earth in the open draw, unable to shift their bodies in any direction lest they draw fire from the enemy in the woods to their front.

If only we knew where to fire artillery, I thought, we could either enable them to move forward or support them in a withdrawal. But it would be too dangerous to fire artillery in the vicinity without knowing the exact location of the squad.

I called battalion to send two TDs to give supporting fire, and I was on the verge of calling for the entire 3d Platoon to move out to assist them, when Sergeant Campbell called me over the radio.

"Butwina's back, Cap'n," he said. "He made it out with one other man. Says his scouts were almost in the woods before the Kraut opened fire, and now all of them are pinned down in the open. One of his scouts is pretty badly wounded."

28

CZECHOSLOVAKIA—AND PEACE

The news from Sergeant Butwina was not good, but I realized it could have been much worse. At least we should be able to fire artillery on the enemy position now that we knew the patrol's location.

"Butwina says to fire Number 201," Sergeant Campbell radioed. "That's the concentration on that little corner of woods you can see on your map. He'll adjust from there."

Lieutenant Reed reached for the telephone and called for the concentration. We waited anxiously for the sound of the big guns going off behind us, and then it came, and the big shells whistled over our heads. We could hear them exploding in the distance beyond the town.

"That was two hundred right."

Lieutenant Reed repeated the correction over the telephone, and we waited again for the sound of the big guns.

Two TDs roared into town from the south, and I sent Private First Class Harry Zellin, of Manhattan, N. Y., one of the platoon runners, to guide them to the patch of firs to provide supporting fire, if possible.

The artillery whistled overhead and exploded again in the distance.

"How was that?" I asked.

"Almost right in there," Campbell replied. "Butwina says reduce the range fifty yards and let 'em have it again. I'm going to adjust after that, and he's going to try to get back to his squad. He's taking my radio. It's got better batteries."

"Roger," I answered and repeated the sensing to Lieutenant Reed.

We heard the whistle of the shells and the explosions. A long pause followed before Campbell gave us the sensing.

"Butwina has started back to his squad," he said, "and I just had a call from him. He says to hold the artillery. Something screwy's taking place. A German just came out of the woods with one of his scouts."

We waited impatiently for a report on the situation. Five, ten, fifteen minutes passed. Finally, it came.

"This is Campbell, Cap'n," the radio said. "I just got another call from Butwina. He says the Germans are bringing out our wounded man, and he's sending one man back with twenty prisoners. The rest of 'em are going on through the woods."

I didn't know what had taken place, but I did know that the patrol was safe now, and that was all that mattered for the moment.

The wounded man was Private First Class Michael Wapner. He had received a serious wound in the side, but the aid men thought he would come through it all right.

The patrol returned shortly before noon, reporting the trail through the woods to Neustadt, the town beyond the ridge, was clear. I pieced together a complete picture of the action after talking with Sergeant Butwina and Sergeant Gettle, who, although he was assistant squad leader, had insisted upon being one of the scouts.

Sergeant Gettle and Private First Class Wapner had been almost inside the woods when the Germans opened fire from dug-in positions on the edge of the forest. Wapner was hit with the first burst. After the first excitement died down, Gettle made his way to where Wapner lay to assist him. The Germans in the woods saw the situation and held their fire. A German aid man came out and helped Sergeant Gettle carry the wounded man to one of the foxholes in the woods where the aid man dressed the wound.

Sergeant Gettle knew a few words of German and began to insist to the enemy lieutenant that he and his nineteen men surrender. The first artillery barrage brought a weakening in the lieutenant's attitude. He began to shake from fright, and Gettle seized the opportunity to pour on the sales talk. The second barrage was almost on top of them, but the lieutenant still did not give in. It was the third barrage that impelled him to surrender, and they moved out of the woods to contact the patrol and have the artillery fire lifted.

The remainder of the day and night passed quietly. I half-expected a call from battalion at any time to report to receive the attack order, but I hoped vainly that the various reports of enemy surrenders *en masse* in other sectors would forestall the attack in the hope of a large-scale surrender in Czechoslovakia. But I was called to battalion the next afternoon, May 5.

Colonel Smith outlined the plan. F Company would attack immediately to take Godrutsch, the little town that lay beside the woods near the church beyond M. Dvorce. As soon as the town was ours, I would send one reinforced rifle platoon to take over its defense for the night, sending a patrol through the woods to investigate a trail leading from Godrutsch to Neustadt. The main attack would come slightly before dawn the next morning with G and E Companies in the assault echelon. G Company's first objective would be Neustadt.

F Company laid down a deafening artillery barrage against the little town of Godrutsch and took it without a show of resistance, although the town yielded seventy-five prisoners. At least half the houses in the town went up in flames from the murderous artillery barrage, and the civilians were dashing madly here and there in an effort to put out the fires when I arrived with the 3d Platoon to take over the town. F Company withdrew, and Sergeant Barnes dispatched a patrol to investigate the trail through the woods.

I waited in the town until almost dark for the return of the patrol. They reported that the trail through the woods was clear.

Captain Byrd called from battalion soon after dark. The news about the burning of Godrutsch had evidently spread among the other villages to the east. The *Bürgermeister* of one of the villages had come into the 3d Battalion's lines and begged that we stop the artillery, claiming there were no soldiers in his town. The officers of the battalion told him to return and spread the information to all the towns in the area—if they displayed white flags prominently from every house and kept the German troops from firing at us when we attacked the next morning, there would be no artillery. I could not avoid comparing the situation, in which we told the Germans when we would attack, with the hectic winter campaign when surprise was an important element.

It was dark when I left with the headquarters group and the 1st and 2d Platoons for Godrutsch the next morning, but it was daylight before we had completed details for the attack. We were getting into formation to move on through the woods when three soldiers in Polish uniforms stepped from the woods.

I turned the three Poles over to Colonel Smith and Captain Byrd when they arrived. They said they were a patrol sent out by their regiment of one thousand men who had been fighting with the Germans against the Russians but now wished to arrange for a surrender to the Americans. They were fully armed and in bivouac twenty-five miles to the east.

The 3d Platoon led our march through the woods along the trail in a close-march formation. The woods were dense, and I expected at any moment to hear the sound of small-arms fire that would mean defenders had moved in during the night, but we progressed without difficulty.

The lead platoons halted at the edge of the woods on a hill overlooking the objective, the town of Neustadt in a broad valley below us. To take the town we must cross six hundred yards of open field to a raised railroad track which ran along the edge of the town and was ideal for defense. On a road which entered the town from the northwest we could see German soldiers working on an antitank roadblock.

We set up the machine guns on the hill and Sergeant Barnes dispatched one squad down the open slope toward the town. If they ran into trouble, we would attempt to level the town with artillery before moving in.

The Germans constructing the roadblock saw the patrol squad and stopped their work to watch, but there was no sound of fire. The squad took the most direct route to the railroad track in an effort to reach the cover it provided before entering the town.

I gave the machine gunners orders not to fire until I should give the signal. I could see no white flags in Neustadt, but perhaps the Germans would not fire if we did not fire first. One shot might set off a blaze of enemy fire-works.

The machine gunners wanted to open fire on German soldiers running and riding bicycles up the sloping hill beyond the town, but the range was too great for their fire to be effective, and I feared the risk of the enemy opening fire.

The battalion staff arrived on the hill, however, and Colonel Smith overrode my objections to firing the machine guns. I did not object because I saw the men from the patrol squad had reached the railroad tracks and four Germans jumped up from their foxholes and surrendered. I knew the town was ours. The other two squads from the 3d Platoon started down the hill, and the 1st Platoon followed.

The six machine guns chattered, their tracers spanning the town in a great fiery arc to burn themselves into the hill beyond. Lieutenant Reed called for artillery on the fleeing Germans.

An enemy machine gun opened up suddenly from the railroad tracks to the right front. The fire was high over our heads and did no damage, but the battalion staff cleared the hill as if by magic. The enemy gunner fired another burst, and I told our own machine gunners to cease firing, almost grateful to the enemy gunner who had fired and cleared the hill of the battalion staff.

I moved down the forward slope of the hill with the remainder of the company, wary lest the enemy gunner open up again, but I found two men from the 3d Platoon at the railroad track covering the enemy gunner and trying to talk him into surrendering. I left a mortar squad with the two riflemen for the purpose of persuasion and continued into the town.

Colonel Smith reappeared in the village to tell me that we should continue the attack to take the next town of Gr. Wonetitz two miles to the east and be prepared to continue to the next two towns. The order was not much of a surprise. I knew that once we had begun the "limited objective" attack we would keep going.

The 2d and 3d Platoons deployed on either side of the road leading east. Over a mile ahead of us up a gently sloping hill was another woods line, and I feared the possibility that it might be defended. My fears proved groundless, however, and we reached the far edge of the woods without trouble. The little town of Wonetitz lay in a shallow draw three hundred yards ahead of us, a narrow draw on our right leading into the town.

The machine gunners and Lieutenant Reed's artillery observers set up almost automatically on the edge of the woods, and I dispatched Lieutenant Whitman's 2d Platoon up the draw on the right. The route offered the maximum of cover in the area, and should his men be fired upon, he would attempt to withdraw and we would plaster the town with artillery, burning it to the ground, if necessary.

We could see and hear F Company firing artillery in another little town several hundred yards to the right and could see fleeing Germans on the roads and hill beyond our objective. The machine gunners begged to fire, but I would not allow them to open up until we knew for certain that Wonetitz was undefended.

I could see Whitman's men following the bottom of the draw on the right leading into the town, and then they were lost from view in a heavy growth of brush. A burp gun chattered suddenly from the buildings at the head of the draw. There was no question now. The town was to be defended. The trigger-happy machine gunners seemed almost glad. Now they could fire.

The machine gunners opened up, and Lieutenant Reed called for artillery. Round after round plastered the edge of the town and then progressed back and forth among the buildings in the rear. A wooden factory building at the head of the draw burst into roaring orange flame. A house began to burn. A round hit an outhouse that must have been a chicken coop. Chickens cackled and scattered in all directions.

One round in each volley began to fall short, and we knew one gun in the battery must be off in its adjustments. We were about to radio to have each gun fire singly to determine which was off, when a round fell dangerously close to where I thought Whitman and his men were. The chatter of a burp gun sounded after the noise of the explosion.

"That one was too damned close," Whitman radioed quickly. "Damned thing hit almost on top of my forward squad. Sergeant Weylandt jumped up to move back and they got him in the side. Looks like he's hurt pretty bad."

The news gave us more incentive to destroy the town, and Lieutenant Reed discovered the gun which was making the error, and continued to fire barrage after barrage. Whitman said he thought he could continue, but I told him to hole up for a few minutes. Battalion wasn't pushing us, and the war was too near over to take any chances.

Lieutenant Reed fired three more barrages. We decided that the next one would be the last. The shells roared into the town, and the 2d Platoon pushed forward toward the flaming buildings. The Germans did not fire another shot.

I moved down quickly with the remainder of the company, and the 2d Platoon finished checking the rest of the town, lining up fifteen prisoners with their faces to a wall and hands high above their heads.

Sergeant Weylandt's wound proved to be more painful than dangerous. I thanked heaven that he had not been killed. My last fatality had been with the knocked-out tank that the first flak-gun positions on the approaches to Leipzig, and I hoped fervently that I could finish the war without another

The civilians in Wonetitz wanted us to withdraw from the town and fire again. They had begged the soldiers not to fight, but the *Bürgermeister* had insisted that they must, and now every house in town had been hit with artillery fire, except ironically, the *Bürgermeister's*.

Battalion ordered us to continue the attack to take the next two towns of Klein Wonetitz and Altsattel. Klein Wonetitz lay a quarter of a mile up the valley to the northeast, and the stream running through Gr. Wonetitz continued to enter the town on the right, providing the only covered approach. The machine gunners set up to cover the advance, and the 3d Platoon moved upon the objective, finding the town completely deserted of soldiers and civilians. I moved forward with the remainder of the company down the main road.

From Klein Wonetitz we could see the rooftops of the larger town of Altsattel beyond a high knolll between us and the objective. I thought the knoll might be defended, so we covered the advance of the 3d Platoon with machine guns again, but they reached the knoll without difficulty.

We set up the machine guns again on the knoll, and I dispatched the 3d Platoon to the right and the 1st to the left of the stream which divided Altsattel in half. There followed the same nervous period of waiting while they moved across the open, but the town was undefended.

The 1st Platoon took three youthful prisoners who said they were fourteen and had been forced into the army only two weeks before, and this was their first action. Their mothers had told them to surrender to the Americans at the first opportunity. They had.

We had already set up our defenses for the night in Altsattel and were delighted to find that the town still had electricity, when Colonel Smith arrived. I was dead tired from the fifteen-mile walk, and I felt that if he said to continue, I would surely fall to the ground exhausted.

He said we would continue to the next town of Prostiborg, however, and I cursed to myself, but there was nothing to do but forget our fatigue and move on.

I assembled the company at the eastern edge of town, and the machine gunners went into position in the last buildings, covering a wide expanse of valley which ended in a high tree-covered ridge which the highway crossed a mile and one-half from Altsattel. According to my map, Prostiborg lay at the foot of the ridge on the other side, two miles from Altsattel.

I sent the 3d Platoon forward initially, deciding it would be foolish to expose the entire company in the open valley until we discovered if the ridge would be defended. The battalion staff arrived and watched with me from a small knoll at the edge of town.

"Have your men push right along, Mac," the Colonel said. "There's nothing out there." The phrase had become so familiar that it was maddening.

As if it had been waiting for the cue, a round of incoming artillery whistled overhead. It was so strange to hear a round of enemy artillery, that we were almost convinced that it was one of our own rounds, but a second round a few minutes later exploded a hundred yards from the knoll and removed any doubt. It was a German gun. The battalion staff cleared the knoll in one dash, and I was left to run the attack without interruption.

"I'll bet battalion thinks we're in cahoots with the Krauts," Lieutenant Reed said, and winked.

The enemy gun continued to fire single rounds, but it was highly inaccurate. The first round had exploded far to the rear of Altsattel, the second near us on the knoll. The others fell in the town or far to the south. I feared that it might be an enemy tank, but someone suggested that it might be a horse-drawn 75mm gun which civilians in Gr. Wonetitz had mentioned having seen pass through.

I dispatched the 1st Platoon to follow the 3d to the wooded ridge, and I moved out a few minutes later with the remainder of the company, keeping alert to dive into ditches along the road should the little artillery piece land a lucky round on our column. But the gun continued to fire to our rear, most of the shells exploding in Altsattel.

"I hope battalion likes the town they ook away from us now," a soldier said. "They sure get me p——d off."

Another said, "I hope the sonofabitch shoots at 'em all night long."

The lead platoons moved unimpeded up the steep ridge, but there was no sign of our objective on the other side. The ridge rose slightly higher after the woods line stopped, and the town was evidently secreted below the crest of the hill.

Far to our left we could see German soldiers alone or in small groups moving into the extensive forests along the hills and ridges, and I knew that the big woods around us were alive with stray Germans. Two enemy soldiers came to the edge of the woods that ran to the right of the clearing in front of us but refused to come out to surrender upon the insistence of men from the 3d Platoon. They did not fire, however, and walked calmly back into the woods. I was convinced that the war would end soon from sheer insanity.

When we reached the open crest of the hill, we could see the steeple of the church in the little town that was our objective. The machine gunners set up again, and the 3d Platoon rushed the remaining distance to the first houses. The other platoons followed, and I allowed the machine gunners to open up on stray Germans moving around in the valley below us. I followed the platoons into the town, and the men rounded up ninety Germans, members of a labor battalion.

The 3d Platoon medic found a Russian girl in one of the houses. She began to sob violently, and the medic comforted her with his arms around her. He looked at me and winked. "She says she had heard that the Americans were coming," the medic said, "and she thought she would be so happy that she would laugh forever, but now that we're here she says she's so happy she has to cry."

The platoons set up their defenses for the night and battalion ordered me to send a patrol to the next town atop a hill at the end of the valley. Staff Sergeant John H. Winter, of Edgewood, R. I., led the patrol of six men from the 2d Platoon shortly after dark, but they returned in three hours with the news that they had entered the town and found no resistance.

E and F Companies jumped off the next morning in the attack, but reports filtering back to us over the battalion radio told us that nowhere was there any resistance. F Company took three hundred prisoners soon after starting out and found the antique 75mm horse-drawn piece which had fired the evening before.

We followed far behind the assault companies and cleared two towns which they had by-passed, but there was no resistance. We reached the pillboxes which had been the old Czechoslovakian defense against Germany, but they were unoccupied.

Regiment ordered battalion to load up on tanks and trucks and continue the assault as rapidly as possible. Resistance had collapsed all along the regimental front. The 3d Battalion had taken the Polish regiment, and the 16th Armored Division had been committed on the highway to our left to take Pilsen.

We loaded on trucks and moved forward, and soon the highway was a confused mass of vehicles. As our column advanced down one side of the highway, a ragged column of Germans in horse-drawn wagons, dilapidated German Army vehicles, civilian automobiles, bicycles and on foot, met us coming down the other side. Some had their families with them. All had thrown away their weapons.

We could not keep from laughing. The German column was so pathetic that it was funny, and also we knew that it must mean the end of the war. The Germans were running from the Russians to surrender to the Americans. This was the last front in Europe, other than the Russian front, and now resistance here had ended.

The traffic became almost a hopeless mass of milling

people. Regiment would take no more PWs—division said their PW cages were overflowing, and would accept no more from regiment. It was up to the battalion to handle the prisoners for the night. Colonel Smith assigned a platoon from E Company to guard them, and more than one thousand assembled in a large open field, not including the fifteen hundred who had already been sent to regiment.

Our column continued forward, and my company shifted to the lead position on tanks. I rode behind the lead tank in the artillery jeep. The little country towns changed into small industrial towns, and we began to notice a scattering of red, white and blue Czechoslovakian flags in the towns in place of the usual white flags of surrender. Civilians waved at us guardedly from behind closed windows.

The scattering of Czech flags should have warned us, but we were totally unprepared for the mad celebration which greeted us in the next town. We had suddenly crossed from the Sudetenland into Czechoslovakia proper.

The houses were a riot of color with red, white and blue Czechoslovakian flags. Civilians lined the streets ten deep, cheering and waving their flags as if their lives depended upon it. Our column was forced to slow down, and the happy civilians pushed into the street and showered us with flowers and cakes and cookies. One old woman thrust a baked chicken into our jeep. Another old woman stood beside the road waving both hands in the air, tears streaming down her wrinkled cheeks. Little children were wild with joy . . . some of them had never known anything but six years of Nazi occupation. The young men wore red, white and blue arm bands and carried German weapons, a part of the underground movement that was even now struggling against superior German forces in the capital city of Prague. Everyone was screaming the Czech words, *"Nazdar! Nazdar!"* and we wondered what they meant.

I looked up and down the column at the soldiers in the company. Brilliant smiles wreathed their faces, and they waved cheerfully at the shouting crowds as if they had just won an election campaign and this was a personal triumph. Hardened, stubble-faced veterans had unashamed tears in their eyes. The unleashed joy of these oppressed people knew no bounds, and it was too much for us.

Suddenly, I began to realize what no one had thus far been able in the war to put into words—what we were fighting for. And I found a lump in my throat which I could not swallow.

Colonel Smith radioed for us to turn south to the small town of Uhice for the night. We were reluctant to leave the cheering crowds, but we moved once again into the country and entered Uhice. The town was predominantly German, so the welcome was subdued, but the few Czechs in the town were overcome with gratitude. Little children gathered around our vehicles asking for chewing-gum and candy as they had in every European country we had visited.

We moved out again the next morning on foot, and in every town the throngs of cheering civilians lined the streets in a spontaneous celebration that had lost none of its fervor with the passing of night. Children dressed in the gay national Czech costumes, old women and old men, pretty young girls, and the young men with the red, white and blue arm bands, cheered us lustily. Our faces became set in answering smiles, and our arms ached from waving back. We were showered with cakes and cookies, and soldiers carried small paper Czech flags in the muzzles of their rifles and bouquets of wild flowers in their hands.

We passed batteries of 88mm flak guns that I knew had been protection for the vast Skoda works in Pilsen, and I could not help but shudder at the sight of the big guns. Even in their helpless state without crews they were frightening.

We swung to the north and came again to the main highway into Pilsen, and the road was lined with armored vehicles speeding into the city. The city had fallen, and veteran war correspondents were describing the welcome as exceeding that at the liberation of Paris.

The battalion halted in Krumiče on the main highway, and we waited among admiring crowds for further orders. Pretty girls appeared suddenly with 2d Division shoulder patches sewed to their sweaters, and others appeared with patches from the 16th Amored.

Someone said that combat action in Europe was over for our division. We laughed. Another rumor. No, we should cease all forward movement. The news was from regiment. It was official! We shook hands wildly and soldiers did impromptu dances around the jeeps and patted one another on the back. Sergeant Quinn said, "Look out, cognac!"

Colonel Smith stopped by my company and told me to climb into his jeep. He was going into Pilsen.

The city was the same cheering, enthusiastic, grateful mass of liberated people as the small towns on the route, only on a larger scale. The streets were packed. Civilians clambered over all the big armored vehicles, and soldiers hugged and kissed beautiful girls while old men and women roared approval. Czech flags were everywhere with a scattering of flags with hammer and sickle on a red background. A few buildings displayed elaborate Czech, Russian, British and American flags, but the civilians were obviously unprepared for liberation by Americans. They had expected the Russians to get there first.

But the festive spirit was not dampened in the least by the lack of proper American flags. It was carnival! It was festival! It was liberation!

The orders had been received when we returned to Krumiče, and G Company was to move a mile to the northeast to the modern little town of Radčiče.

As we moved on foot toward the town old men and women working in the fields saw us coming and dropped their work to run to meet us, grasping us around the neck and kissing us on both cheeks, tears of gratitude streaming down their faces.

The town was ready for us when we arrived. Little boys and girls preceded their elders and ran to meet our column, thrusting bouquets of flowers into our hands and shouting, "Nazdar! Nazdar!"

When the excitement had died down, and one of the Slavic-speaking men in the company explained that we wished billets for the night, I was besieged by requests for soldiers to stay in various homes. I found myself unable to consider tactical disposition of the company. Soldiers scattered in all directions, hustled along by the enthusiastic civilians. I found the lump in my throat bigger than ever.

The news came by radio that the war was over. There was no defining our joy. Sergeant Quinn brought out the treasured keg of cognac. The next day, May 8, would be VE-day.

The townspeople in Radciče held a dance for us the next night in the town guesthouse. One of the artillerymen was escorting a young girl whom he had met the night before, and she had told him that her friend, Leibe, would like very much to attend with the captain.

The small guesthouse was crowded with dancers, and the older men and women sat with the young children at tables around the sides of the room. The male dancers were predominantly GIs, but a few Czech young men were present. The orchestra reminded me of the circus bands in the US as they played the waltzes, the polkas and the mazurkas. The Czechs would join in often to sing the songs enthusiastically even as they danced.

At the insistence of the band leader, Leibe agreed to sing, and the notes came forth in a clear, sparkling soprano. When she had finished, she made a brief speech which the Slavic-speaking soldier told me said that the people would now sing their national anthem. It would be the first time they had sung it in public in six years.

The people rose as one, and every boy, girl, man and woman joined in the singing with clear, lusty voices that made goose-pimples rise on my arms. Some of the older people cried, and it was all I could do to keep the tears from my eyes.

When the song ended, the orchestra struck up a rousing song which my interpreter told me was the equivalent of our own "For He's a Jolly Good Fellow," and they were singing it for me. I felt warm and foolish inside, and I wanted to leave the room, but then I realized that they were singing to me only as a symbol for all the men in the company.

The band broke into a fast polka, and the floor suddenly cleared of dancers. This dance, I was told, was for me. I should choose a girl and dance the number alone.

I felt very self-conscious as I motioned to Leibe and we moved out on the dance floor, but I found myself imitating Leibe's spinning turns and gay, vivacious laughter. The others in the room formed a large circle around us and beat time to the music with their hands.

When it was over, the soldiers began to cry, "Speech! Speech!" and the civilians caught on and applauded. I stood upon a chair in the center of the room trying to think of something to say. I mumbled a few words of sincere gratitude for the wonderful reception these wonderful people had given us, and a soldier translated for Leibe, and she told the people what I had said. They applauded warmly.

Leibe and I walked outside into the cool night air. In the distance we could see fireworks exploding in the air above Pilsen, and we knew that they too were celebrating VE-day. I looked around me and saw that light streaming from the windows, and Army vehicles driving on the highway with their headlights on, and I heard the gay music and laughter from the dance in the background. I suddenly realized that I could light a cigarette once again in the open and not be afraid of drawing enemy fire, and I did. It was a simple thing, but it gave me a wonderful feeling that life was worth living again.

I put my arm about Leibe's waist, and she pointed to the multi-colored fireworks display, and laughed, *"Dobri! Dobri!"* I had learned that *"dobri"* was *"good,"* and I said, *"Dobri, dobri."*

I looked away in the distance, and I seemed to see the faces of the men from Companies I and G who could not see this great day because they had died to obtain it. And then their faces were gone, and I saw the mud and ice and snow of the Siegfried Line, and the exploding fireworks became bursting artillery shells in the Ardennes and bursting flak at Leipzig. But then, the terror was gone, and I saw two companies of men marching by, and there was I Company and G Company, tired, dirty, weary, but with smiling faces, and somehow the faces of the men who had been killed were in the background, smiling and waving bravely to those who marched on.

Leibe looked up at me as if to ask what I was thinking, and I said, *"Dobri, dobri,"* and Leibe squeezed my hand and laughed.

Yes, *dobri, dobri.*

EPILOGUE

—and that is the end of my story.

But perhaps you would like to know that my company moved on five miles north of Pilsen to Tremosna, and there we met another group of tired, dirty infantrymen, who called themselves Russians. A month later we were loaded on a big boat at Le Havre, and on July 20, 1945, we sailed into New York Harbor and received the cheers of grateful America and saw a tall lady with a torch that brought tears to our eyes.

The characters in my story were destined to be sent to help finish another war in another part of the world where another group of American infantrymen were fighting a dirty, miserable war. But a miracle happened, and the other war came to an end.

Most of my characters are wearing civilian clothes again now, but I know that wherever they are they have a hollow place in their hearts for those who will not be changing to civilian clothes again—ever . . . those GI Joes who, that others might live, were cut down in a harvest for the devil.

BANTAM WAR BOOKS

Introducing a new series of carefully selected books that cover the full dramatic sweep of World War II heroism—viewed from all sides and in all branches of armed service, whether on land, sea or in the air. Most of the volumes are eye-witness accounts by men who fought in the conflict—true stories of brave men in action.

Each book in this series has a dramatic cover painting plus specially commissioned drawings, diagrams and maps to aid readers in a deeper understanding of the roles played by men and machines during the war.

FLY FOR YOUR LIFE by Larry Forrester

The glorious story of Robert Stanford Tuck, Britain's greatest air ace, credited with downing 29 enemy aircraft. Tuck was himself shot down 4 times and finally captured. However, he organized a fantastic escape that led him through Russia and back to England to marry the woman he loved.

THE FIRST AND THE LAST
by Adolf Galland

The top German air ace with over 70 kills, here is Galland's own story. He was commander of all fighter forces in the Luftwaffe, responsible only to Goëring and Hitler. A unique insight into the German side of the air war.

SAMURAI by Saburo Sakai with
Martin Gaidin & Fred Saito

The true account of the legendary Japanese combat pilot. In his elusive Zero, Sakai was responsible for downing 64 Allied planes during the war. *SAMURAI* is a powerful portrait of a warrior fighting for his own cause. (May)

BRAZEN CHARIOTS by Robert Crisp

The vivid, stirring, day-by-day account of tank warfare in the African desert. Crisp was a British major, who in a lightweight Honey tank led the British forces into battle against the legendary Rommel on the sands of Egypt. (June)

REACH FOR THE SKY by Paul Brickhill

The inspiring true story of Douglas Bader. The famous RAF fighter pilot who had lost both legs, Bader returned to the service in World War II as a combat pilot and downed 22 planes in the Battle of Britain. Shot down, Bader survived the war in a German prison camp. (July)

COMPANY COMMANDER
by Charles B. MacDonald

The infantry classic of World War II. Twenty-two-year-old MacDonald, a U.S. infantry captain, led his men in combat through some of the toughest fighting in the war both in France and Germany. This book tells what it is really like to lead men into battle. (September)

Bantam War Books are available now unless otherwise noted. They may be obtained wherever paperbacks are sold.